"Once upon a time there were women who wrote together"

WOMEN
OF THE
FAIRY TALE RESISTANCE

WOMEN OF THE FAIRY TALE RESISTANCE

The Forgotten Founding
Mothers of the Fairy Tale and
the Stories That They Spun

JANE HARRINGTON   ILLUSTRATED BY KHOA LE

Black Dog
& Leventhal
Publishers
New York

Copyright © 2025 by Jane Harrington
Interior and cover illustrations copyright © 2025 by Khoa Le

Cover copyright © 2025 by Hachette Book Group, Inc.

Hachette Book Group supports the right to free expression and the value of copyright. The purpose of copyright is to encourage writers and artists to produce the creative works that enrich our culture.

The scanning, uploading, and distribution of this book without permission is a theft of the author's intellectual property. If you would like permission to use material from the book (other than for review purposes), please contact permissions@hbgusa.com. Thank you for your support of the author's rights.

Black Dog & Leventhal Publishers
Hachette Book Group
1290 Avenue of the Americas, New York, NY 10104
www.blackdogandleventhal.com
BlackDogandLeventhal @BDLev

First Edition: August 2025

Published by Black Dog & Leventhal Publishers, an imprint of Hachette Book Group, Inc.
The Black Dog & Leventhal Publishers name and logo are trademarks of Hachette Book Group, Inc.

The Hachette Speakers Bureau provides a wide range of authors for speaking events. To find out more, go to hachettespeakersbureau.com or email HachetteSpeakers@hbgusa.com.

Black Dog & Leventhal books may be purchased in bulk for business, educational, or promotional use. For more information, please contact your local bookseller or the Hachette Book Group Special Markets Department at Special.Markets@hbgusa.com.

The publisher is not responsible for websites (or their content) that are not owned by the publisher.

Print book cover and interior design by Katie Benezra

Library of Congress Cataloging-in-Publication Data
Names: Harrington, Jane (Writer), author.
Title: Women of the fairy tale resistance : the forgotten founding mothers of the fairy tale and the stories that they spun / Jane Harrington.
Description: First edition. | New York, NY : Black Dog & Leventhal, an imprint of Hachette Book Group, 2025. | Includes bibliographical references and index.
Identifiers: LCCN 2024030751 (print) | LCCN 2024030752 (ebook) | ISBN 9780762488704 (hardcover) | ISBN 9780762488711 (ebook)
Subjects: LCSH: Women authors, French--17th century--Biography. | Fairy tales--France--History and criticism. | Salons--France--History--17th century. | French literature--Women authors--History and criticism. | French literature--17th century--History and criticism. | LCGFT: Biographies. | Literary criticism.
Classification: LCC PQ149 .W63 2025 (print) | LCC PQ149 (ebook) | DDC 398.2092/520944--dc23/eng/20241031
LC record available at https://lccn.loc.gov/2024030751
LC ebook record available at https://lccn.loc.gov/2024030752

ISBNs: 978-0-7624-8870-4 (hardcover), 978-0-7624-8871-1 (ebook)

Printed in China

APS

10 9 8 7 6 5 4 3 2 1

*To the matriarch, Kathryn Jeanne, who gave me life.
And to Zaza, full of fairy magic, who saved it.*

CONTENTS

INTRODUCTION: *NOT A FAIRY TALE* · ix

MARIE-CATHERINE D'AULNOY · 1

FÉLINE · 9   BELLE-BELLE · 32

HENRIETTE-JULIE MURAT · 59

IRIS · 68   ANGUILLETTE · 69

CHARLOTTE-ROSE LA FORCE · 85

DUNAMIS · 94   PERSINETTE · 115

MARIE-JEANNE L'HÉRITIER · 123

FINETTE · 131   BLANCHE · 140

—

CATHERINE BERNARD · 155

FLORINDE · 160

—

CATHERINE DURAND · 169

BRILLANTE · 174   OGILIRE · 181

—

LOUISE D'AUNEUIL · 187

PATIENTINE · 193   QUEEN OF FLOWERS · 200

—

ACKNOWLEDGMENTS · 207   BIBLIOGRAPHY · 208   INDEX · 217

NOT A FAIRY TALE

Once upon a time—the mid-1600s, to be specific—there were some women in Paris who created a social club they called the *salon*. There they had conversations about the latest news and entertainments of the day, much as you might in a coffee shop or pub, a student union or sorority house. But these women didn't have those kinds of places to gather in because they were barred from educational institutions and public spaces, as all women in their society were. In addition to being denied the same opportunities as men, they were not allowed to control their own money, to travel freely, or—*this* bothered them the most—to love and be loved. Many were in arranged marriages (to men frighteningly older than they were), and while their husbands were allowed to have affairs as they pleased, the women were bound by law to be faithful. Even in the case of abuse, which was common, they didn't dare file complaints because they ran the risk of being labeled "unruly" and sent away for long spells. So, obviously, they had a lot to talk about. The salons were very popular.

Not with the government, however. The ruler of France at the time was the boy king Louis XIV, whose regime considered the salons hotbeds of radical thought that spurred agitation among the populace. And, well, they were. And did. It wasn't difficult to spur agitation, though, as citizens of nearly all economic levels felt that their livelihoods were being drained to fund wars and other aggrandizing ventures to benefit the patriarchy. As Louis XIV grew to be a man—one who liked to be called the "Sun King," so brilliant did he deem himself—the atmosphere only got more tense, the government clamping down on the people of France whenever the king got nervous. Among the casualties were the salons, which were basically shut down.

Fast-forward a few decades, through much of Louis' lengthy reign, to a time when his sun is just beginning to set, you might say. It's the

INTRODUCTION: NOT A FAIRY TALE

※

1690s, and a new wave of women friends are looking for a place to gather, so they decide to open a new wave of salons. These women call themselves *conteuses*, female storytellers. They know there will be scrutiny from the government, even spies in their midst, but they're not worried. They're merely creating fairy tales, playing harmless games. One example: A theme is offered to the gathering—say, metamorphosis—and then each salongoer tells a story rooted in that idea. The telling might be improvised or practiced ahead of time, but the resulting tale always reflects its social origin; the storyteller's presence is palpable, the tone conversational. When satisfied with their works, the conteuses send them out for publication. The manuscripts have to go through the royal censor, of course, but a story with *fairies* in it? These won't warrant a serious read from the busy censor. He probably won't get past the first page. *This* the women are surely counting on.

The tales are subversive, you see. The fairies? Symbols of female empowerment, avatars of the conteuses themselves, who refer to each other as "modern fairies." The very writing of these stories is an act of liberation, an exploration of love, femininity, masculinity—themes they feel are tragically misunderstood in their culture. The plotlines push against a prevalent viewpoint that women are weak and of limited intelligence, a viewpoint that favors men as public beings while women are expected to keep hidden. The conteuses are fighting for change: for recognition, power, sensible policies. Many of the tales are romances in which the female protagonists go through trials for lovers of their choosing. They rule over queendoms and exact revenge on despotic kings, something that alone can risk a work's censorship, the law barring even indirect criticism of Louis XIV or his policies. The women do throw a little praise for the monarch into their tales, small flatteries and references to his greatness, in an attempt to stay out of the Sun King's glare. Many of them fail at that, but in spite of dispiriting punishments, their tales become an absolute sensation. These women produce, altogether, more than seventy stories, which are collected in volumes and published across Europe. They coin the term "fairy tale," or *conte de fée*. There are seven conteuses whose names are most celebrated: Marie-Catherine d'Aulnoy, Henriette-Julie Murat, Charlotte-Rose La Force, Marie-Jeanne L'Héritier, Catherine Bernard, Catherine Durand, and Louise d'Auneuil.

Well, you may be thinking, *if they were so popular, then why haven't I ever heard of them? And*, you may also be thinking, *why would the movies and storybooks I grew up on claim that Charles Perrault and the Brothers Grimm were the fathers of the fairy tale if that weren't true?*

INTRODUCTION: NOT A FAIRY TALE

Good questions. Let's start with Charles Perrault. He was a regular visitor to the conteuses' salons and a participant in their fairy tale games. He wrote down a few stories and published a small collection anonymously—sort of. He put his son's name on it. It's not clear why Charles Perrault didn't own up to this work, but some possible reasons are that (a) the men who went to the salons were looked down on by those in society who thought it too feminine a pastime, and (b) he wanted to be remembered for his more serious writings—essays and dialogues, the kinds of pieces men were trained to produce in the academies. But irony being the power it is, Charles Perrault is not much remembered for any of that "serious" writing. He's remembered for being "Mother Goose," the persona that became attached to his book of tales. Perrault is widely thought of as the originator of such classic characters as Puss in Boots and Little Red Riding Hood and Sleeping Beauty. But that's . . . a fairy tale.

Take Perrault's "Sleeping Beauty in the Wood" as an example. This is a retelling of a story by Giambattista Basile, a well-known Italian writer whose works had been published many decades earlier. Basile hadn't claimed to make up that story; he had attributed it to women of the countryside, anonymous spinners of yarns. Perrault, in his version, replaced wise men and astrologers with fairies (seven of them, interestingly) and did some toning down—taking out a description of the sleeping girl being raped, for one thing—but he otherwise followed the Italian storyline very closely, even including the entire second half, which involves a cannibal queen who decides to eat the princess's babies, with gourmet sauces to enhance the flavors. (More detail about those stories is unnecessary to this discussion, but if curiosity is getting the best of you, both Perrault's and Basile's are easily findable online. Basile's version is called "Sun, Moon and Talia" from his collection titled, believe it or not, *Entertainments for Little Ones*.) The point is that Charles Perrault is no more the parent—goose or otherwise—of the fairy tale than was Basile, or, for that matter, the famous Brothers Grimm. They were, however, instrumental in creating the myth surrounding Charles Perrault.

The Brothers Grimm never actually met Perrault, of course. Aside from being in different parts of Europe, there were more than eight decades between the death of Perrault and the births of the brothers. But the Grimms were scholars, so they would have been steeped in the history of the fairy tale. Which makes their disregard of the conteuses' once wildly popular tales a pretty clearly purposeful act.

INTRODUCTION: NOT A FAIRY TALE

They called the women "inferior imitators" of Charles Perrault, which is absurd given that the women founded the fairy tale salons and that Perrault's little book actually came out *after* the first of the conteuses' many volumes of tales. Assertions the Grimms made about the story they called "Rapunzel" also defy logic. In the notes that accompanied their tales, they claimed that they had gotten their version from a man named Friedrich Schulz, but it doesn't take much digging to discover that Schulz had really just translated that story from the French "Persinette," one of the conteuses' tales from more than a hundred years earlier. The translation was nearly word for word, something that would have been obvious to anyone who read the two stories and certainly to language historians, which the Grimms were.

The Brothers Grimm insulted the memory of the conteuses in more personal ways as well, their criticisms suspiciously similar to those that had come from a notorious band of male writers who were known for their woman-bashing at the time of the salons. The writings of these men compared women to animals, warned of their dangers—their lustful gazes and cackling voices—and railed against the depravity of the salons and their popularity with gay and trans people. A man named Pierre de Villiers was one of the most caustic critics and the first to take on fairy tale writers specifically. His book was entitled *Êntretiens sur les contes de fées . . . pour servir de préservatif contre le mauvis goût*, which translates to *Interviews on Fairy Tales . . . to Provide a Condom Against Bad Taste*. (While there is some debate about whether he actually meant *préservatif* to mean "condom," after running the word through multiple translators and determining that condoms did in fact exist at the time he wrote that, I've decided to take him literally.) Villiers preferred, he wrote, Aesop's fables, with their "wit" and "delicacy" and "all the knowledge of an excellent philosopher." It is too much of a temptation not to share one of Aesop's fables here as an example of what Villiers favored:

"The Camel Who Shat in the River"

A camel was crossing a rapid river. He shat and then saw his own dung floating in front of him, carried by the current. The camel puzzled over this. "How is it that that which was behind me I now see pass in front?"

Moral: Sometimes the idiots hold sway over the sensible.

INTRODUCTION: NOT A FAIRY TALE

Not saying it's bad, not at all. Enduring message, for sure. But "delicacy"? "All the knowledge of an excellent philosopher"? Even Aesop's still-famous Tortoise and Hare might be intimidated by such praise. The shortness of the fables could have had something to do with Villiers' high opinion of them. One of his recurring complaints about the conteuses' tales was that they were too long, though he never provided any details in those reviews, so one might get the idea that he didn't actually read any of them. Same goes for the Brothers Grimm, who parroted this very complaint and praised Perrault's stories, arguing that his voice mirrored much more accurately (and here is irony wielding its power again) that of *real* female storytellers—those illiterate "old wives" of yore who stayed home and did their chores. Regardless of the brothers' reason, or lack thereof, the end result was that they did not include—or at least credit—any of the conteuses when they compiled works for their *Grimms' Fairy Tales*, as the tome would become known around the world. Never mind that few, if any, fairies flutter through the hundreds of stories the Grimms collected.

That's a word worth repeating: "collected." The Grimms were collectors, transcribers, recorders of a tale-telling past. And they were proud of that fact; they didn't claim to be otherwise. But what we're made to believe from the covers of our favorite picture books and the opening credits of Disney films is that the Grimms were "authors" or "creators" of most of the classic fairy tales. Not that the picture book publishers, or even Walt Disney, necessarily knew they were spreading misinformation. A falsehood oft repeated does have a way of beginning to resemble fact. But a simple time-travel back to the Grimms' first edition in 1812 will allow us a visit with just one example of the truth: Snow White, or Sneewhittchen, as the brothers called her. They plainly stated in their notes that they'd heard many versions of this story from the various gatherers they employed to help them with their research. As for the version they chose to publish, they named in the notes the people who had shared it with them, and the brothers produced the story as close to verbatim as they could, as that was part of their mission. Those are hardly the acts of "creators" or "authors" of original stories.

Before leaving Snow White behind, it's also worth pointing out that the Grimms' tale is curiously different from the storybook and movie versions that we are so familiar with and that bear the brothers' names. Here are a few highlights from the original version of the tale published by the Grimms:

INTRODUCTION: *NOT A FAIRY TALE*

- The queen is Snow White's biological mother, not stepmother.
- The girl is seven years old when the huntsman is summoned to kill her and bring back her lungs and liver so her mother can cook them, with salt, and eat them.
- The mother tries thrice more to murder the child, until finally Snow White ends up in a glass coffin, where she stays for a long time without rotting (a point explicitly made in the Grimms' text) before a prince happens by and takes possession of her.
- The prince's servants have to carry the coffin around all day because he is obsessed with looking at her, but eventually they get sick of this and open the coffin to yell at Snow White and hit her, thus dislodging the piece of apple from her throat.
- The couple marry the next day, and they invite Snow White's mother to the festivities so they can execute her there by strapping fire-hot iron shoes to her feet and watching her dance in pain until she dies.

Not a great choice for bedtime reading, you may be thinking, but there's worse in the Grimms' collection. In "The Robber Bridegroom" a young woman is sent off to marry a prince who turns out to be part of a band of thieves that kidnaps women and kills them, something she witnesses while hiding behind a barrel, when a finger that has been chopped off a woman lands in her lap. In "The Juniper Tree" a mother gets upset with her son and decapitates him, then sets her daughter up to think she was actually the one to kill her brother, and then the mother cooks the boy into a stew that she feeds to the unsuspecting father. I'll stop there, even though that just scratches the surface of the brutality—mostly against children and women, and mostly with no discernible moral—in the tales the Grimms judged worthy of publication.

You may be wondering at this juncture if the Grimms intended their stories for children. Most of what's written about them claims they didn't. But here's the title they gave their collection: *Kinder- und Hausmärchen*. In English, that's *Children's and Household Tales*. Not sure how else to interpret that except that they thought their stories appropriate for children. The conteuses' tales, however, the Brothers Grimm argued, were definitely *not* for children. They deemed the women's tales too complex for a child's simple mind and, further, maintained that the women hadn't

INTRODUCTION: NOT A FAIRY TALE

intended them for children. As to the first claim, the conteuses did use bigger words than did the Grimms, and in stark contrast to the brothers' blunt stories, the women's tales had actual plotlines and even character development. But too hard for a child to understand? You can soon answer that question for yourself.

As to the claim that the conteuses didn't intend their stories for young people, it is probably true that the greatest market for their books was women. But here's a question: How would "woman" have been defined at that time? In the twenty-first century, we think of a fourteen-year-old as not a woman but a teen girl. However, in the time of the fairy tale vogue, fourteen-year-olds were regularly sent off to marry and have babies, so it can be assumed that they were considered women. The fairy tales would have been written with these very women in mind, as theirs were the plights the conteuses had experienced themselves and were trying to combat with their pens. Furthermore, over the time that the tales remained popular and were reissued in numerous editions, these women would certainly have read them to their growing children. In these stories, there was no explicit sex (à la the earlier tales by Basile) or violence (as would come later with the Grimms). These were quest tales with brave and clever protagonists who were not punished for their curiosity or their wanderings nor rewarded for blind obedience and silence. These fairy tale princesses didn't sleep through the action; they *were* the action. The conteuses would not have had it any other way.

In this book you'll rendezvous with each of the seven salon sisters, their life stories pieced together from the fragmented records and flawed histories that survive them. You'll also find in these pages a selection of retellings of their tales, all based on the original French publications (late 1690s to early 1700s) or English translations from the eighteenth and nineteenth centuries. Although some whittling and reshaping occurred in the writing process, I always felt a "modern fairy" at my shoulder as I worked to retell these stories, keeping me true to the conteuses' voices and to the spirits of the young heroines—all, like the writers who first imagined them, women of the fairy tale resistance.

MARIE-CATHERINE D'AULNOY

Marie-Catherine d'Aulnoy was the conteuse who started the fairy tale craze. She is credited with penning an impressive twenty-five tales. More impressive still, she also wrote novels and poetry and "pseudo memoirs," which were travelogues and recollections fictionalized to make them more exciting. Perhaps she thought a true account of her life would be dull. You be the judge.

Born Marie-Catherine Le Jumel in 1652, she came from nobility on both sides—her father's family was "of the robes," or judicial sorts, and her mother was related to Henri de Beringhen, the first *premier écuyer*. Although the job description that came with that title may seem lowly—manager of the stables—it was a big deal. The premier écuyer position brought the bearer tête-à-tête with the king, riding alongside him and even subbing for him at the gambling table. Henri held the position for some decades and made a reputation for himself as "the wisest man of his time" before passing the title down to his son, Jacques-Louis, a cousin and contemporary of Marie-Catherine. Keep him in mind for later.

That Marie-Catherine was a spunky kid with a passion for literature is more than apparent from scribblings she left behind in the margins of one of her favorite plays. In looping cursive (translated here from the French) she warned any future possessor of the book, "If you do not mind what is inside, I hope you get ringworm, impetigo, fever, plague, measles, and a broken neck." Demonstrating either further proof of a sardonic sense of humor or a desire to tone down the harshness of what she had just written in permanent ink (my bet's on the former), she signed off with "May God help you against my curses."

WOMEN OF THE FAIRY TALE RESISTANCE

Her mother, Judith-Angélique, known for her fierce criticism of gender-based power imbalances under the patriarchy, raised her daughter to value independence and protect herself by whatever means necessary. These were traits that Marie-Catherine would need throughout her life and certainly from the age of thirteen, when, as the story goes, a band of masked men swooped into her boarding school and kidnapped her. Among them was François de la Motte, the Baron d'Aulnoy, more than thirty years her senior and—she would quickly figure out—her betrothed in an arranged marriage. Many accounts point to her father as the instigator of the arrangement and even the perpetrator of the kidnapping, but that's unlikely: It appears her father was dead by that time. This would mean that her mother made the arrangement. Seems hypocritical for a feminist, but perhaps some sense can be made of this by flipping back to an earlier chapter of François de la Motte's life, one that, in the parlance of the fairy tale genre, would be called a "rise tale," a.k.a. a "rags to riches" story.

Probably while still in his teens, la Motte, who had no fancy pedigree to boast of, was taken under the wing of the rich and powerful Duke of Vendôme. La Motte was put into service as a footman at his residence (the Place Vendôme in Paris), then became a valet and moved up the household ladder from there. Around about the time Marie-Catherine would have been learning to walk, the duke was helping the thirty-something la Motte purchase the barony d'Aulnoy, which gave him a fortune of his own as well as entry into social circles he'd never known. This is how he became friends with Judith-Angélique, who found him charming and was impressed with his assets—not only the value of the barony but also the influence that came with connections to the House of Vendôme. Which, by the way, was cheekily referred to on the streets of Paris as the "House of Sodom" because of the duke's unabashed homosexuality. (This openness was fairly common for men—King Louis XIV's own brother was gay and didn't hide it—but as you'll see when you meet the next salon sister, *not* so common for women.) That la Motte had long had male lovers is pretty clear from the record, and there are no references to be found of his having any romantic relationships with women. So why, you may wonder, did he suddenly, at age forty-six, want to get married? The answer to that is also pretty clear. In the year prior, the baron had slipped into serious financial straits. By then, the Duke of Vendôme had died and couldn't help him out. Marrying into wealth was a means to save the barony. We can assume that he kept the extent of his money woes from Judith-Angélique until after the ceremony, but there is still the question of why she would deem a much older man with a demonstrated preference for his own sex a desirable match for her daughter. One possibility is that she may have actually thought these to be points in favor of the union—that is, a man set in his ways and lacking sexual interest in her might just give the debuting Baroness d'Aulnoy the freedom to enjoy her new social milieu without the usual interference that came with marriage bonds. Of course, it's impossible to know what Judith-Angélique was thinking, though one thing *is* certain: She came to rue the decision, as evidenced by the calamitous events that would soon unfold.

But back to the newlyweds.

Marie-Catherine despised her spouse from the get-go and was known to run away from him, often in disguise, every chance she got. By her seventeenth birthday she'd had three babies, two of whom she'd had to bury, and she was pregnant with her fourth. (It's worth noting here that she was known to adore her children, to play with them as if she were a child herself, and even to breastfeed her infants, which was not the norm for an aristocratic mother.) She lived in fear of the baron's temper, which grew inversely to his shrinking wealth, and he was now gambling away all the money she had brought into the marriage. There was nothing she could officially do about it, though, as this was not illegal behavior for a husband. However, she began to take notice that there *was* illegal behavior he was engaging in: *lèse-majesté*, to be specific, or bad-mouthing the king. The baron blamed his debts largely on the policies of the monarchy, and the more he became unhinged about his plight, the more he ranted about King Louis, not only at home but sometimes in public. Lèse-majesté was no petty crime; it was a capital offense that could result in execution. If Marie-Catherine had any compunction about bringing to light her husband's high treason, one can assume that her mother, who took the lead on this project, had no qualms. Judith-Angélique's feelings for her son-in-law, as per multiple sources, had by this time turned to "hatred." Mother and daughter hatched a simple plan: They would hire a couple of cavaliers to befriend Baron d'Aulnoy, witness his crime, and turn him in. What could go wrong?

Well, just about everything. The details could fill a book, but here is a truncated version. The baron did get arrested for lèse-majesté and was thrown into the infamous Bastille prison, but he managed to convince the authorities to arrest the men who had set him up, and they were tried for the same crime (it seems it was also high treason to coax someone to say bad things about the king), and soon the cavaliers were put to death. But not before they gave up the names of their co-conspirators. Marie-Catherine was still recovering in bed, just weeks past childbirth, when members of the King's Guard burst in to arrest her. She asked permission to attend to hygienic matters before being taken away, but while they waited outside her boudoir, she escaped via a back stair and slipped into a nearby church, where she hid under a velvet-curtained coffin set up for a funeral mass. Eventually she managed to make her way to the home of extended family, where she hid out for a few days before being turned in by a relative she had trusted (thought to be her brother-in-law, but she refers to him in later writings only as "my Judas").

Here is where the aforementioned cousin, Jacques-Louis, the premier écuyer, comes into the picture. Or presumably so, as his influence with Louis XIV is really the only explanation for how differently Marie-Catherine and her mother were treated compared with the cavaliers they hired. It certainly wasn't just because they were women. That was not a thing, as will be borne out in a bit. By the time Marie-Catherine was arrested, Paris was abuzz about the crimes, so, to avoid whatever the equivalent was of paparazzi in the seventeenth century, she was taken to the city courthouse and jail, the Conciergerie, in the dead of night. She had a babe in arms, and a trunk of necessities was brought in behind her to a room that she later described as comfortable and a relief. She had expected worse. For the length of time she was there—which is unclear because no official records were kept from her detention, and her own writings on the subject are incomplete—she was watched closely at all times (and that means *all*), because her earlier escape had been such an embarrassment to the King's Guard. They weren't going to take any chances while they waited for the king to decide what to do with her.

Meanwhile, Judith-Angélique was being dealt with elsewhere. Histories align on the fact that she agreed to become a spy for France and Spain in exchange for her head, and it appears she was banished for life, as she never set foot in France again. She spent most of her remaining years in Madrid, comfortably outfitted with a pension from the king of Spain. That last part, it seems to me, lends credence to a particular claim that she actually became a double agent, working, in the end, against the interests of the French monarchy.

MARIE-CATHERINE D'AULNOY

Marie-Catherine was banished as well, but historians argue over whether spying was part of the deal. Consider this, though: During her time away, which lasted more than a decade, she lived in a number of European cities, including Madrid, mingling with the upper echelons of society. When she finally returned to her homeland, she was granted a legal separation from Baron d'Aulnoy and set up in a house on a smart boulevard in Paris—all part of a "reward for services rendered to the Court," as records show. Hard to imagine what "services" those could have been if not espionage.

Wait, you may be thinking, *Baron d'Aulnoy was still alive? Shouldn't he have been executed for saying mean things about the Sun King?* Yes and yes. The baron's old Vendôme connections likely came into play to save him. He was, however, saddled with hefty court costs that he couldn't pay, and he spent time in prison for that. But for much of his wife's exile he was a free man in Paris, left to plot from afar new ways to make her life miserable. He accomplished that, in spades, not too long after her return. Their eldest daughter was getting married, and of course he had no money for the dowry. So he promised his new son-in-law what was left of Marie-Catherine's inheritance. Sadly, there's no record of how she specifically reacted to this, but it had to have been colorful, given the response from King Louis XIV himself, who banished her once again, this time for *mauvaise conduite*, a crime that basically meant misbehavior by women. She was incarcerated in a convent (it may seem strange today, but at that time convents were commonly used as women's detention centers), where she had to stay for years—yes, *years*—something she seemed to endure by wield of pen. During this period of isolation, she generated a lot of tales, most filled with strong young women who battle forces out of their control and are saved in unexpected and imaginative ways or by deus ex machina, a device Marie-Catherine often employed to rescue her protagonists from tyranny.

It is tempting to give her a happily ever after at this point in the story, but there is one more thorny episode that merits attention, this one starring a very close friend of hers: Madame Ticquet, wife of a legal adviser to the king who was known for his brutality. Perhaps he kept his abuse within legal limits (the law allowed a man to beat his wife so long as the weapon's diameter did not exceed that of his thumb), but whatever the reason, he was never made to stop. Then one night on the street, he was shot in the gut by an unknown male assailant. He survived the attack. Madame Ticquet was arrested for attempted assassination. She claimed innocence until she was subjected to torture by "water pot," a standard practice in the day to elicit information. It went like this: The prisoner was stretched naked over a stool at the small of the back, hands and feet tied and pulled in opposite directions, then forced to swallow four pots of water (a total of about six quarts), and then, if that didn't work, the prisoner was bent back over an even higher stool and four more pots were forced down. After her "confession" Madame Ticquet was taken to the executioner, a young man, new at the job, who got flummoxed when she kissed his hand and then gracefully set her neck on the chopping block. It took him three tries with the sword, blood spurting everywhere, before he successfully severed her reputedly beautiful head, which was then propped up on the platform, facing out, as a cautionary tale to all wives in the crowd. Yes, there was a crowd—all of Paris, according to the newspapers.

Though it's said Marie-Catherine was initially implicated in the scheme, and some accounts even claim she was banished (yet *again*), I choose, given no bona fide proof of that, to leave her in Paris for the remainder of her days, hosting her famous salon on the rue Saint-Benoît. She would have had her writer friends for company—though some had disappeared by that time, as you'll see—and her adult daughters. Baron d'Aulnoy eventually died, leaving her finally free of marital shackles. For five years, anyway, which is as long as she would outlive him, unfair as that seems given the age difference.

But Marie-Catherine did achieve acclaim for her work in her lifetime. From the moment she returned to France after her first exile, she wrote popular books with an international flavor that appealed to readers across Europe. She was even admitted to Italy's Accademia dei Ricovrati in Padua, one of the first literary academies to accept women, where she was nicknamed Clio after the Olympian Muse. Her fairy tale collections met with great publishing success, starting with the first volume, *Les contes des fées*, or *The Fairy Tales*, in 1697. Undoubtedly to help secure royal privilege—that is, approval by the censor—she dedicated the book to the Duchess of Orléans, Louis XIV's sister-in-law and the highest-ranking woman in France at that time. (If you are wondering why the king's wife, i.e., the queen, was not considered the highest-ranking woman, it's because she—a second wife whom he'd married secretly after the death of his first—was not of his social stratum and thus was an "unofficial" ruler. More on her to come.) Marie-Catherine's tales were not only read widely but also performed onstage, including at the Palace of Versailles,

where a national decree required "Knights of the Order" to act out fairy tales for the dauphin, the king's eldest son and heir.

One tale that would surely have been in that mix was "The White Cat," her most popular and enduring tale, retold here as "Féline." It is the story of a creature who has long suffered under a spell that can be broken only by a human who falls in love with it as it is—a beauty-and-the-beast tale, in other words, but with a beast in the form of a female cat and a beauty in the form of a prince. This was written more than forty years before the "Beauty and the Beast" we know so well (that, too, is by a French writer, and one who would have certainly grown up on the contes de fées of the renowned Madame d'Aulnoy), so Marie-Catherine was no, eh, copycat. Among the points of divergence between the two is the inclusion of a nested tale in "The White Cat," a story within a story, that explains the underlying curse. This narrative comes from the cat herself, who, after returning to her human form, steps into the role of storyteller to inform her new beau of her past—one that includes her abduction as a child, an arranged marriage to a monster, and a parade of punishments for her rebelliousness. This may sound suspiciously like autobiography, but Marie-Catherine does give her protagonist something that always seemed to elude her: a happy ending.

Transformation also figures into another one of her tales retold here, but this transformation is of the gender variety. "Belle-Belle" features a teenager who bravely puts herself in danger to keep her father safe. (If you are again thinking of "Beauty and the Beast," remember who got there first.) Belle-Belle disguises herself as a man in order to go to war in her father's place. While a cross-dressing warrior was not entirely new in literature of the era, Marie-Catherine put hers, and *herself*, closer to the battle lines. At the time she was writing this tale, a very popular form of entertainment was political satire, distributed via pamphlets, which poked fun at Louis XIV, making him appear weak and stupid or excessively vain and immoral. He *hated* these things (the way late-night comedians are hated by certain pols today), and he would have had all the authors rounded up for lèse-majesté, but they wrote anonymously to avoid that whole decapitation business. Shift the spotlight now to our writer, Marie-Catherine, scratching away at a manuscript in a cramped room in a convent during banishment number two. Onto the page appears Belle-Belle—or Chevalier Fortuné, the name she dons with her enchanted male attire—riding her steed to the palace of a king who is not only a military failure but also a leader whose power is overshadowed by that of his tougher sibling, a woman. Not wanting to give too much away, I'll just add that Belle-Belle saves the day. Clearly, Marie-Catherine was taunting King Louis, a rather unwise risk to take given her situation. But you'd have to agree that that woman did have balls. And so, you'll see, does her gender-bending Belle-Belle.

MARIE-CATHERINE D'AULNOY

FÉLINE

ONCE UPON A time there was a king who feared that his three sons would be seized with the desire to reign before his death. He was a distrustful sort, the king. And selfish. And scheming. So he hatched a plan to divert his sons with promises he could escape fulfilling. He summoned them one day and said, "My dear children, you know that my advanced age does not permit me to attend to state affairs so closely anymore, and I fear my subjects may suffer."

(The king was a liar as well. He wasn't too terribly old, he was certainly clear of mind, and he cared little about his subjects' sufferings.)

He went on: "I wish therefore to give one of you my crown, but it is only fair that in return for such a gift you should seek ways of making my retirement pleasing. It seems to me that a clever, pretty, and faithful dog would be a pleasant companion. I declare that whichever of the three of you brings me the finest dog shall be my heir."

The princes were surprised at their father's request for a dog, as he had never shown much interest in pets. But they gladly accepted the commission. The king gave them money and jewels, adding that in a year they must return, and on the same day and at the same hour bring him their dogs.

Before their departure they repaired to a keep about a league from the town. There they brought their friends and had a great feast, at which the brothers swore eternal friendship, that they would act without jealousy, and that the successful one should share his fortune with the others. At length, they set out, deciding that on their return they would meet at the same place and go together to their father.

Each took a different route, but we shall follow only that of the youngest. He was of a happy disposition, considered handsome, and skillful in all exercises befitting a prince. He sang pleasantly, played charmingly on the lute, and he could even paint. He was also recognized for his honesty and gallantry.

A day scarcely passed that he did not buy dogs: big, little, greyhounds, bulldogs, boarhounds, harriers, spaniels, poodles. As soon as he had a very fine one, he found one still finer, and therefore let the first go and kept the other. In this manner, he traveled far. One night, walking without knowing where he was going, he was overtaken by thunder and pelting rain. He could see a light ahead, wavering in the distance, and he made his way toward it, thinking it a house where he could take shelter till morning.

He walked for quite a while through the storm, the light seeming to only grow in magnitude ahead of his path. This was no mere house, he finally saw, but a castle built entirely from gleaming gemstones in a palette of colors he had only ever seen through prisms. A stag's foot hung at the entrance, and he pulled on it. In an instant the doors opened, and a dozen hands, all bodiless, ushered him in with torches, leading him through room after room, pushing him from behind until he reached a great salon where a commodious armchair slid across the floor quite on its own, stopping abruptly in front of a fireplace that at the same moment lighted itself. More hands appeared and, setting him in the chair, began replacing his wet clothes with dry ones, these more magnificent than any he had seen in his own court.

When he was powdered, curled, perfumed, adorned, and made more beautiful than Adonis, the hands led him into a hall resplendent with fine furniture. A table was laid for two. He perceived cats (yes, *cats*) taking their places in a little orchestra. One held a book in which was written the most extraordinary music imaginable, and the rest had small guitars. Suddenly, each began to mew in a different key and to strike the strings of their guitars with sharp claws. It was quite awful, the prince thought, and he was trying to work out how to plug his ears without appearing rude, when a little figure entered the hall. It was covered in a long black veil and was attended by two cats with swords at their sides.

The prince did not know what to think. The little figure approached him and raised her veil, and he saw in front of him the most beautiful white cat that ever was or ever will be. She looked very sad, and she began to mew so softly and prettily that it went right to his heart. Then she said to him, "I am Féline. You are most welcome in my home."

"It is very kind of you to receive me so cordially," said the prince, "but you do not appear an ordinary animal. Your gift of speech and your castle are strong proofs to the contrary."

"I beg of you to leave off making me compliments," she said. "Come, let supper be served."

The bodiless hands waited table. First two dishes were put out, one of young pigeons and the other of fat mice. The sight of the one prevented the prince from eating the other, imagining the same cook had prepared them both. But Féline, guessing by his expression what was passing in his mind, assured him that his kitchen was separate, and that he might eat what was given him without worry. The prince felt quite sure that she would not deceive him, and so he ate. The meal was delicious.

He noticed that Féline wore a miniature on one paw. He asked her to show him and was astonished to see in the tiny portrait a young man that resembled him most incredibly. He looked inquisitively at her, but she just sighed and became more melancholy. Fearing he had upset her, he changed the subject to news of the world, prattling on about this and that, and finding her to be surprisingly well informed on matters one would not expect a cat to care about.

After supper Féline invited her guest to enter a hall containing a stage on which twelve cats danced a ballet. Their leaps and capers were peculiar, but soon the prince found the dancers enjoyable to watch. When they were done, Féline bade her guest good night, and the hands that had heretofore been his guides took charge again and led him to a most unusual bedroom, where the floor was carpeted with butterfly wings and the feathers of rare birds, the bed was of gauze fastened up with ribbons, and there were large mirrors that reached from ceiling to floor, a hundred cupids smiling from gilded frames.

The prince was awakened in the morning by a confused noise. The hands took him out of bed and dressed him in hunting costume. He looked out into the courtyard and saw it filled with cats, some leading hounds on the leash, others sounding the horn. Féline bid him to come down and join them. A wooden horse awaited him, and while he at first resisted mounting the awkward-looking thing, the hands persisted in placing him in the saddle. He found that it moved better than a real horse, and on it he followed Féline, herself in a tricorn hat and riding a monkey. It was quite a successful hunt; the cats ran quicker than the rabbits, and

the birds, too, were scarcely safe, for the cats climbed trees. When it ended, Féline blew a horn, and the procession returned to the castle. She put on again her black veil and supped with the prince.

The days went on this way, with entertainments of all manner, and soon he forgot about the dog he was to take to his father. Indeed, he forgot his country, and cared only about being with Féline.

But she remembered his obligations and said to him one evening, "Do you know that your father is expecting you in three days?" Seeing the sudden anxiety that came over him, she added, "King's son, do not vex yourself. I am your friend. You can stay here another day, and although it is far from here to your country, the wooden horse will easily take you there in time."

"I thank you," the prince said, "but it is not enough to return to my father. I must take him a dog."

"I know," Féline said, passing an acorn from her paw to his hand. "This contains a dog more beautiful than the dog-star."

"Oh!" cried the prince. "You are laughing at me."

"Put the acorn to your ear," she said. "You will hear it bark."

And so he obeyed, and he heard the little dog and was assuaged. He wanted to open it right then, but she convinced him to wait until he was with his father. He thanked her, and tenderly said, "I regret leaving you. Although you are queen here and the cats that form your court are more intelligent and gallant than ours, I do wish you would come with me."

Her only reply was a deep sigh.

When the prince arrived at the keep to meet his brothers, they were surprised to see a wooden horse that performed better than all those in the riding schools. They also wondered why he had no dog at his heels. So he showed them the acorn, and they looked at each other, confused but also secretly glad for such foolishness. There was no denying the desire that had been growing in the two older brothers to be the winner of their father's competition.

The next day they went on together in the same coach. The older brothers brought their little dogs in baskets, so delicate that one scarcely dared to touch them. When they reached the palace they were greeted by all, and when the king set eyes on the two dogs, he did not know which to favor, for they were equally impressive. And then the youngest brought out of his pocket the acorn Féline had given him. He opened it, and there was a perfect, silken dog lying on soft wool. The king found it impossible to find anything to say against the tiny animal. He held it in his palm and seemed quite mesmerized.

But remember, the king had not the least desire to give away his crown. So he told his sons that he was pleased with their labors, and since they had succeeded so well in the first thing, he wanted them to prove their skill further before he fulfilled his promise. He said he would give them a year to look by sea and land for a piece of linen so fine that it would pass through the eye of a needle.

The two older brothers were visibly disgruntled and departed quickly, without so much affection for the youngest this time, as his showing them up with the superior little dog had greatly cooled their love.

So the prince mounted his wooden horse and steered himself away. He stopped at many places, in search of spinners and weavers, hoping to procure the prize his father sought. But soon his longing to again see Féline led him back to her castle. He found there the windows and doors flung open in welcome, and the hands ready to serve him. But nowhere did he see Féline, until finally, in the evening, in a dim corner of her room, he found her curled onto a pillow. She seemed in a state of neglect, her usually lustrous coat matted, her claws untrimmed.

"Dear one," he said softly, "what is it that has happened to you?"

Hearing his voice, she perked up, and stretched, and answered, "Whatever reason I had to hope you would return, king's son, I dared not expect too much. I am usually so unfortunate in the things I want that this event surprises me."

"But of course I would return," he said. "Why would you think otherwise?"

She looked down at the paw on which she wore the miniature, then back up at his face, and though she seemed on the brink of saying one thing, she said another: "Tell me about your journey."

And he related the events, and what was next expected of him by his father. "I think the task impossible," he concluded.

"We'll see," she said, and she leapt from her perch and led him to a gallery that extended along the river, where the cats of her court had taken to shooting off fireworks each day when darkness fell, to cheer her up. This night it would be to celebrate the prince's return. The rockets were such that he'd never seen before, lighting the hills so brightly it was as if they had been touched with fire.

The days that followed were the best of the prince's life, for he had only to think of something he wanted and it was immediately brought to him by the hands. Féline was so charming to be with and talk to, so versatile of mind. "You are not natural," he said to her one evening as they dined. "Tell me what miracle has made you able to think and speak as if you attended the most famous academies."

"Cease your questions," she replied, her eyes going from his plate to her own, from the grilled fish to the skewered mice. And then, again, she let out that deep sigh that signaled she would say no more.

The second year passed as quickly as the first, and though Féline again had to alert him to his impending departure, she assured him that he needn't be anxious. She had commissioned a most wonderful piece of linen, she said. And further, she told him, he would have a more stylish equipage for this journey. Beneath the window of the salon where they stood, he saw now twelve horses harnessed in velvet and attached to an exquisitely enameled carriage. Footmen awaited him, their uniforms decorated in coats of arms that depicted Féline, crown on head.

"Go now," she said to the prince, "appear at the king's court in so sumptuous a manner, and he shall not refuse you the crown." She handed him a walnut, saying, "Do not crack it until you are before him. It contains the piece of linen."

"No," he said, "I am so deeply satisfied here that I would rather spend my life with you than amid any glory I might receive from my father."

But she was almost out the door by then, creeping off in the direction of her rooms. "I shall not forget the affection you showed a little white cat," she said, without turning her head to look back.

Though the horses were meant to get the prince to the keep early for his rendezvous with his brothers, he found himself stalling, lingering at water holes and taking walks through poppy fields. Still, he arrived with enough time to have proceeded to the castle with his brothers as planned, but they had gone off without him, delighting in the calculation of their father's wealth divisible now by two. Thus their exasperation was palpable when they approached the castle to find that their younger brother was waiting at the gates for them, and the brothers' mouths were agape at the elegance of his entourage.

The first and the second pieces of linen offered to the king were indeed fine enough to fit through the eye of a needle. But the king, with barely a pretext of apology, said it was a different, *smaller*, needle that he had had in mind all along. A

particular one that he instructed his magistrate to produce. It was barely visible to those who looked upon it. The two brothers began grumbling in protest, but the youngest pronounced that his would surely go through the eye of that needle, and in so saying he took the walnut from the box in which he carried it and cracked it open.

The king chuckled, and then so did the brothers, for it was no piece of fine fabric in that walnut but a cherry stone. The prince cracked that open to reveal a grain of wheat, and in that a millet seed. By now the courtiers were laughing, too, but the prince ignored them all and split the tiny seed. Out popped a piece of linen a hundred hands long, so wonderful that all the birds, beasts, and fishes were painted on it, and every plant of the earth, and shells of the sea, and the sun, moon, stars, and planets of the heavens. The needle was brought forth, and the piece of linen was pushed through it easily. The king and the brothers fell into a dismal silence, the beauty and the rarity of the linen compelling them to finally say that no linen in the world could be compared to it.

The king, turning to his children, then said, "Nothing consoles me more in my old age than your deference to my wishes." (Remember, he is a liar, this king.) "I therefore will put you to a further proof. Go and travel for a year, and at the end of that time he who brings back the most accomplished companion will be crowned king on his wedding day."

Our prince did feel a pang of injustice, for the little dog and the piece of linen were deserving of laurels. But he did not oppose his father. Instead, without delay, he climbed into the carriage and sped off—this time directly for the castle of Féline.

When he arrived on the grounds, he found the road strewn with rose petals, and perfume burners smoked on all sides. All the cats climbed up to the gutters to welcome him with a chorus of mewing. He waved and thanked them, never letting on how dreadful he thought the sound.

"Well, king's son," Féline said when he entered the gallery, "you have again returned without a crown?"

"Madam," he replied, "your kindness has certainly given me the best chance of gaining it, but I am convinced that my father would have more trouble in giving it away than I should have pleasure in possessing it. So I will take no part in his latest challenge."

"But I will help you find an accomplished companion to take back to him," she said, adding before he could lodge the protest that was plain on his face, "so come and let us amuse ourselves. There is to be a naval battle between my bravest cats and the terrible rats of the country. Cats do fear the water, but their ships of cork are superior to those of the rats, so it should be an equal fight. Things in life ought be fair, after all." A statement that elicited simultaneous sighs in the both of them before they retreated together to the terrace that overlooked the sea.

Now and again over the course of the next year, the prince could not help asking Féline fresh questions about her enigmatic existence. But she always refused to answer, saying their time together was precious and should be spent in play. She was, in fact, exceptionally cheerful that year, her melancholy seemingly in hiding until the final days before he was to return to his father.

"There is something you must do for me," she said to him on the eve of his departure, after they had finished a game of chess.

"Anything," he said, for he did love her dearly.

She told him what she wanted him to do, her instructions as simple and calm as if she were asking him to return the chess board to its shelf: "You must cut off my head and my tail and throw them into the fire."

He jumped to his feet. "If you are testing me, please do not!"

"I am not testing you. I know your merit."

"But I cannot bear to hurt you."

"Then be swift," she said. "I am not afraid."

"I would miss you too much. I have never had such a friend."

"*Please*. It is neither you nor I who rule our fate in this matter."

"But I *love* you," he cried.

"Then that," she purred, "is why you must do it."

He continued to try to dissuade her, but she was obstinate in her replies, urging him so ardently that he finally drew his sword, and with shaking hands cut off Féline's head and tail and threw them onto the burning logs in the fireplace.

For a time, he could not see for the tears, could not hear for the screaming (his own, it was), until a gentle, calming hand touched his shoulder. He looked up to see a young woman he did not recognize. "King's son, you have broken the spell," she said, in a voice he *did* recognize: the white cat's.

WOMEN OF THE FAIRY TALE RESISTANCE

He became aware, then, of a parade of lords and ladies entering the room, all with cats' skins thrown over their shoulders. One by one, they bowed low to Féline, as joyful at seeing her again in her natural state as she was upon seeing each of them. Finally, she asked if they wouldn't mind leaving her and the prince alone for a time.

And she told him her story:

> My father ruled over three kingdoms. My mother loved him very much, but she also had a passion for travel and often planned trips without him, as he did not share her wanderlust. And so it was that, some months before I was born, she set out to visit a certain mountain of which she had heard the most wonderful accounts. On the way she was told that they were passing near an ancient fairy castle and that the garden was reputed to have the best and most delicately flavored fruits ever eaten.
>
> My mother was seized with a violent urge to taste them and directed her entourage to go to the castle. Once at the gates, she knocked in vain, her desire for the fruit increasing by the minute. She sent for ladders so they might get over the garden wall, but every time one of her attendants made it to the top, the wall shot up to a greater height. Ladders were then tied together, but still the wall rose. Many climbers fell from the precarious height, until it was clear that they would never get over that way.
>
> From a nearby hill she could see some of the trees inside the garden, loaded with fruits. She felt that she must taste them or die. She ordered tents to be pitched on the hill, and she and all the court remained there for weeks. She neither ate nor slept; she did nothing but think about the fruit in the inaccessible garden. She fell dangerously ill, and no one could cure her. All of her officers were greatly distressed.

Only weeping and sighs were heard while the dying queen repeatedly asked her attendants for fruits.

One night she became aware of a tiny woman seated on a stool by her bed. She introduced herself as the Fairy Viole and said, "My sisters and I do not appreciate Your Majesty so obstinately wishing to eat our fruits, but since your life is in danger, we have agreed to give you as many as you can carry away, and as many as you like while you remain here. Provided you make us a present."

Pulling together what strength she still had, my mother cried, "Anything! I will give you one of my family's three kingdoms, my heart, my soul!"

The fairy shook her head and said, "We desire the daughter shortly to be born to you. At her birth, we shall come fetch her away and bring her up among us. We shall endow her with all the virtues, with knowledge and beauty. In short, she will be our child and we shall make her happy. You will not see her again until she is married. If you like the proposal, I will cure you at once and open the orchards for you."

My mother closed her eyes and let out a long breath. "Although your conditions are very hard," she said, "I accept them rather than die, for it is certain I have not a day more to live. Cure me, wise fairy."

Viole touched her with a small gold wand, saying, "May Your Majesty be freed from the sufferings that keep you in this bed!"

It felt to her immediately as if she had taken off a very heavy gown. She popped out of bed and called her ladies-in-waiting, who were shocked to see her looking so well. They helped her dress and brought her to the gates, where the fairy was waiting with her two sisters, who were not quite as small as Viole and were identical to each other in appearance. My mother begged them to take her at once into the garden and show her the trees. The fairies reminded her of her promise before letting my mother choose the fruits she wished off the branches of the trees. She stayed in the garden for seven days and seven nights, and then she gathered so much to take with her that it filled the carts of hundreds of mules.

My father was delighted at my mother's return. There were balls, masquerades, and banquets at which the fairy fruits were served. He did not know the treaty my mother had made with the fairies, and he often asked her the name of the land from which she had brought such good things. She was vague on that point, and this puzzled him. So he questioned those who had accompanied her, but as they had been forbidden to tell of the adventure, they dared not speak of it.

As the time of my birth drew nearer, my mother became acutely anxious about her promise to the fairies. Soon she was pale and ill-seeming, and my father became distressed and urged her to tell him what was wrong. With great difficulty she told him what had passed between her and the fairies, and how she had promised their child to them.

This infuriated my father, who would not even try to understand the desperation she described. He overwhelmed her with a thousand reproaches, then shut her in her room and surrounded it with guards. He never went in to see her, and directly after I was born he had me brought to a wing of the palace where he could personally watch over me. My mother remained a most unhappy prisoner in her room.

The fairies knew everything that was going on, and they were angry at my father, not only over the broken promise but also over my mother's captivity. They began inflicting evils on his kingdoms, and then they let loose a fearsome dragon that poisoned water, burned forests, and devoured whole families.

My father fell into the depths of despair over the dire fortunes that had taken hold of his realm. He consulted all the wise men of his kingdoms, but they had no good advice. Then he sought out a fairy who had protected him when he was a child. She was very old and frail and scarcely ever left her bed. He asked her if she could resolve his family strife and smite the dragon that was terrorizing his subjects.

"You have annoyed my cousins," the old fairy whispered in a scratchy voice, "and the little princess belongs to them. You have imprisoned the queen, but what is her crime except the weakness of being born to the human race? Fulfill the promise she gave. That is the only hope that good shall come."

Seeing no other way, my father agreed to trust her. He would give me to the fairies since they had vowed to treat me well. And he would set my mother free. He needed only to be told how to deliver me to my new guardians.

The elderly fairy said, "In a week's time, you and the queen must carry her in her cradle to the mountain of flowers. You can remain near and see what will happen."

When he returned to the palace, he released the queen. She was so dejected and changed that he would hardly have recognized her if his heart had not assured him that it was the same woman he had so deeply loved. He entreated her to forget the troubles he had caused, assuring her that they would be the last she would experience from him. She replied that she had brought them on herself by her imprudence in promising their daughter to the fairies. My father then told her he intended to deliver me to their keeping. It was now my mother who objected. She wept and groaned without obtaining her desire, for my father was too well aware of the fatal consequences, and our subjects continued to die as if they had been guilty of the faults of our family.

I was put into a cradle ornamented with everything pretty that art could imagine. It was hung with festoons of flowers carved from precious stones, the colors dazzling so in the sun's rays that one had to look away from them. Twenty-four princesses of the blood carried me on a litter, and the whole court followed, each in his rank.

While we ascended the mountain, the sound of a symphony could be heard coming nearer, and at length there appeared the three fairies to whom my mother had promised me. Each was seated in a pearly shell that rested on the back of the dragon who had so recently wreaked mayhem but now was subdued and obedient, bridled with diamond reins that the Fairy Viole held in her grip. The other fairies held olive branches to signify that my father's submission found favor with them.

The fairies each in turn took me in their arms, kissed me, and bequeathed me with many precious qualities. When they placed my cradle between them on the dragon's back and the enormous beast unfolded his scaly wings, my mother began uttering loud, wretched cries. Taking pity, the fairies promised her that I would remember her face and know all she and my father had been through, as if I had witnessed all. And I am glad for that promise, for fate would have it that I was never to set eyes on my parents again.

My new guardians had built a tower for me on a hill overlooking the fairy castle and the orchard of my mother's ill fate. In the tower they'd constructed apartments for all the seasons of the year, each containing the greatest of comforts, splendid clothes, and art and literature. A high terrace garden, with a fountain and arbor, provided shade in even the hottest months. The fairies taught me everything that belonged to my age, and there was scarcely anything I did not understand with the greatest of ease. They arrived each day on the back of their dragon, who left them off at a window in the top of the tower. They could not come on foot, for the tower had no door.

The fairies were attentive and treated me lovingly, for the most part. Viole was strict. Not mean, but often suspicious, though she had no need to be. I behaved perfectly. And when by myself, I occupied my mind with all that can be found in books. I also had a parrot, one endowed with reason and speech, who kept me company. I enjoyed looking out the window, the views vast and ever changing under the sun and the moon. From my vantage point in the tower, I could see but one road, deep and full of ruts and trees. I had never witnessed anyone traveling it. Not until the day the knight appeared.

Except in pictures from my storybooks, I had never seen anyone like him. Having no idea that danger can attach to the satisfaction of contemplating a pleasant thing, I leaned out the window to look at him, and the longer I looked the more pleasure I felt. He made a low bow, and then tried to speak to me, but the distance between us was too great for his voice to travel intelligibly. That did not stop us from gazing upon each other, which we did until darkness began to fall and he parted.

In the morning, I was agreeably surprised to see the knight again at the foot of the tower. He held by his side what looked like a long trumpet, but it soon became clear that it was a speaking horn he had fashioned in order to communicate with me. He held it to his mouth and pointed it at the window, and I could then, just barely, hear his voice. He wondered aloud why I was up there, but he knew I could not answer, having no such device as his. He said that upon seeing me in the window of the strange tower he had been gripped by feelings he had never had in his life. He said that he would like to come every day to see me, at the same time, and if I agreed I should throw something down to him.

I could hear from the castle the rumblings of the dragon, who one or another of my fairy guardians would soon be mounting to come to the tower for a visit. And so I waved my arms frantically, signaling that the knight should go. But he didn't move, not until I took from a flower box on the ledge a handful of blossoms and dropped them out the window. Then, with a sweet, melodious *adieu*, he headed back to the neglected road and was out of sight before the dragon swooped over from the castle.

It was Viole who slid down the dragon's crepe wing and into the window that morning. The first words she said were, "I smell the voice of a man here."

I was paralyzed with fright lest she instruct the scaly beast to find the knight and turn him to ash. But I fought to keep fear from my face and said, "What a splendid joke, dear Viole. We all know voices don't have *smells*. The science books are clear on that." And I made myself laugh as if it had only been her intention to elicit my mirth.

She looked about the room with her untrusting eye, then shrugged and handed me the distaff she had brought with her. "Spin," she said. "You don't spin enough." And she shrugged again and summoned the dragon and climbed up onto its scaly back and was gone.

I was too distracted to spin, though, so I rested the distaff against the wall of the tower room and descended the few steps to the garden terrace. I had a spyglass there through which I often surveyed the countryside. I could see now, on a hill not far away, something I hadn't seen before: a pole tent with a table under it, and people milling about. Walking now in their direction, up a rise, was the knight. He had set up a camp to be near me, I came to realize, which both flattered me and filled me with alarm. He did not know of the dangers my powerful guardians posed, that their dragon could destroy him with a breath.

"Worry not," my parrot said to me. "I will go and warn him away." And she lifted off her garden perch and flapped her wings hard until, as I watched through my spyglass, she landed on the shoulder of the knight.

She remained there long, the two of them engaged in conversation until finally he pulled something from his pocket and tied it round her leg. When she returned to the terrace, I saw that it was a little portrait of him, a miniature. She said he had asked her a dozen questions about me, and that he now well knew the treachery he would face if caught. But no matter her warnings, he was determined to risk everything rather than give up the pleasure of seeing me.

He came each morning, early, before the fairies made their first visit of the day. He spoke through his horn, and my parrot facilitated my end of the conversation. After a fortnight we had become so comfortable with one another that it was as if our hearts beat as one. I lived each day to talk to him, distracted and nervous during all the hours in between.

The fairies had taken notice of my change in spirit and decided among themselves that it was time for them to arrange my marriage. "I pity you," my parrot said after she told me what she had overheard, that I was, in nine days, to marry a famous fairy king. She dipped her head to show her unhappiness at the choice.

"You have seen him?" I asked.

"I once shared a branch with him," my parrot said. "For, yes, he has claws for feet! He is a chimera. A bird, ruminant, and fairy all a one. And he has a temperament that matches his ugliness."

I looked into the portrait of my knight, which I had been wearing on my wrist but hidden under my sleeve. And I wept.

The next morning when he came, I told him of my fate, how I was resigned to it, the powers too much to fight against. But he insisted that he would not live without me, and implored me to find means to get out of the tower, or for him to enter it. I did not think it possible, but I so wanted him away from the tower and safe, that I promised I would find a way if he promised not to return until my parrot called for him. He went away hopeful.

I wracked my brain, but I had come up with nothing by the time I was paid a fairy visit. Thankfully it was not Viole but her sisters, who beamed and said as one, "How exciting it will be for your mother and father to come to the wedding!"

I hadn't yet thought of that, how my parents would finally get to see me after all these years, but only to witness my marriage to a hideous beast. At the idea of it, I broke into loud sobs.

Flummoxed, they tried to calm me, but to no avail. They reached for the distaff on the floor and held it out to me. "Spinning relaxes."

I almost swatted the thing, but then an idea began to form. It was no foolproof plan, but it was *something*, and that was better than nothing, even if it required lying on my part, something I had never done in my life. "Instead of spinning, I would like to make nets with which to catch the birds who are ever pecking the berries in my garden. May I have some twine?"

"We will bring you a mountain of twine!" they cried, stroking my hair. "If it will make you happy."

"That is my fervent hope," I said, that part no lie.

It was a rope ladder I was making, and I worked night and day, hiding it when the fairies came and asking for more and more twine, as it would have to be such a long ladder to deliver me from the window to the ground below. The two fairy sisters were not of a suspicious nature, but they questioned all the same why I needed such a great amount of twine for a few nets. "I want them to be perfect," I explained, "and so I destroy any that are not exactly right."

I did not finish my ladder until the morning of the final day before I was to wed the chimeric king. The ceremony was scheduled for the deepest night, the hour before dawn, as that is when fairy weddings take place. That gave me enough time to get a message to my knight by parrot. But it was a very confusing day, with so many interruptions by the fairies, who were constantly primping me or changing their minds over some detail or another. And I had had so little sleep. This is all to say that there is probably a logical reason for what went wrong. I do not blame my parrot or my knight. I used to blame myself, but with all the time I have had to think, these eons since that fateful day, I know I did the best I could. Maybe I did not give the right instruction to the parrot, the *complete* instruction: that my knight was to wear black clothing and arrive just after dark but before the moon rose, and wait for me to climb down. He did wear black, and he did arrive just after dark and before the moon rose, but for whatever reason, when he saw the ladder I had dropped from my high window, he climbed it instead of waiting for my descent.

I realized the tragic error as soon as I set out to make my escape. I had been delayed due to an earlier argument the fairies had had over the fit of my crown, and so it wasn't until they left that I could make the switch out of my wedding dress and into clothes suitable for the long climb. When I slipped my bare foot onto the first rung of the ladder, I could tell I wasn't alone on it. And I could see it was my knight when the sky lit up from the fiery chariot that was headed to the castle, my betrothed's arrival. Then came the rustling of the dragon's wings unfolding. It was time for the fairy trio to retrieve the bride. My knight climbed over the ledge and into the tower room with just minutes for us to embrace. For the first time. For the last time.

Fairy Viole was so angry to see the knight in my arms that she pried us apart herself and ordered the dragon to devour him. I tried to throw myself after him, wishing to be taken too with the one I loved best in the world. But the fairy sisters held me back, and Viole spat, "We must reserve you for longer torment." She touched me with her small gold wand, and I at once became a white cat.

They brought me to this palace, one that belonged to my father but that they appropriated as punishment to him for his daughter's sins. They changed the lords and ladies into cats, too, and left the attendants with nothing but hands. Then they decreed that I could only be delivered from my fate by the love of a man who should exactly resemble the knight they had torn from me, and that he must perform the prescribed act of cruelty as means to my release. All quite impossible, they were certain, and thus the sentence they intended: that I would remain for all eternity a lonely beast, banished from humankind.

She looked down at her wrist now, at the delicate miniature there. "You," she said to the prince, "not only possess the same features, same expression, same tone of voice, but your love for me is equally pure and your trust in me equally strong. My troubles are at an end."

"And so mine," he said, throwing himself at her feet. Her human feet.

Her attendants in the meanwhile had prepared a coach to take them to his father's kingdom. With the fairy magic at an end, there were no tricks to get them there more swiftly than horse hooves allowed, thus no time to waste. The smallest of their coaches had been hooked to a retinue of the fastest steeds, and with the wind at their backs the entire way, the couple arrived at the king's road just as the prince's brothers turned their own carriages in the direction of the castle. The brothers rode in elegant barouches of azure, and their horses wore feathers on their heads. Beside them on satin bench seats were women of great physical beauty. Through their open windows, the brothers snubbed their noses at the simple carriage their brother steered, and asked in an amused way how his year had gone. The curtain was drawn and they could not see who accompanied him.

"It went wonderfully!" the prince cried, speeding by them.

The courtiers hastened to announce that the three princes had arrived. The king looked down from his throne as his sons approached with their prizes from the year-long quest. The king had initially intended to make good on his third promise, but in the end he'd decided to weasel out again. He had had his court historian design a contest of knowledge so difficult that no one would be able to succeed, and *especially* no woman, sans education in the academies. It was made up of questions dug from the oldest texts that could be found in the farthest reaches of the shelves of the royal library, and the subjects were so obscure that they would likely not even be known to the greatest scholars. Indeed, one would have to have lived long ago and spent most of their time reading books in order to answer even one of the questions posed. There were ten in all.

"How fine and elegant you all look!" the king said in greeting, though his eyes lingered for a moment on the woman his youngest son had escorted up the aisle. Her dress, while not shabby, was, well, antique. "We have a little quiz for our guests to enable me to choose the one of you who is most accomplished. Whoever can answer the questions correctly will be named queen to rule beside one of my sons."

The two older brothers began to protest loudly, for they had not chosen their companions for their learnedness but for their bearing and beauty. The king ordered the trumpeter to drown out their complaints, though, and the contest began. Not surprisingly, the only one of the three who knew the answers, *all ten*, was the one who had, in fact, lived long ago and spent most of her time reading books:

Féline. The king was the one protesting now, stumbling over his words, trying to find the magic ones that would justify his keeping his lands and his crown.

"Father," the prince interrupted, "we have not come to take from you a throne. My friend, Féline, has a fine castle where we will live."

"Three, in fact," she said. "My inheritance. So keep yours, sire. And allow me to give one to each of your sons."

The king was speechless for some moments. Then he uttered two words that tasted strange in his mouth, for they were heartfelt: "Thank you." And the older brothers, remembering again the fondness they had felt before their father's trials, were gracious from that day forward. Indeed, the entire family lived happily ever after.

WOMEN OF THE FAIRY TALE RESISTANCE

BELLE-BELLE

ONCE UPON A time there was a king who wished only for peace. His kingdom had been forever at war. Or so it seemed to him, his father having clashed for many years with a violent emperor whose penchant for combat had grown only more ferocious upon the young king's rise to the throne. So much so that, at the point where this tale begins, the emperor had laid siege to the capital city itself. In the bloody battle, the king scarcely survived, pulled away against his will by the queen dowager, who had ordered her own guards to steal him off with her to safety.

The queen dowager was his sister. She was not aged or a widow, the usual preconditions for the title; she just liked it and called it her own. Not that there was any real authority granted a queen dowager (or any female heir, so long as there was a male heir to be in charge), but she was resigned to this power imbalance, even if she was quite sure that she would have made a better ruler than he. She had nerves of steel, and in the opinion of many a heart to match, while the king was a highly sensitive man, prone to bouts of sorrow. This was why she had taken it upon herself to get him out of the besieged capital before he witnessed what was surely next to come. The army of the empire had, in waves, killed almost all of the king's soldiers, then carted away the gold and jewels, then driven the livestock through the southern gates. It was only a matter of time before their pillaging reached into the narrow lanes, the homes, the attics where parents clung to their children. *Oh no*, she thought, *the king should not witness that, should not hear the screaming.* He would have fought to his death. And that she couldn't abide. Hard heart or not, she loved her brother dearly.

The king didn't resent his sister for saving him. It was not in his nature to be resentful. And his mind was far too busy, in any case, with its dark imaginings of his kingdom's suffering. He was plagued by guilt and would have locked himself away and taken no food, but he knew his people looked to him for strength, and so he held steady until he and his sister were able to return to the capital, abandoned

now by the emperor, ransacked and silent. No cannon fire, no heaving grunts or swishes of spears, no pounding boots on the cobbles. No bickering and bartering at market stalls, no clicking of stick puppets, no children's laughter. He assembled what soldiers he could from among the crestfallen, but the resultant force was far too meager and weak to march on the emperor's citadel, which the king knew he must do. And so he published a decree throughout the kingdom that every man of title must serve in his army or send a son in his stead, or else be subject to a heavy tax or imprisonment.

In the far eastern reach of the countryside, near the sea, lived an old, infirm nobleman. He had once been a man of court and had possessed considerable wealth, but he'd long ago been reduced to a living that bordered on poverty. He had three daughters, who endured it with him patiently. If by chance they even spoke of their misfortune to their father, it was to console him rather than to add to his troubles. They were living a quiet life under their rustic roof when the king's edict reached the ears of the old man. He called his daughters and said, "What are we to do? The king commands my service or that of a son in the battle against the emperor, and I cannot provide either. What can come of this but ruin?" His three daughters entreated their father to take heart, because they felt sure they would be able to find a remedy.

The next morning the eldest sought her father, who was walking dejectedly in his orchard. "Sir," she said, "I come to beg you to let me join the army. I am of tall stature and fairly strong. I will outfit myself as a man and pass for your son."

The nobleman was opposed to the plan, but she firmly pressed the case until he consented. It was then merely a matter of providing her with a costume from his own closet that would be suitable for the part she was to play. He also gave her the best of the horses that served the farm.

After traveling for several days, she passed through a meadow bordered by hedges. She saw a shepherdess in trouble, trying to get one of her sheep out of a ditch into which it had fallen.

"Alas!" cried the shepherdess. "I'm trying to save my sheep from drowning, but I have not strength enough to pull it out."

"I do pity you," the oldest daughter said. But she was determined to stay true to her mission and not get waylaid, so she went off without helping her.

The shepherdess at once called out, "Fare thee well, girl!"

The oldest daughter, surprised, thought, *She scarcely saw me for a moment and she knows I am disguised. I shall be recognized by everyone! And if the king finds me out, he shall think my father a coward who tries to avoid danger.* Upon this reflection, she thought it best to return home.

Her sisters and her father had been fretting since her departure and so were relieved to see her enter the house. She told them of her failing, and the second daughter said, "Father, I might have a better chance of success, as I am tougher in spirit than my elder sister. Let me go and you shall not regret it."

Nothing the old man could say in opposition was of the least avail. He therefore consented to her departure. To ensure she wouldn't suffer the same fate as her sister, she wore a different costume and rode a different horse.

Passing by the same meadow as did her sister, she too saw a sheep at the bottom of a ditch and the shepherdess occupied in pulling it out.

"Unfortunate that I am!" the shepherdess exclaimed. "Half of my flock has perished in this manner. If someone would help me I could save this poor animal, but everyone avoids me."

"It is not a wonder," the second daughter said. "You take such little care of your sheep, letting them fall into the water." And without offering further consolation she put spurs to her horse.

The shepherdess shouted with all her might, "Fare thee well, girl!"

The second daughter stopped the horse in its tracks and thought, *How unlucky! I, too, am recognized. It would be ridiculous for me to join the army with so feminine an appearance that everybody would know me to be a woman.* She at once returned home.

Again, the family had been fretting and were relieved at the sister's return. They listened to her story until, quite suddenly, the father pushed himself from his chair and proclaimed, "Let's not speak of all this again! I do not fear my fate. And now if you'll excuse me, I spotted a case of apple rust in the orchard and I must spend the remains of the day inspecting my trees." And with an odd cheeriness that did little to convince his daughters of his claim regarding his fear, or the existence of apple rust for that matter, he tottered to the door and was gone.

He was trying to avoid the inevitable: his youngest daughter's entreaty to be sent on the quest. He was especially attached to Belle-Belle (for that was what she was called) because she took care of him so well. She read him interesting stories, attended him when he was ill, and always provided meat for him to keep up his strength.

"You know, Father, the skills I have developed in the hunt will be useful in war," she said now, easily catching up with him on the path.

He sighed.

"And my great desire to lessen your troubles will endow me with courage, so I am not afraid."

He sighed again. "Please don't leave me, dear. Even if fortune favored you and you returned covered with laurels, I should not have the pleasure of seeing your triumph, for the lack of your presence would end my days."

It was her turn to sigh now. "*Really*, Father, my sisters are quite capable of attending to your needs. And perhaps I shall not be gone long. The war cannot go on forever."

He could not sway her, try as he might, and so she departed the next morning with her family's blessing. She strode off on the most wretched horse and in the poorest of suits, as that was all that was left for her.

At the same meadow where her sisters had turned around, she found the same woman, who was again trying to pull a sheep out of the ditch.

"What are you doing, shepherdess?" Belle-Belle asked, in a deeper register than she normally used. She had practiced sounding like a man in the days she had been traveling.

"Since dawn I've been busy with this sheep," replied the shepherdess. "Every day some new misfortune happens to me, and no one comes to my assistance."

Belle-Belle dismounted, leapt over the hedge (in a deliberately unladylike manner), and with great effort heaved the sheep out of the ditch.

The shepherdess, elated, said to her, "You are the truest of your sisters! Your kindness has been shown to someone who will not be ungrateful."

"Oh, *no*," Belle-Belle muttered, not bothering this time to disguise her voice, "I *too* am recognized."

"Worry not about that," the shepherdess said. "I know all about you, where you wish to go, and what you wish to do. If it is your desire to pass as a man, I will help you." And the fairy (for that was what she was, no shepherdess) touched the ground with her shepherd's crook, and Belle-Belle's ragtag steed changed in front of her into a muscular stallion.

"Yours was too scrawny," the fairy said, then tapped its back, where there appeared a cloth of green velvet and a saddle of the finest leather. She tapped the horse's neck and a polished bridle materialized.

Belle-Belle, delighted but not entirely surprised, as it was a time when fairies were not so unusual, cried, "Thank you!" Then, realizing she had used her regular voice, she lowered it and said, "He is stunning."

"He is far more than just pretty to look at. His name is Comrade, and he's long been in our service. You'd be wise to follow where he leads. He knows what's needed."

Belle-Belle peered into the stallion's eyes. *Yes,* she thought, *you've got some intelligence in there. Perhaps not that of a human, but*—She was interrupted by a sloppy sneeze from the horse and wiped her face with her sleeve.

"Do be careful what you think, dear," the fairy said, turning her full attention to Belle-Belle now, to the simple tunic and riding pants that did little to hide her shape, to her hair unconvincingly tucked under a tattered cap. "We can do better than this," she said, striking the ground again with her crook. A rift opened in the grass near their feet, and out popped a trunk with a gold key protruding from its lock. The fairy turned it and lifted the lid, and inside was a full set of clothes in the most tasteful style. "The right garments do make the man! Whenever you wish a new wardrobe, stamp your foot and the trunk will appear."

"Quite nice," Belle-Belle agreed, but she couldn't help but wonder how this new outfit would be any more effective at concealing her identity than the one she currently wore. And her identity was, of course, her overriding concern, her fear that she might be discovered to be a woman. She had to admit, though, that the quality of the clothing was alluring, and the homespun she wore felt suddenly very scratchy. She reached into the trunk and ran her hand over the fine linen of the breeches, the supple chamois of the belt. A tingle went up her arm and through her body. Not like the tapping of a nerve, not a shock, she thought. The word "beauty" popped into her head.

The fairy, who had begun waving her crook in the air like a wand, said to Belle-Belle, "You can dress now. You're liminal."

"Liminal?"

"Neither here nor there," the fairy said, "not one nor the other."

Belle-Belle squeezed her own arm and looked around the meadow. She was very much there, she thought. She gave the fairy a quizzical look, which was returned with a gaze that seemed to go right through her.

"You're not *visible*," the fairy clarified, "even to *moi*."

"Ah, I get it," Belle-Belle said. Still, she looked toward the road and was glad to see no travelers happening by. Just a wood rat peeking out of the dirt, a falcon on a wind current high above, a few sparrows hopping from branch to branch in a linden tree, and the stallion nibbling buttercups in its shade. "What about Comrade?" Belle-Belle asked. "Can he see me?"

"Hm," the fairy said. "I can't recall if the enchantment applies to animals."

The horse snorted and turned away, his raised and swishing tail pointed at Belle-Belle now.

So she leaned against the tree trunk and pulled off her boots and woolen socks, then let her tunic drop, and soon enough she was plucking the clothes from the trunk, and with each piece she donned (*Oh, how fine the fabric, how soft against the skin*) she felt a strange reflex, a squaring of her shoulders when she buttoned the shirt, a heightening of her stance when she pulled on the jacket. Her thighs seemed more solid when she slid the breeches up, her neck thicker when she tied the cravat. By the time she'd buckled the scabbard round her waist, something inside had altered. It was palpable, this something.

"Have you quite finished changing?" the fairy asked.

"I have," Belle-Belle said. And if she hadn't been so at peace (*Yes, that is what the something was, peace*) she might have startled. For her voice, without any affectation on her part, was of a decidedly masculine register.

The fairy waved her crook again in a wide circle, then looked Belle-Belle up and down. "How well you fit the part of chevalier! Now all you need is a name. What do you think of Fortuné?"

Fortuné (for so we shall call her now) replied, "I accept that," and he (for we shall use masculine pronouns now) thanked the fairy sincerely before mounting the stallion and taking to the capital road.

By midday they had entered a forest, where Comrade immediately took a sharp turn off the path. Fortuné pulled at the reins, trying to get him back on course. But then he recalled the fairy's counsel: *Follow where the stallion leads.* It was soon apparent that he was leading to a vast clearing, in the middle of which sat

a woodcutter. He was surrounded by fallen trees, perhaps hundreds of them, cut into logs.

"Sir," Fortuné said, "where are all the people who helped you fell these trees?"

"I did it myself," the woodcutter replied. "And I intend to carry it all out of here myself."

"But how?" Fortuné asked, for there was not even a mule anywhere in sight.

"On my back."

"How many trips does that take?"

"One! That is why they call me Strong-Back."

"That's quite a gift!" Fortuné said, as Comrade gave him a nod and a side-eye. "Do you make a good living at it?"

The woodcutter guffawed. "We are all poor in this part of the country."

So Fortuné offered him a share of his future earnings as a soldier if he would leave off his work and come with him. Strong-Back agreed, knowing he could not do better selling his wood.

When they passed out of the forest, they came to a great open grassland. Comrade now steered them to a man who sat on a ledge of granite. He was tying his legs together with ribbons, leaving so little space between them that it appeared impossible for him to walk.

Fortuné said to him, "Why are you doing that?"

"I am preparing for a hunt. My natural pace is so swift that when I chase a stag or hare I outstrip it too quickly and cannot make my catch."

"That is remarkable," Fortuné said. "What is your name?"

"Fleet-Foot."

And soon, happy with the same deal offered him, he joined the travelers as well.

Comrade stopped next at the edge of a marsh and tipped his head in the direction of a man who was sitting on a rock. The man had a bow at his side and was putting a scarf over his eyes.

"What are you doing?" Fortuné asked him.

"I see too clearly," he said. "My sight is such that I can make out the fluttering of a wing four leagues off. It is troublesome to shoot game that is that far away, because retrieving it is most onerous. So I dim my vision in order to see only the birds that are closer to me. It is more practical that way."

Fortuné made his offer to the man, who refused several times before agreeing to go. In the course of the negotiations, he managed to improve the deals for the other hirelings as well, so Good-Shot, as he was aptly named, was welcomed warmly by his mates.

They arrived at the gates of the capital city just before sunset. When Fortuné introduced himself and his company as new recruits for the king's army, they were led by a guard to the palace, its fire-blackened turrets casting long shadows over the city. The entourage wound through narrow streets that were eerily quiet though teeming with people, most hunched under makeshift roofs or crowded into hovels created from the ruins of buildings that had been hollowed out by cannonballs.

"It is worse in other places," the guard said as they moved haltingly to avoid ruts and debris. "The emperor's forces are still in many towns, and so the people escape and come here or else are enslaved."

"I see for myself why the king needs an army," Fortuné said, the gazes of the masses seeming to follow him. He was surprised to see a spark in their eyes. *Is that hope I see?* But then he cast the thought away. *I am imagining that.*

Comrade neighed loudly, shaking his head, and turned a final corner and onto the palace grounds.

The day's new soldiers were assembled in a courtyard, and the king and the queen dowager were on the landing at the top of a stone stairway, finishing their blessing of the troops. Fortuné tried to remain respectfully in the rear, but Comrade ignored his tugs on the reins and took them to a position in the front, which immediately caught the attention of the royal siblings. After they had uttered their amens and sent all the soldiers off to the barracks, the queen dowager called down to Fortuné, "But not *you!*" and descended the stairs.

Fortuné cursed his horse (in a deliberately ungentlemanly way) and braced for the worst. But when the queen dowager stood before him, she merely smiled and asked who he was.

He dismounted, made a bow, and then told her of his father, his years of loyalty and service to the crown, his modest circumstances, his ailing health. "I have come to represent him in the fighting force, Your Majesty," he said in conclusion.

"I remember that nobleman from when I was very young." It was not the queen dowager who offered this but the king, who stood now beside her. He shared his sister's features and could almost have passed for her if not dressed as he

was, which was kingly, but not in an ostentatious way. In truth, he made it a point to dress plainly in deference to the humble people he ruled. "My father respected him. Took his counsel."

"Don't you think, brother, given his gallantry in filial duty, that we should reward this chevalier?" the queen dowager asked, stepping close to Fortuné and touching a finely manicured hand to his cheek. This made him fearful of being found out in this first true test, and he trembled at her closeness. "Rather than let this lovely face be scarred by war," she went on, "let's keep him in the service of the capital. I hear the office of the knights' esquire has just become vacant."

The king let out a pained breath, for news of the esquire's ill fate had arrived just that morning. A sniper, it had been, while he was on a reconnaissance mission. "If you wish it," the king said to his sister, and he approached Fortuné and asked if he would be agreeable to the position.

Fortuné again trembled, but it was not fear that gripped him now. If the queen dowager hadn't seen through his guise at such close inspection, then he felt confident no one would. It was something else that made him tremble, something he could not yet identify. "Sire," he said, "I am at your pleasure."

The king nodded in thanks, then looked at Comrade. "Your stallion is the finest I've ever seen. I should worry about him in our stables if I were you. I admit to turning a blind eye to the disappearance of a horse here and again. There is such scarcity of food, such hunger in the city."

At this, Comrade tossed his head and pushed forward with his nose the three men who had hitherto been listening to the proceedings from behind him.

"Who are *they*?" the queen dowager asked, a grimace on her face as she surveyed the rough-looking, unusual trio.

"Gifted men, Your Majesty," Fortuné answered.

"*Gifted?* At *what*?" she asked.

Good-Shot piped up. "I can shoot game all day from atop the city's walls."

Fleet-Foot added, "And I can run all day to retrieve it."

"All day, you say?" the king asked.

"And night," said Good-Shot.

"I'd suggest taking on extra kitchen help," Fleet-Foot said.

"My, my," the queen dowager chirped, "is that a *smile* I see on my king's face? It appears that our good Fortuné has pulled him from his latest malaise."

The king's mien had indeed lightened at the prospect of increased provisions for his people and the growing fighting force.

"And what can *you* do?" the queen dowager now asked Strong-Back.

In answer, the burly man hoisted Comrade on his back.

"You may take charge of the livery stable, then," the king said, and he actually *chuckled* as he pointed in its direction and watched Strong-Back bounding off with the stallion still on his back, as sprightly as if he were carrying nothing at all.

Over the weeks that followed, they all acquitted themselves admirably in their positions. Fortuné discovered that the trunk now provided clothing and gear for all of them, so his gifted friends began wearing enchanted attire, too. It did not transform them, or at least not in the way it transformed Fortuné, but the garments infused in them a sense of comfort. They had never been to a city, not even once before in their lives, and so they would have been uneasy with the wind rattling gutters instead of whistling through tree branches, with walls surrounding them instead of horizons, with grief-stricken sobs in the night instead of the chirping of crickets. The fairy's magic saved them from such troubles, and thus they were as carefree as they had been in their bucolic existence.

Fortuné, on the other hand, *was* struggling. It wasn't that he minded the city so much. And it wasn't his duties that vexed him; the king was profusely appreciative of the work of his new esquire. No, Fortuné's struggles were with his heart, for the more time he spent in the capital, the greater was his yearning for the king. (Yes, that is what *that* something was: *yearning*.) Fortuné had from the start of his tenure been struck by the king's empathetic nature, and it distressed Fortuné to see the king slip into such a low frame of mind whenever the news of the day was fraught, as it so often was, or when there was no news at all of the state of the imprisoned, the missing. The children. Fortuné had begun lingering about the palace after meetings of the knights, and the king seemed to appreciate this, and began asking him to stay and talk or sit quietly with him. And so a bond had developed between the two.

What a fate! Fortuné thought one morning while out on an early walk in the palace gardens. *I am falling for someone who cannot return my feelings, who cannot even guess that I suffer.* He sat on a bench under a camellia that pushed out the most glorious pink flowers amid leaves still curled from the smoke of the emperor's siege. One

of the blooms, too heavy to remain on a thin branch, dropped onto the bench next to him.

Behind the glass of a window above, the queen dowager was troubled as well. She had become quite obsessed with a longing for Fortuné. Especially so since the other young ladies of the court were also drawn to his charm. He was inundated daily with love letters and gifts from them, to which he showed only indifference. She had concluded, especially given his increasing melancholy, that he had a true love back home.

But he can be cured of that, she thought as she looked down at him, at the way he picked up that soft blossom, cupped it in his hand. And she made a decision right then and there: Fortuné would be her husband. Never mind that his social status would not allow him to marry a queen dowager. She would give up the title for him! They could move to a lovely duchy together, live as duke and duchess. What good was her presence in the capital, anyway? It was true that she had a great many good ideas, some that she was sure would even stop the war, but who would listen to them? Ideas without power meant nothing. And the city had become so dreary since the siege, so depressing. Yes, *this* was the solution. Fortuné would not be able to resist such an improvement in his standing and wealth. And so, with a lightness of spirit she hadn't felt for some time, she hurried down a side stair to avoid her lady-in-waiting and emerged into the garden just as the object of her desire was rising to leave.

She feigned surprise at seeing him. "Well, isn't it nice to happen upon my brother's esquire. Please, accompany me on a stroll through the gardens."

"The king will expect me," Fortuné said, though this was not entirely true. Yes, he was expected, but not just yet, for the king had gone south on a predawn scouting expedition to the borderland and had not yet returned.

"The king will *expect* you to not let his sister walk alone in the gardens. You never know where treachery lurks."

And so he agreed, as he knew he must, taking her offered arm and following her lead, which took them onto a path that soon was not a path at all but a stand of old-growth trees. She rested her back against the smooth bark of one and said, "I was awakened this morning by the birds' delightful singing. How happy they are to fly off wherever they wish to go! Alas, they know only pleasure. Melancholy does not trouble their lives."

"With all due respect, Your Majesty," Fortuné replied, "birds are not entirely free from care and anxiety. They have always to fear the fatal shots of the hunter."

"Ah, the hunter, yes," she said, nodding, her cheeks flushed with desire at being so near Fortuné.

"And when winter covers the ground with snow, birds die for want of seed," he added, in a nervous voice, for she was gripping his arms with her hands.

"But in the spring," she said, "the earth is yielding. What could possibly challenge their happiness then?"

"They must find a new mate each spring," Fortuné said.

"You think that a problem? Why, there are men who delight in doing so a dozen times a year," she said. "You seem surprised! Your heart is then made of different stuff?"

"I do not know, for I have never had a lover."

"*You* have never *loved*? How can you say such a thing to a woman who reads in your eyes and on your countenance the passion that occupies your soul?"

"My words are true."

This seemed only to increase her hunger and delight. She pulled him against her, her eyes now closed, her lips quivering until the moment they met Fortuné's.

He would not push her away. She was the queen dowager, and he deemed it best to comply, to endure this indignity. In the future, he would just do a better job of avoiding her. This was what was going through his mind as she was kissing him. And of course, because a kiss takes two, it was not long before she realized his disinterest and pushed *him* away.

"You *heartless* creature," she spat, her face reddened now from bruised pride rather than desire. "You don't know what you have missed."

It was then that they both heard the royal trumpet announcing the king's return. "I am needed in service," Fortuné said. "We must go."

But she stayed rooted for some time, ignoring him, seeming to study with the toe of her shoe the dappled light that reached the forest floor. Then she pushed herself from the tree trunk and said, "I could tell my brother how you didn't behave on our private little walk. How you showed no *respect*." She walked ahead of him between the towering trees. "I *could*, you know."

They crossed paths with the royal scouting party as soon as they emerged from the wood. The king steered his horse their way, saying, "Well, look who are out on this fine morn."

"Yes, brother," the queen dowager said, "we've been for a walk. I've news."

"Me, too," he said. "We've discovered something this morning. The emperor's hubris is such that he has taken to keeping the gates of the citadel wide open. That doesn't mean we can send cavalry, of course. His mercenaries would spot our troops approaching and have them mowed down before they got anywhere near. But a spy mission might succeed." He looked down at his sister, who was scowling. "Are you all right?"

"No," she said. "I must inform you that it was not my idea to walk in the wood this morning. The esquire you place so much trust in asked me to go. He told me he had a desperate yearning that burned inside him."

Fortuné braced for the worst, but the queen dowager stopped there. She seemed to be working something out all of a sudden.

"Brother," she said finally, "did you just say that anyone can walk into the citadel?"

"Apparently," the king responded.

She nodded slowly, and then an *Ah-hah! Even better!* expression came over her face. She cleared her throat and adopted a concerned tone. "In the wood, Fortuné confided in me that he wants, more than anything in the world, to recover all the treasures of our kingdom: the jewels, the furniture, the sculptures, the paintings, the tapestries, and the precious metals."

"And the children?" the king added.

"Yes, yes, the children," she said.

"And our imprisoned soldiers?"

She nodded impatiently and continued. "Fortuné begged me to ask you to allow him, *without* an army, to go to the emperor and demand the return of it all, forthwith. He boasts of a plan he has been designing, and since he is so wonderfully clever and wields arms with so much dexterity, I was not altogether surprised at his proposal. He does put that much confidence in himself."

"Surely my esquire was meaning to amuse," the king said, adding with a smirk, "or else he has gone mad."

"No, brother," she said. "He was as serious as a man can be. He is by nature earnest, as you well know by now. Why do you hesitate to allow him to bring such honor to our kingdom?"

"Because I fear he would lose his life," the king said. He was not smirking any longer. His demeanor was one of decided consternation.

"I'm afraid," the queen dowager said, with a forced sigh of resignation, "that his life may be lost either way. For he assured me, on bended knee, that if you oppose his zeal and refuse him permission, he will languish and die."

"Is this true?" the king asked Fortuné.

Fortuné looked at the queen dowager. He could not have predicted her capacity for deceit. But he also could not accuse a crowned head of lying. "It is true that I would find honor in such a quest and that I would willingly lay down my life for the kingdom."

"What do you need by way of provision?" the queen dowager asked, not meeting his eyes.

"Just my men and mounts," Fortuné said. "I will leave this day."

The king peeled off his gloves and set them on the saddle in front of him. "I consent, then, but with immense regret." He extended a hand to his esquire.

It took a moment, but Fortuné realized he was meant to kiss the king's hand, and so he stepped forward and took it into his own and held it to his lips. When he let go, he dared not look up, for his eyes were brimming with tears. Had he, he would have seen the same in the king's eyes. He didn't see, either, the queen dowager's face, contorted now with heartsickness and rage upon witnessing the passion in Fortuné's kiss, a passion she had been denied. She turned and left before anyone could see her own eyes brimming.

When Fortuné got to the stables, he leaned against Comrade's stall. *I am done,* he thought.

The horse neighed, shaking his head.

"The emperor shall have a rope around my neck as soon as I ask for the king's treasure."

The stallion nuzzled him as if to say, *We will go with you, your helpers and I. And if we perish, we shall perish together.*

The trunk provided all the accoutrements that Fortuné and his companions needed for the journey. As for their mounts, Strong-Back chose the most excellent ones from the livery for himself and Good-Shot and Fleet-Foot, horses that were made even more remarkable by having gifted riders. And so they all seemed to be flying as they traveled to the citadel.

As the king had said, the gates were open, so they trotted right in. Their first impression was that the city was massive. Their second was that it was anything but splendid. Spilling from every door and window were downcast people with mean looks and crazed manners. Fights broke out on every corner. This was not what they had expected of a wealthy metropolis. Fortuné was surprised, too, at how easy it was to be granted an audience with the emperor. He merely told a guardsman that he had a message from the king, and a few hours later he was asked to disarm and dismount, and he was shown into the palace. Alone.

The throne room was cavernous, and it had a powerful stench that came from the myriad incense lamps that protruded from the stone walls. The ceiling dripped, though there was no rain outside. The dais was equally bleak, with thrones that looked as if they were made from driftwood planks and tarnished metal scraps that had been dropped into piles from above. There were three, and they were occupied by the emperor, the empress, and their daughter, a teenage girl who seemed to be the only one of them with concern for her outward appearance. While her parents wore long, lumpy robes that made them look more like boulders than people, the daughter looked as though she had been chiseled from stone by a sculptor for the gods. The three were engaged in conversation, but they broke off as Fortuné neared, and upon the emperor's orders that his family vacate the room the empress took her leave. The daughter also got up to go, but spying their visitor, she stopped and looked him up and down, then said, "Perhaps you shall want my counsel for this one, Father."

"I don't expect so," he said. "Run along."

But she sat back in her throne and crossed her arms.

The emperor coughed, as if clearing away the insolence, and said to Fortuné, "What do you want?"

"Your Highness," Fortuné said, taking off his hat and sweeping it forward as he bowed (something he'd practiced during his wait). "I have been sent on an official errand by your neighbor the king."

"I know, I've been told that. I'm busy. Get to it."

Fortuné let out a long breath, then stood straight and looked him directly in the eye. "I am here to ask you to return to me all that you took from our kingdom."

The courtiers erupted in cackles and sniggers but promptly fell silent at the emperor's glare. Then he said to Fortuné, "If you were at the head of five hundred thousand men, I might listen. But I hear there are four of you."

"I have not undertaken to use force, sire, to restore my king's property but merely my humble remonstrances."

"Whatever that means, you won't get what you want. Go away."

Fortuné bowed again and prepared to leave. He was alive, he thought, and that was more than he had expected to be. He would go back to the kingdom and admit failure. The king wouldn't mind. But then Fortuné thought about the queen dowager. She would just come up with some other way to torment him. If he could manage to get *some* of their wealth back, maybe she would forget her vendetta.

The emperor looked down at him. "Why aren't you gone yet?"

"Sire, I am wondering whether there is some kind of trial I could go through to, uh, gain my objective?"

"No," he said. "*Go.*"

"Father," the daughter said, "you know I have beaten all who have entered into athletic competition with me. Tell the king's emissary that if he can beat me in a footrace, you will give him the treasure."

"Definitely not," the emperor said.

She leaned closer to her father and spoke under her breath, though all of what she said echoed around the stony chamber. "You think I will *lose*. You *always*

think I will lose. How am I supposed to have any *faith* in myself if my own father always thinks I will *lose*?"

"Shhh!" the emperor said. "Shhh!"

"Stop *shushing* me. I want to know. What chance do I have of becoming a world-class *anything* if my father controls the challenges I face? Self-confidence is built from challenges. And besides, what need do you have, *really*, for all the stuff you steal all the time? You're like a five-year-old who has to have all—"

"Yes, dear, quite right!" the emperor said loudly, trying to drown her out. Then, addressing Fortuné again, he said, "I have decided that you will be running a footrace against my daughter. Tomorrow."

"In a week," the daughter said. "*Training.*"

"In a week," the emperor said to Fortuné. "And if you win, you can take your king's loot. If she wins, you leave and tell him that if he sends another emissary or tries in any way to take back what is rightfully mine, I will send a squadron of dragons to burn what is left of his kingdom."

"Thank you, Highness," Fortuné said. "May I choose a champion in my stead?"

"No," he answered.

The daughter leaned in again. "Why not? I want to race the *best*. You always think you have to be *strong* on people, and for *random* reasons, too. It's like a tic with you. For instance, you know we don't have any *drag*—"

"Good points you make!" he bellowed, patting her leg. Then he again turned to Fortuné. "I've decided that you may choose a champion. Be in the orange grove in one week's time. At noon."

"At dawn," the emperor's daughter said.

"At dawn," the emperor repeated. And he dismissed the court and bolted from his throne.

Back in the capital city, with each passing day the king grew more certain that Fortuné had been vanquished. His gloom grew heavier by the hour.

"You're pushing your food around your plate as you did when you were a child," his sister said as they sat for a midday meal on the third day since the band had gone south. "And like when you were a child, you're being a terrible conversationalist."

She left a pause, but he didn't fill it. "Maybe that's what we need around here. A child. You should think about getting married. What ever happened to that woman you danced with last Whitsuntide? She fancied purple."

He let out a long sigh, perhaps the fifth sigh of the meal and said, "Did he ever say what part of the countryside he was from?"

"Who?" she asked.

"I think he said something about the east, maybe near the sea."

"Oh, *him*," she muttered, pouring herself a second cup of tea. "What does it matter?"

"His father will need to know."

"Yes, I suppose a message will have to be dispatched if things don't go well. But how do you know Fortuné is not having the time of his life, rolling under the covers this very minute in an imperial bordello?"

"We can do a search," he said now.

"You don't mean of the bordellos, I hope."

He pushed his chair out and got up. "There should be a record of where Fortuné's father went when he moved from the capital. I'll ask the archivist to check the books." He stumbled into the doorframe as he left the room.

"Have you even *slept*?" she called after him.

He had not. Not since Fortuné left.

And neither had Fortuné himself. As if the distress over unrequited love and impending doom were not enough to cause insomnia, the emperor's accommodations were vermin infested. Rats chased each other across the floorboards and rafters all night long. As she listened to them, she thought a lot about the king. (And, yes, we use the feminine pronoun here, because when Fortuné removed his charmed attire at night and settled into bed, he was as he used to be.) She thought, too, about what would happen after the race. She knew Fleet-Foot would win it, but then there was the matter of whether the volatile emperor would be true to his word or just slaughter them all for sport. If they did survive the ordeal and by some miracle recover the kingdom's treasure, she had decided that she would, or *Fortuné* would, ask to be released from his duties upon their return to the capital. Given the feat, the king would be sure to agree. That's about as far as her plans, her imagination, went, as she listened to the scratching and scurrying of the rats. For she wasn't sure she would go home, no matter how much she missed the countryside, the sea air, and her family. She felt too changed to go back to the way things were.

The day of the race finally came, and the onlookers gathered at the site in the dim light of early morning. The grove of orange trees was three leagues in length and so well raked that you could not see a pebble as big as a pin's head. The emperor's daughter was already there, warming up with high kicks and sprints, when Fortuné and his companions arrived on horseback. Strong-Back took the mounts to tie them up, and Fortuné and Good-Shot hastened to the finish line to take up posts there. Soon enough, the emperor and the empress took their seats in the grandstand midway down the track.

"Let's get on with this, I haven't had my breakfast." The emperor yawned, then took up a horn and yelled into it: "Champions! To the starting line!"

Fleet-Foot took his place next to the emperor's daughter. She held out a small cup to her race-mate. "I take an energy drink before I run. It's just an herbal, entirely harmless. I insist you do the same so no one thinks I've cheated."

Fleet-Foot, being of an amiable nature, nodded and drank it back as she did the same. It seemed little more than water to him, it was so weak. And, yes, it was entirely harmless. At least to those with normal constitutions. The gifted, however, can have unpredictable reactions to the most innocuous things. And so it was that when the starting bell rang, Fleet-Foot was quite sound asleep.

The emperor's daughter, focused intently on her own performance, took off in a tear without even noticing that he was slumped over his starting block. And as she expected nothing less of herself than to remain in the lead until the very end, she ran on with grace and swiftness, never cognizant of what had occurred. None of the viewers at the sidelines dared observe aloud that she was the lone runner on the course.

But Fortuné did. For when she came into view of the finish line, he saw no sign of his champion. "We are lost!" he cried. He could not see the starting line, as the terrain of the course rose and fell in such a way that it was hidden from view. And in any case, it was too far away for Fortuné to have made out more than a lump where Fleet-Foot lay.

"He's asleep," Good-Shot said from above. He had scaled an orange tree and sat on a branch that hung over the track. He now pulled an arrow from his quiver and set it in his bow.

"You're not going to *shoot* him," Fortuné said.

"No. The fly that is crawling on his ear." And Good-Shot let go the arrow, and it whizzed through the grove and split the insect in two.

The close shave woke Fleet-Foot, who jumped to his feet and in one stride broke through the tape at the end of the course, his competitor's bare toes but a hairbreadth away from the win.

The emperor was so astonished at what he saw that he became convinced that the gods were helping Fortuné and thus he had an unfair advantage. So when the contestants and viewers had gathered on the track for the announcement of the winner, he loudly proclaimed that it was not the king's champion who had won but his empire's.

His daughter stood as close to the grandstand as she could get. She had her hands on her hips and spoke under her breath: "Do you think, Father, that giving me the medal will make me a better athlete? Well, here's some news for you: *Winning isn't everything*. But do you know what is? Your *word*. A powerful ruler who breaks his promises is no better than an ogre or—"

"What good advice!" the emperor shouted. "The win goes to the king's champion!"

The emperor's daughter then gave Fleet-Foot a respectful nod and winked at Fortuné before taking to the track again for her cooldown.

"My guards will show you where the spoils are stored," the emperor said.

"And the children?" Fortuné asked.

"Yes, them too."

"And the soldiers?"

"Yes, them too."

"Thank you, Your Highness."

"There are, of course, some reasonable conditions," the emperor said, looking off for a moment to make sure his daughter was out of earshot. "You are limited to what you and your men can carry away. Today. In one trip. And don't even ask for carts or carriages, for I never promised those. I am going to eat my breakfast now, and you'd better be gone by the time I'm done." He left then, motioning impatiently for the empress to follow.

They wasted no time, and because Strong-Back was able to carry every last bit of the kingdom's treasures, including the largest of the bronze statuary, the

greatest pieces of gilded cabinetry, the hundreds of children in bondage, and all the soldiers who had been captured, they had left the citadel before the emperor had even drained his second cup of coffee.

They were a sight coming over the hills, Strong-Back's load reaching into the clouds as he moved along as lightly as if he were carrying a bundle of fleece. It was dusk when they came into view of the capital city, their first witness the guard at the southernmost post on the wall. At first he couldn't understand what he was looking at. So he lifted his spyglass, and then he nearly fell from the high perch in astonishment.

The king and queen dowager were in the vaults at the time, for the royal archivist had called both of them there. He'd found, after days of searching, the book that the king had asked for. It was now set on a high oaken stand.

"You were right, Your Majesty," he said. "The nobleman in question did move east. A footnote on his family's lineage and histories page is very specific on that point. There should be no difficulty in sending him a message."

"Then what *is* the difficulty?" the queen dowager asked. "Surely you didn't call us here to a room full of book lice to tell us that."

The archivist placed his index finger on a branch of the family tree.

It was at this moment that the clarions blared to announce the return of the heroes. They passed through the city to roaring celebrations, tearful reunions, and passionate thanks for their bravery. Strong-Back unburdened himself in the royal courtyard, creating a mound that filled the entire space that had, on the day they first arrived in the capital, been filled with soldiers. The king appeared on the same landing where he had stood on that first day. The queen dowager took her place next to him, and, looking down at the diamonds and emeralds and rubies and crystal and gold and platinum, all glistening in the twilight, she gasped.

Fortuné dismounted from his stallion and bowed as the royal siblings descended the stone stairs.

"Thank you," the king said, but the distress in his voice stood at odds with the joyousness that surrounded him. "I can never repay you for this."

"What a true statement, as those who commit crimes are not exactly entitled to rewards," the queen dowager said. The archivist was behind her, and she ushered him to open the book. "Let's see, what does it say here . . . The nobleman you claim as your father had three children. And how many of those were sons, O scribe?"

"None," the archivist answered.

"Well, isn't that a *shame*, dear Fortuné," the queen dowager said, without making eye contact. "At least fraud is not a capital crime, so you needn't be executed."

"Is this true?" the king asked of his esquire. "That you were not born of the nobleman?"

Fortuné could see now how the king had been suffering, the hollowness around his eyes. "The nobleman is my father."

"Liar!" the queen dowager cried. "Perhaps *that* is a capital crime, lying to the king. Scribe, look it up, tout de suite!"

The archivist closed the book, bowed to the queen dowager, and ascended the stairs to the palace doors.

"Can you prove it, Fortuné?" the king asked.

Fortuné nodded. "I can." But he didn't move, just stood there, his eyes cast on his boots. *Oh, how smooth the leather*, he thought. He sure liked those boots. Comrade, still by his side, stamped a hoof on the pavement once, then again.

"You can?" the king repeated. Then he cocked his head curiously, as if he were hearing a far-off voice or catching an aroma he knew from childhood. Or witnessing an arrival.

"Then prove it," the queen dowager said, with a cluck meant to convey an indulgence of fantasy, an allowance of a moment of entertainment before the accused would be taken to his cell. But now she cocked her head, too.

The sounds of celebration emanated from the streets, the plucking of épinettes and tapping of tambours, the singing, the laughter. Hardly a soul had remained in the courtyard, just the royals and their guard, the champions and their steeds, and now, seemingly out of thin air, a woman. A shepherdess by her appearance, a crook in her hand. She struck the ground with it and out of a rift appeared a small trunk, a golden key protruding from its lock.

"This is the part where you and the king live happily ever after, Belle-Belle," the fairy said, turning the key and lifting the lid.

"What?" The king looked at Fortuné, whose eyes were still on his boots.

"He, rather *she*, is a *daughter* of the nobleman, dear brother," the queen dowager said. "Which explains quite a lot," she added, relief palpable in her voice. "But one could argue that a crime was still committed. Impersonation."

"And how else," the fairy said to the queen dowager, "might she have saved her family from wreck and ruin? I ask you, how would Belle-Belle have been received in the king's fighting force?"

"You make a powerful point," the queen dowager said.

"And you might consider making a powerful apology," the fairy said.

"I am sorry for accusing Fortuné of a crime."

"Just for that?" the fairy asked her pointedly.

The queen dowager sighed. "All right, I'm sorry for it all," she said. "Will you forgive my abysmal behavior?" she asked Fortuné.

He nodded absently. His attention was on the open trunk.

The king stood before it, looking down at the neatly folded clothing. On top was a cloak made of lambswool that Belle-Belle had sheared and carded herself, using her finest brushes for days and weeks. She'd woven the cloth, too, and dyed it with indigo. The king ran a hand over the cloak and bunched the soft cloth in his palm. A tingle went up his arm and through his body. The word "beauty" popped into his head.

"Go on, Fortuné, get changed," the fairy said, raising her crook in the air to cast the spell of liminality.

"Please, not yet," Fortuné said. He stepped over to the trunk.

"If you put this on, you become Belle-Belle?" the king asked Fortuné, holding the cloak up.

Fortuné nodded.

"But I don't know Belle-Belle," he said. "Where would Fortuné go?"

"That troubles me, too," Fortuné said.

The fairy lowered her crook now. "No need to rush things. How about I send you two on a holiday to get to know each other? Where in the world would you like to go?"

"I can't leave my people," the king said. "The emperor is sure to retaliate, and I must formulate a strategy and prepare the soldiers."

"You know what, brother?" the queen dowager said. "You've never been so good at all that. Neither was our father, to tell you the truth. Too sensitive, the both of you."

"I don't refute that," the king said. "I often wish I had been endowed with your gutsiness, sister. In my darkest nights, when I am not sure I will make it to morn, I imagine the kingdom in better hands left to you."

"Well, you needn't perish for that to happen," she said. "A simple abdication will do. Just give up your throne! I could, say, make you a duke, and you could take Belle-Belle as your duchess. Or Fortuné as your, uh, co-duke. Whatever your pleasure."

"I know of a lovely duchy in the east, by the sea," the fairy offered, raising her crook again and waiting for a nod from Fortuné and the king. "It is a place of peace."

The king, his fingers still caressing the soft wool of Belle-Belle's cloak, said, "Can we, uh—"

"Take the trunk with us?" Fortuné finished.

And so it was done. And in time the families were joined, and a great wedding was had in the capital, where the people, now living in peace, danced and ate, the children laughed. And that is where our pretty tale ends.

HENRIETTE-JULIE MURAT

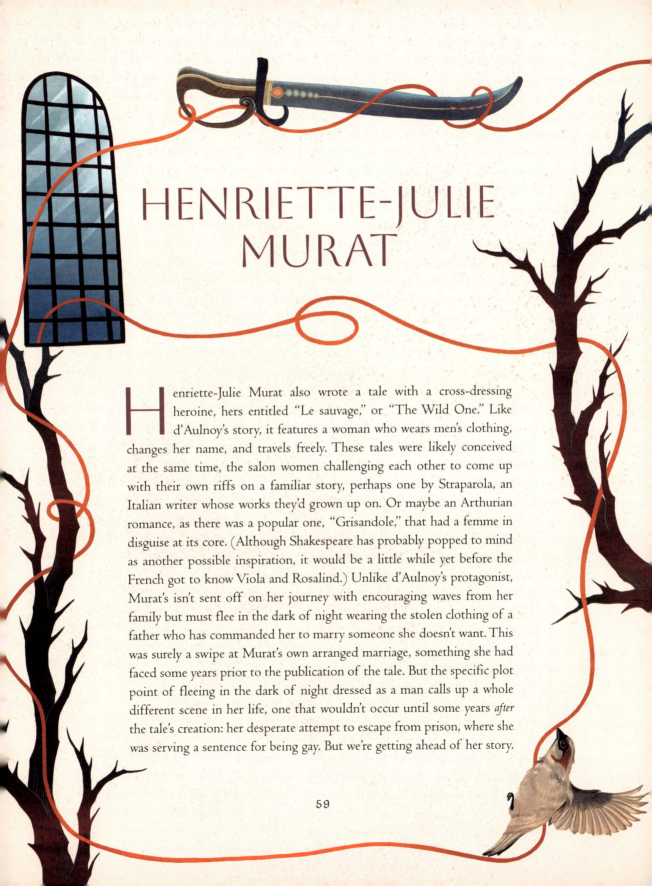

Henriette-Julie Murat also wrote a tale with a cross-dressing heroine, hers entitled "Le sauvage," or "The Wild One." Like d'Aulnoy's story, it features a woman who wears men's clothing, changes her name, and travels freely. These tales were likely conceived at the same time, the salon women challenging each other to come up with their own riffs on a familiar story, perhaps one by Straparola, an Italian writer whose works they'd grown up on. Or maybe an Arthurian romance, as there was a popular one, "Grisandole," that had a femme in disguise at its core. (Although Shakespeare has probably popped to mind as another possible inspiration, it would be a little while yet before the French got to know Viola and Rosalind.) Unlike d'Aulnoy's protagonist, Murat's isn't sent off on her journey with encouraging waves from her family but must flee in the dark of night wearing the stolen clothing of a father who has commanded her to marry someone she doesn't want. This was surely a swipe at Murat's own arranged marriage, something she had faced some years prior to the publication of the tale. But the specific plot point of fleeing in the dark of night dressed as a man calls up a whole different scene in her life, one that wouldn't occur until some years *after* the tale's creation: her desperate attempt to escape from prison, where she was serving a sentence for being gay. But we're getting ahead of her story.

WOMEN OF THE FAIRY TALE RESISTANCE

Henriette-Julie de Castelnau was born in 1668 in Brittany. Both of her grandfathers had served in the role of marshal of France, which meant the family was considered "sword nobility," or *noblesse d'épée*, high aristocracy. At the age of eighteen she was presented in the court of Louis XIV and caused a stir, as is commonly reported, by appearing in the traditional dress of her Breton homeland. By all accounts she thrived on the thrum of Paris, attending balls and soirées with her cousin Charlotte-Rose La Force (soon to be a fellow conteuse) and was part of a social circle that included the Princess of Conti, King Louis' eldest legitimized daughter (that is, one of his mistresses' children whom he approved of). Henriette-Julie somehow managed to enjoy this lifestyle as a single woman into her twenties, until her family insisted she marry.

Count Nicolas de Murat was a widowed military colonel with a lineage as prestigious as her own. Clearly there was no desire involved—she is described in multiple histories as a reluctant bride—so it's safe to assume that this was yet another transactional coupling. Families such as these were finding it hard to maintain their lifestyles because of the economic repercussions of the king's constant wars and his lavish expansion of the palace and grounds at Versailles, so they found some benefit in consolidating riches through marriage (think corporate mergers, I guess). Thus it's not a huge surprise that Henriette-Julie didn't live with her husband very long, although few facts can be gleaned about the circumstances of the split. Some say she left their marital home outside of Paris shortly after having a baby boy and never returned, preferring the city and her former life there. That was about the time the new wave of salons was taking shape, and she was known as a regular at the renowned Madame Lambert's, a precursor to the fairy tale salons and a place that celebrated women writers. This seems to be where she met all the other salon sisters and when her literary career took off.

Henriette-Julie's first book may shed some light on her marriage woes, although you'd have to read between the lines, since it was one of those fictionalized memoirs. Titled *The Defense of Women* in contemporaneous translations, it was written in response to a widely read book that had come out the prior year, *Female Falsehood; or, The Life and Adventures of a Late French Nobleman*, a pseudo memoir itself by Pierre de Villiers (author, you may remember, of *Interviews on Fairy Tales . . . a Condom Against Bad Taste*). Henriette-Julie's book, treated by its readers as a feminist manifesto, was republished multiple times in France and elsewhere. In it, she makes the audacious points that wives are often justified in leaving their husbands and that women's troubles in the world have more to do with bad luck than "unruliness." The main character in the story laments that "as soon as a woman lives separated from her husband, she gives [people] weapons against her" and is attacked by society. In the protagonist's case, she is even attacked by her own family members, who are complicit with her husband, and their accusations include her having a same-sex relationship. A son she loves also figures sadly into the story. All of that does track with the author's life, but whether she meant it to be read as a mirror is unknown. One thing can be said for sure: The broad appeal of this book reflects a loosening of at least some gender-based constrictions that women were enjoying at that moment—a resumption of intellectual gatherings in salons, some measure of choice in living situations and thus bodily autonomy, and the freedom of voices such as Murat's—even as the shadow of the king's hardening religious views was beginning to spread over them. The celebration of this book, indeed of all Henriette-Julie's works, would, unfortunately, be short-lived in France. But not before she rocked the world with her contes de fées.

She published, all with royal privilege, three collections of fairy tales between 1697 and 1699. In contrast to d'Aulnoy's deus ex machina approach, in which the protagonists are unexpectedly saved, her tales demonstrate the maxim that magic fails when it comes to matters of the heart, giving her stories a dysphoric air. Until the oft-tragic endings, though, her characters are filled with youthful exuberance and engage in passionate quests. For instance, in a tale called "The Fortunate Punishment," a young queen seeks out a fairy for help, which takes her on a labyrinthine path described in lengthy, lyrical passages that illustrate not only the author's appreciation of the natural world but also (surely) her intent to lull the censor to sleep and leave him snoozing under a bush while the woman arrives at her destination, where the fairy's beauty "melts her heart" to such an extent that the queen sends her attendants away and stays alone with the fairy for three nights. (This would definitely *not* have been okay with the royal censor.) In the same tale, Henriette-Julie also manages to insert what can only be interpreted as her true feelings about marriage, even as she allows two young lovers to be wed. "However joyful this day must have been," the narrator tells the reader, "I will not describe it, for whatever happy love promises, a wedding is almost always a sad celebration." In another tale, "The Palace of Vengeance," she also allows lovers to join at the end,

but she leaves them in a cursed castle made of glass, where they are "condemned to see each other forever." These dénouements are not atypical of the dozen-plus plots Henriette-Julie contributed to the fairy tale boom.

The dedication in one of these collections, *Sublime and Allegorical Stories*, is titled "To the Modern Fairies," which is where we first see this term of endearment that the conteuses used for each other. In the dedication, Henriette-Julie imagines them as the chic fairies of their own tales, living in enchanted castles, concerned only with "great issues," and spreading "grace by gentle influences." She contrasts them with the "ancient fairies," those "ragamuffin" domestic deliverers of lore who stayed home to tend the fire and whose tales were meant to scare children into submission. She's being playful, yes, but also staking a claim in a debate that had been going on for much of the century, the Quarrel of the Ancients and the Moderns. Women's literature had always been part of this debate, those against it on the side of the "Ancients" and those for it on the side of the "Moderns." In her tongue-in-cheek introduction to the newest contes, Henriette-Julie was reminding detractors (among them Villiers, who, no surprise, was invested in this debate) of the cultural power the conteuses were wielding with their success.

Her other two collections were dedicated to that daughter of King Louis, the Princess of Conti. These dedications, which are in verse, speak of how "destiny" has given the princess "the most charming of all goods" and how the author wishes not to be rewarded for her tales with "treasures nor grandeur" but only the "gift of pleasing you." About the same age as Henriette-Julie, the princess, like the fairy in the labyrinth, had a reputation for melting hearts. She was known to have many lovers, both male and female—the latter, it seems, spoken about only in whispers. In contrast, as already alluded to, male homosexuality was not legal but was accepted. There was an actual handbook in some circles (entitled something like "A Brotherhood of a Special Kind") that set out standards by which gay men should conduct themselves and their love lives. For women, the rule seemed to be that as long as same-sex relationships stayed behind closed doors, everything was fine. Until it wasn't.

It is unclear when Henriette-Julie became aware that she was under surveillance, but police reports show it started in 1698, when she was at the height of her fame. She was being inducted into literary academies with fellow salon writers and was receiving awards, including Toulouse's Floral Games prize for a volume of

poetry. A madrigal was dedicated to her that same year, published with royal privilege in a collection that recognized the most important women of Louis XIV's court. But a police lieutenant named René d'Argenson had a different opinion of her, which he described in a series of correspondences addressed to Versailles that he titled "The Disorders of Madame de Murat."

In the beginning, d'Argenson thought that the mere idea of being surveilled would scare her straight and make her "more submissive," as he put it (though, of course, in French: *plus soumise*). This didn't seem to work out, however, so he stepped up his spying, reiterating in subsequent memos to the king her "monstrous attachments to persons of her sex" and claiming she was guilty of "tribadism," a specific sex position set out in the criminal code. He had no evidence to support this, he admitted, but he was quite certain it was occurring in the privacy of her home. From the one-sided reportage that still exists, it would appear that the king wasn't initially too worried about all this, but d'Argenson stuck with the project, documenting every bit of "shocking conduct" he witnessed Henriette-Julie and her friends engage in, including "impudent conversation removed from both modesty and religion," "dissolute songs," and "execrable oaths proffered while gaming." Basically, behavior of the typical libertine male. He also noted her "insolence to piss out a window," which may sound like a precarious and unlikely thing for a woman to attempt until you consider who was probably standing *under* that window.

At some point, getting little help from Versailles, d'Argenson began confronting Henriette-Julie in person to pressure her to leave Paris. In one of these encounters she told him she couldn't go because she was five months pregnant, something he reported back to the king as, curiously, proof of the "debauchery" he'd been accusing her of. He asked that she be detained immediately, adding that he thought she would not object "if her delivery were to be hastened." I can think of only one way to interpret that suggestion in a world with no neonatal intensive care units, which comes across as pretty base behavior for a man claiming righteous shock at women cussing and gambling. Fortunately, though, as a follow-up report reveals, she probably made up the story that she was pregnant to mess with him. She was determined to stay in Paris. It was her home, and she had a partner, a woman named Nantiat. Also in Paris was a child from her marriage, a boy who was just seven years old at the time of the incident. This, however, didn't seem to give the lieutenant a moment's pause in his dogged pursuit, which would finally end after *four years* of surveillance. Whether the king ordered Henriette-Julie's arrest to be rid of her or of him is a fair question.

As to how the arrest went down, all we have are some euphemisms with which to paint the picture: She was taken with "a great deal of caution and care." (If you want the French directly from the administrative record: "beaucoup de circonspection et de mesnagement." That last word by itself also translates to "housekeeping" or "cleaning," but apparently "care" is favored in that phrasing.) There was no formal charge or trial—no witnesses to any crime, remember—so accounts of what happened postarrest are sparse to nonexistent. Histories on the subject tend to conflate or confuse the reason for her punishment with a libelous piece of writing she had supposedly crafted a few years prior about the king and his "unofficial" wife, but that claim doesn't make much sense. If there is any truth at all to Henriette-Julie's libel, it was probably just repurposed as a red herring to throw posterity off a track that would have tarnished the reputations of "noble" families at a time when the monarchy was making a sharp turn toward ultraconservatism. It's more than clear what this arrest was about: women loving women. For this infraction, Henriette-Julie was given what amounted to a permanent exile from Paris and an open-ended prison sentence at the Château de Loches. Yes, "château," as in castle.

Loches was, indeed, a majestic sight, a medieval fortress with a massive keep and round towers rising from a gently rolling heath. But up close, this was no fairy tale setting. (Unless you're thinking of Henriette-Julie's Palace of Vengeance, which may well have been on her mind, too, as she approached it.) A king in the fifteenth century had turned the castle into a prison, outfitting the towers with dungeons that extended four stories below ground, including a torture chamber renowned for its "iron cage," a metal box where those who really got under the king's skin spent months or even years crouching. Though the dungeons were still in use at the prison in 1702 when the coach carrying Henriette-Julie went through the gates, there's little chance she ever saw the inside of those. But that's not to say her detention wasn't cruel.

Upon her arrival, the commander of Loches was instructed by King Louis' secretary of state, the Count of Pontchartrain, to restrict her visitors, especially women, whom (he wrote in all seriousness) "she has long known to use for purposes that modesty does not allow me to explain." After she was found to be writing letters to family and friends, including Nantiat—or, as Pontchartrain put it, the one "most implicated in her disorder"—she was effectively cut off from all written communication. A subsequent memo notes that she was being fed with "utmost frugality." By two years in, one can conclude that she was self-harming, as the commander was told to "take all necessary precautions for her personal safety." She was, at the same time, begging to be allowed to go live with family in Brittany, a plea to which Pontchartrain responded directly, telling her in a letter that only when her husband "asks for this grace, it will be granted." He didn't ask. Skip forward another two years, and she was plotting her escape.

It's unknown how she acquired the outfit, but it was impressive: a man's shirt, jacket, wig, hat, stockings, shoes, and even a sword and scabbard. And while she was unsuccessful in her attempt to get away, she did force an extensive search before being found in a church on the prison grounds. She had holed up in a grotto under a shrine that contained a relic said to have belonged to the Virgin Mary, the "Holy Girdle," which Henriette-Julie may have hoped would provide some protective power. No such luck. Her captor bearing down on her, she swung her sword, missed, and then bit him on the thumb, hard enough that it was mentioned in the report of her capture. That probably also explains why the memo from Pontchartrain that accompanied her on the resultant transfer to another prison said that she was a "très vicieuse" woman and that she must be kept under close watch and treated "with great care." (And there is that word again, "care." To borrow a line from Inigo Montoya in *The Princess Bride*, I don't think it means what he thinks it means.) There are no records of her stay at the second prison, or at the third prison, which she was soon transferred to, but it can be surmised that the conditions were severe. She began having serious health problems during this stretch, which likely prompted her return to Loches and a change in the terms of her incarceration.

Now under what amounted to a city arrest, Henriette-Julie was allowed to move freely but still had to live at the Château de Loches, in what she called "my blue room" in her prison journal. Yes, after six years of being silenced, she had finally been given back her pen. She wrote every day, the pages a patchwork of quotidian descriptions and creative pieces, all addressed to a cousin she missed very much. She described a small circle of women with whom she'd created a literary "academy," organized walks in a marsh that she pretended was the Tuileries, invented dances and songs, and stayed out late on summer evenings. In the midst of a harsh winter, she wrote that she had "invented the fashion of putting red coats over [their] clothes, and immediately all the ladies put them on and they were even worn to church!" She recounted bedtime stories told to the children of friends—"We cannot laugh more or tell more extraordinary tales"—and then described dreaming of fairies and princesses. "Oh, what a lovely thing to have fun with."

But as the diary progressed, more and more space was devoted to her illness, which appeared to be kidney disease. "My heart marks time in a different way than the sun," she lamented in one entry; she described fevers and vomiting that kept her up all night—"I didn't sleep, like an owl"—and passing stones as big as olive pits. "I want to enjoy the moments of my health as others enjoy those of love," she wrote, while her days were being consumed by acute pain. And though this diary was very much focused on the present—no descriptions of her prior prison years, for instance—she did, in the throes of distress, reminisce about her life in Paris, about her friend Marie-Catherine d'Aulnoy's "lively and cheerful conversation" and the "animated ambiance" of her salon on the rue Saint-Benoit: "She wrote, as I do, out of fantasy, in the midst and noise of a thousand people who came to her house." Marie-Catherine had died while Henriette-Julie was in prison, shortly before her escape attempt.

Eventually she was allowed to go live in Brittany with an aunt, on the condition that she not leave home. There she wrote her final book, a novel about a haunted castle. It wasn't until Louis XIV died in 1715 that she was finally granted complete freedom, but it was never realized because Henriette-Julie herself, though only in her forties, was dying. The *Mercure galant*—a fashionable magazine that had showcased her literary works and championed all the fairy tale writers not so long before—published a death notice, obviously written by a relative, that was more ancestral braggadocio than obituary. In its eight full pages, there was not one mention of her professional accomplishments, no listings of her books or accolades. No kind words, even, unless you count a reference to the moment of death, when, according to the writer, her "delicacy of mind and the elevation of her genius were particularly evident." That seems to be as close as Henriette-Julie's family could get to honoring her life.

HENRIETTE-JULIE MURAT

Though most of the poetry she wrote has vanished, I found one poem sandwiched between the stories in her collection *The New Fairy Tales*. She labels it a conte, but it reads more as autobiographical verse. She titled it "The Happiness of Sparrows," though in my retelling I've given it the name of its heartsick character, Iris. The original poem rhymes, something that my skills at translation are not up to tackling, and I've fiddled with the form a bit. But I'm confident that I've captured the intended pathos, and so I offer it as a more respectful tribute to this woman's life.

A full-length tale is also retold here, "Anguillette," named for the fairy who figures prominently in the story. She is obviously modeled after Melusine, a character in popular French legends who was cursed by her mother to periodically turn into a fish from the waist down. (If this strikes you as a menstruation metaphor, you'll see that Murat must have had the same thought.) Melusine is variously depicted in folklore as a water sprite or mermaid, and some consider her the seventh member of a legendary league of women that includes Queen Titania, Queen Mab, the sage Viviane, Urgele, Anna de Bretagne, and Morgan le Fay. Though we don't learn much about Anguillette herself in the tale, she is one who cares (in the true sense of the word) for the young people whose destiny is in her hands. Unfortunately, her powers are limited and—like the writer who conceived her—she can't avert tragedy.

IRIS

Two young lovers, their wishes filled,
Tasted the sweetness of a
   charming mystery.
They took great care to please each other,
Saw such beautiful fires growing in
   the sky.
What more is needed to be happy?

But alas, unfortunately for them,
Young Iris had a mother to tear her from
   her desire.
What a trying fate to have no
   lasting pleasure!
All that love can do to despair
In these tender lovers was vividly seen.

To bear such misfortune
Iris went every day to a solitary wood,
Dealing with the pressing pain
We suffer when we lose what we love.
There are no torments that cost so
   many tears.

One day after singing her desperate sadness
To the trees, the streams, the echoes around,
She saw on a branch two sparrows,
A hundred times happier than she,
Who freely followed the transports of love.

"Little birds," she said, "flee!
Your ardor would soon be disturbed
If by misfortune my mother were to see
You are in love, passionate and faithful.
Alas! She would send one of you far away."

HENRIETTE-JULIE MURAT

ANGUILLETTE

ONE CANNOT BE acquainted with fairies and be ignorant that the most skillful among them have failed to discover a charm that would secure them from the misfortune of being compelled, for a few days each month, to change their shape into that of some animal, terrestrial, celestial, or aquatic. During that dangerous time, they are at the mercy of mankind.

There was one such fairy who changed herself into an eel and was unfortunately taken from the river by a fisherman and flung into a small pond in the midst of a meadow, where fish required for the table of the king of the country were kept. Anguillette (as this fairy was named) found in her new abode other fine fish destined, like herself, to live but a few hours.

The younger of the king's two daughters, Plousine, was walking at the time in the meadow. She approached the pond to amuse herself. The sun shone brilliantly on the water, making the skin of Anguillette glisten in the rays like all the colors of the rainbow. Plousine ordered the fisherman to scoop out the eel for her. He obeyed, and the fairy was placed in the hands of the person who would decide her fate.

Contemplating Anguillette, Plousine was touched with compassion. She ran to the riverside and put her gently into the water. This service filled the fairy's heart with gratitude. She appeared on the surface and said, "I owe you my life." Seeing that Plousine was now afraid, she added, "Don't fear! I am a fairy and will prove the truth of my words by heaping favors upon you."

As people in those days were accustomed to beholding fairies, Plousine recovered from her first alarm and listened with attention to Anguillette's instructions. "Go, young princess, and return to this spot tomorrow morning. Think, in the meantime, what you would wish for, and whatever it may be I will grant it." After these words, Anguillette sank to the bottom of the river.

That night Plousine leaned on the window ledge of her bedchamber, her thoughts occupied with what her choice should be. Her room was at the back of the palace and just high enough that she could see the meadow beyond the gates and the reflection of the moon rippling in the river. She thought the sight so beautiful that she almost chose beauty for her wish. But in the end, she came to a different decision.

Rising with the sun, Plousine hastened to the riverside and found, on the spot where she had seen the fairy, a column of the purest marble. An instant later, the column opened. The fairy emerged from it, no longer a fish but a majestic woman. Only her robe and headdress were reminiscent of the eel, sparkling, as it had, in all colors known and unknown to the human eye.

"I am Anguillette," she said. "I've come to fulfill my promise. You have chosen intellectual perfection, and you shall possess it from this very moment. You shall have so much sense as to be a marvel to those who till now have flattered themselves they were specially endowed with it."

At these words, Plousine felt an alteration taking place in her mind. She was unable to conceal her own astonishment at her new skills, and she thanked the fairy with an eloquence that she had heretofore been a stranger to.

Anguillette smiled. "I am so pleased with you for making the choice you have," she said, "that I will reward you by adding the gift of loveliness you have so prudently forgone. Return hither tomorrow at the same hour. I give you till then to choose the style of beauty you wish to possess."

Plousine, even more impressed with her good fortune, went back to the palace. Oh, her mother's surprise, and that of the king and all the court, at hearing the elegance and fluency with which Plousine spoke! As for her sister, Ilerie, she was impressed, too, but it also brought out in her an envy that she had never known before, the two siblings having been all their lives the most kindred of souls.

Night came. Plousine, occupied with the new expectation of becoming beautiful, could not sleep. She instead wandered a hall hung with portraits of several of the queens and princesses of her family, painted in the form of Greek goddesses. She indulged a hope that they would assist her in deciding on a style of beauty worthy to be solicited from a fairy. The first that met her sight was Hera. She was fair and had a presence such as should distinguish the queen of the gods. Athena and Aphrodite were beside her, for the subject of the picture was the Judgment

of Paris. The nobleness of Athena excited Plousine's admiration, but Aphrodite's loveliness was even more captivating.

Nevertheless, she passed on to the next picture, a frame that contained Artemis, attired as the poets depict her, with a quiver slung behind her and a bow in her hand. She was pursuing a stag and was followed by a band of nymphs. Plousine had all but decided that this would be her new look when she spied a small painting over the mantelpiece. The subject of this one was Hebe, daughter of Zeus and Hera. She was lit by a heavenly light. Her tresses were the fairest in the world, the turn of her head was most graceful, her mouth was charming, and her eyes appeared much more likely to intoxicate than the nectar with which she seemed to be filling a cup.

"I will wish," decided Plousine, "to be as the youthful Hebe." And then she returned to her bedchamber.

At dawn, she hastened again to the riverside. The fairy kept her word. She appeared and threw a few drops of water in the face of Plousine, who became immediately as she had imagined. She looked at her reflection in the water and almost did not recognize herself.

"I have fulfilled all your wishes," said Anguillette. "I'm sure you are content, but I shall not be unless my favors exceed your desires. In addition to the intelligence and beauty I have endowed you with, you have but to wish for wealth and at the same moment you will acquire it, not only for yourself but for all those you may deem worthy."

The fairy disappeared again, and Plousine returned again to the palace. Her family was again astounded, and she admitted to them that a fairy had endowed her with her new charms. The king and queen were pleased at these attentions, but Ilerie's envy only grew. And even more so as Plousine's beauty drew the attention of all the young men of the kingdom.

Ilerie's reaction troubled Plousine, and so she wished for her (and a wish was the same as giving) a wealth of gorgeous gowns and spectacular jewels and rouge powders and colorful wigs and all manner of stylish accoutrements from every corner of the world. Ilerie appreciated Plousine's gifts, as did their parents, whose palace and kingdom were also showered with new riches from their daughter's generous wishes.

But for all Plousine's power, for all the hearts she touched or inflamed, her own heart remained unaffected. She soon grew weary and began spending long periods at a retreat she had wished for, a short distance from the capital. It was not opulent but had a charming simplicity. A forest surrounded it, with paths intersected by brooks that formed natural cascades. She often walked these paths, sighing, and one day her heart felt more than usually oppressed, so she seated herself on the grass beside a rivulet whose gentle murmur courted meditation.

"What sorrow is it," she asked herself, "that comes thus to trouble me? What princess in all the universe is blessed with a lot as perfect as mine? The beneficence of the fairy has accorded me all I could wish for. I cannot imagine whence arises my ennui. I shall go back to the riverbank and try to find the fairy to ask her why I sigh."

But before Plousine even rose, Anguillette, again an eel, for it was one of those days of the month, poked her head from the rocks of the narrow brook and said, "You lack love. That is why you sigh."

"Then I shall only have to wish for it," Plousine said, perking up.

"But that is a dangerous proposition," the fairy said. "For if you ask me in the future to deliver you from such passion, I cannot. I can only bestow wealth. I cannot take it away."

"So be it," Plousine said. "What is the use of beauty and intelligence if it does not bring happiness?"

Anguillette, her colors flashing in a sunbeam that penetrated the woods, said resignedly, "You must wait a few days, but you will fall in love." And the eel slithered between the rocks and was gone.

Plousine's mood improved immediately with this new hope, and when a courier appeared at her door and summoned her back to the city to meet a foreign prince, her melancholy dissipated entirely. This, she was sure, was her wish granted, and so she returned to the palace with such lightness that she felt as if she were flying through the air.

Her family received her with great pleasure. Her parents informed her that the prince and his entourage had been staying with them for the past week, and so they had decided to have a fête on the morrow to introduce him to the kingdom. Plousine asked what he was like.

"I've never seen anyone who could compare," Ilerie answered.

Plousine couldn't help but notice how happy her sister seemed, and this only served to buoy her own spirits. "Describe him."

"He is such as they paint heroes," replied Ilerie. "His form is graceful, his demeanor noble."

"You draw a most amazing portrait of him," said Plousine, her heart swelling with emotion. "But is that not a little flattered, your description?"

"No," replied Ilerie, blushing now. "It is why I fell in love with him at first sight and have agreed to our betrothal."

Plousine was startled, but then she told herself that she must merely have been mistaken. Surely it was not this prince who was stirring her heart if he had promised himself to Ilerie. *It is someone else I'm meant to meet at the fête*, she told herself, *plain and simple*. She threw her arms around Ilerie. "Congratulations!" she said, and she felt in return a warmth that she had not known from her sister for some time. She was grateful for that, for she had missed their previous closeness.

In the morning, Plousine was utterly consumed with what she should wear to the festivities. She had never before experienced more than a twinge of angst over her appearance, and here she was practically paralyzed by vanity. She changed into every possible outfit she could assemble from her closet, until she realized she was late and dashed out of her chambers and to the palace gardens where the fête was being held. The music and dancing had already commenced.

Instead of joining with the merriment, she stayed under trees decorated with garlands of pink roses, surveying the attendees. There were many young men in attendance, some she recognized from her own kingdom. But these were not of interest to her. The strangers, those were the ones she focused on, the ones in attire whose styles and weaves were foreign to her own country. *It will be one of them*, she said to herself, and then her eyes landed on him. She had no doubt, not a bit. Why else would she feel so lightheaded? Why would one satin-slippered foot move involuntarily in front of the other in a beeline toward him? The yearning that filled her was nearly painful.

He was in profile, standing on the sidelines, too. She recognized tenderness in the way he reached a hand out and cocked his head, mouthing a thank-you to someone who passed him a glass of cordial. Plousine was close enough now to see the etching in the ruby-red crystal—Cupid with his bow and arrow. *Of course*.

"My dear sister, you have finally arrived!" It was Ilerie, who Plousine could now see was the deliverer of the refreshment. "This is my Atimir."

The prince bowed graciously, his eyes not yet meeting Plousine's, not yet going through that change: one moment in love with one sister, the next in love with the other. Ilerie would be the only witness to that metamorphosis. For by the time Atimir stood up from his bow, Plousine was blinded by her own tears.

She fled from the garden as fast as she could, through the grounds and into the meadow, and she threw herself onto the riverbank. "Anguillette!" she wailed.

The marble column rose from the turf, and out stepped the fairy. "I am sorry," she said. "I could not stop Ilerie from falling in love with the young prince."

"So let *me* stop loving him," Plousine pleaded.

But Anguillette sadly shook her head and reminded the princess of the limits of her power. "You have now experienced that fatal pleasure that I would never willingly have accorded to you. Matters of the heart are too unpredictable."

"Then I wish to die, right here and now," Plousine sobbed.

"I cannot, and would not in any case, deliver your demise," the fairy said. "But I have someone else for you. Someone deserving."

"Will I feel this same way for him?"

"No," Anguillette said, kneeling, her hand on Plousine's silken hair. "You will know something else. Tranquility. But you must go far away to live. I am ready to take you."

"How can I leave my home, my family, my—"

They both lifted their heads now, at a sound from across the meadow, a tormented cry of "Plousine! Plousine!" and there was Atimir cresting a hill and racing toward them, then throwing himself onto the riverbank, too. He had followed her, and her sister had followed him, as Plousine and the fairy could see now, though Ilerie was yet in the distance.

"I yield to a passion a thousand times stronger than my reason!" Atimir cried.

Plousine knew what torture he was feeling, for the same force, ardor and wretchedness as one, moved through her being as she gazed down at his face. She could practically taste the saltiness of his tears. She reached out a fingertip. One touch, that's all she wanted.

"There will be no going back if you do that," the fairy warned. "You are but mortal."

Plousine looked to the hill again, to her sister's now-stumbling form, and then back to Atimir. "Ilerie is the one who is deserving," she said to him, through heaves of sobs. Then she nodded to Anguillette, and she and the fairy rose above the meadow, the forms below getting closer to each other as they shrank away and were gone into the clouds.

When Plousine could see clearly again, she was far out at sea, descending alone into a small cabin in the fore of a ship. It was a small but comfortable room, and on the wall was a single painting, a landscape with a young man at its center. He was cutting nets to set loose a great number of birds, all with the most marvelous, striking plumage.

On the ship, Plousine passed her days struggling between her love and her desire to forget. She walked often on deck, where the sailors were dressed in rose-colored silk that matched the sails. They often held their arms out and let the sea air billow through their blouses, such was the sense of freedom the seafarers imbued.

One day, she saw land ahead. It appeared to be a very lovely country, with trees of surprising height and gracefulness. As the vessel neared the shore, she saw that they were covered with birds of the same variety and brilliance as those in the painting, and their songs were enchanting, their notes soft.

When the ship dropped anchor, the princess disembarked. And the moment she set foot on the shore and breathed the island's air, her heart seemed to rest and she fell into a deep slumber.

This place was called Peaceful Island. The fairy Anguillette had conferred upon it, for two thousand years, the power of recovery from unfortunate attachments. (Some assert that it still possesses this power, but the difficulty is in finding the island.) The prince who reigned during this period was named Chares. He was, on this day, taking an airing in the woods that fringed the shore, and the sleeping princess attracted his attention. He approached her and was struck by her beauty.

She awoke then and opened her eyes, and she, too, was struck by the nature of the prince. Not by his beauty (though he *was* beautiful) but by his style of dress. His tunic was woven from an assortment of feathers that Plousine could not have identified, except to say that they were all of soothing hues. The mantle that fastened at his shoulders was made from swan's down. The only part of his attire that was not feathered was the thin saber he wore at his waist.

"You must be Plousine," he said as she stared. "Anguillette told me about you."

He continued to speak to her in a cheerful, if jittery, sort of way (*That, too, is birdlike*, she found herself thinking) until at last he asked her if she'd like to see his palace.

"Please, I would," she said, for she felt strangely at ease.

He extended a delicate hand and helped her up, and they walked a short distance, soon reaching an avenue bordered by canals of flowing water, at the end of which was a castle built entirely, and artfully, of woven branches and vines.

His guard was lined up at the entrance. They, too, wore feathers, and each, like the prince, sported a fencing sword at his or her waist. (For on Peaceful Island, as in most charmed places, men and women have the same opportunities and liberties.) Everyone on the island was well trained in swordsmanship and took pride in the care of their weapons, but no one used their swords in battle, for there was no war on Peaceful Island.

The court was numerous enough, with merry and gallant men and women. And though the courtiers, like everyone else Plousine had so far seen on the island, wore little other than feathers, they evinced so much taste that the effect soon seemed quite natural to Plousine.

That evening Chares gave a banquet in her honor, which was followed by a concert of flutes, lutes, theorbos, and harpsichords. The music was lively, the voices sweet. Every song was a love song with an enchanted ending.

At the end of the night, Chares walked her to an apartment that had been selected for her. It was the most comfortable room she'd ever been in, and there were many amiable attendants to help her get settled. After they had gone and she was in bed, she said to herself, "Who could have believed it? I can think of Atimir and my family without pain. Is this a dream?"

"No," said Anguillette, who was standing over her bed.

"But it is such a strange place," Plousine said. "Everybody is happy. They seem so free."

"They are happy *because* they're free," Anguillette said.

"What do you know about Chares?" Plousine asked.

"He has been unlucky in matters of the heart, too, which is how he came to be here. No prince in the world is more worthy to be your partner."

"Though I cannot say I feel *love* for him," Plousine said, "I am more than sure that I could stay here with him forever and know the tranquility you spoke of."

"So reign, then, fair Plousine, in his heart and over this island," the fairy said. "I will wed the two of you in the morn, for I must leave tomorrow. Another empire under my protection is in need of my attention now."

The next day, Plousine opened her wardrobe and found there a number of dresses. A few were as feathery as those of the islanders, but others were exactly the style she was used to wearing. Still others were in-between, with feathers limited to the trim or a sash. It was one of these she chose (and with not a bit of angst in the selection), a gown the blush color of a mourning dove's breast.

She descended to the promenade to meet the prince. As they walked he told her, with sincerity, how sorry he was for the troubles that had brought her to his dominion. He knew not the particulars, as she knew not his, only that there had been love and loss. He told her he would be always devoted to her. And with no hesitation or misgivings, she promised the same.

When they reached a place called the Cove of Sacraments, they climbed the steps to an altar that was perched over a deep channel. The island's inhabitants gathered at the edges of the cliffs, and from the willowy trees surrounding them came a chorus of angelic birdsong. An arch had been set up over the altar, made of olive branches and palm fronds interlaced with white poppies, under which Anguillette stood waiting, a crown of crane feathers on her head.

"Unlike the marriages in most kingdoms," the fairy began, her voice echoing through the cove, "the unions of this island are fair and faithful. In that promise we join Plousine and Chares in eternal bonds." She went on to read the sacred vows, which they repeated in earnest. And then the wedded couple kissed for the first time, under the arch, with all looking on.

Though it was not a lustful kiss, not on either side, it was true. And, yes, they were happy. Anguillette bid them adieu with relief, and the newlyweds spent the day and night in joyful celebration. Their pleasure in each other was such that the next morning Plousine sighed contentedly upon waking and said, "I wish the whole world could hear of my good fortune."

Chares laughed. "We haven't that many messengers!"

Plousine laughed, too, but then her expression became more serious. "Can we at least send word to my parents? It would alleviate their worry to know I am settled and content."

"Of course," Chares said, for he, like Plousine, saw no harm in that. None at all.

Her loving note arrived in but days by way of a winged ambassador, who read it aloud for the royal family. They were, indeed, consoled by the news, for they had been deeply troubled since the unexplained disappearance of Plousine. When Ilerie and Atimir had returned from the meadow that fateful day, they had decided to say nothing of the spectacle they had seen, for they knew it was a sort that mere mortals could not effect. And Atimir, once his eyes were deprived of Plousine, soon recovered his feelings for her sister. It was not so much that he was fickle by nature but that the effects of the wish lived more strongly inside Plousine, for she had been the one to whom it was granted. That didn't mean that Atimir, upon listening to Plousine's words read by the feathered messenger, didn't feel a burning inside him. He did.

"They must come for your wedding, Ilerie!" the queen exclaimed, and she dictated a message for the ambassador to take back to the couple, informing them that the nuptials would take place in a fortnight. Had she not been so excited, the queen might have noticed the rising fear in Ilerie's face and the flush that had come over Atimir's. But she had not a clue, and so she sent the messenger away and continued with the busy preparations for the wedding, only now with the pure joy of knowing her family would be together again.

The invitation was met with mixed emotions when it arrived on the island. Chares rarely left the bounds of his realm, and then it was usually to visit similarly remote and enchanted places on matters of commerce. But he felt that Plousine should not miss her sister's wedding if she wished to go, and so he kept his trepidation to himself. On her part, Plousine was nervous. It was one thing to think of Atimir in the abstract, but the anticipation of actually seeing him caused an undeniable fluttering within. Her initial impulse was to decline the invitation, but between Chares' encouragement and her mother's expression of longing to see her, she agreed to go. More than once during the packing and arranging, she thought about Anguillette and whether she should try to reach out and ask her advice. But she knew that Anguillette would tell her not to go, and so she pushed the fairy from her mind. She was not a child, she told herself. Regardless of the fluttering, she was happy with Chares and would honor her vows, no matter the strength it took.

To be clear, Plousine would not have gone if she hadn't been sure of that.

Their travel from the island was not as swift as the messenger's had been, for this trip necessitated a carriage and a retinue of attendants. They took first to the sea, and then winged horses lifted them from the deck and through cloud cover that was thicker than anticipated, because of cyclones along the route. Finally, they landed at the palace with but a few hours before the wedding, and the guard received them with speed and wonder.

They were brought to the great hall, where Plousine's mother and father nearly suffocated her with hugs, and they also warmly embraced Chares, whom they immediately saw was a loving and devoted husband. His exotic dress and the feathers that their own daughter now included more generously in her wardrobe did not make them inordinately curious. Nor did hearing of their arrival on winged horses. They'd grown used to spells being cast over their daughter's life.

"Where is Ilerie, my dear mother?" Plousine asked.

"She is cloistered with her ladies-in-waiting until the ceremony. But look! Here is her fiancé now!"

Atimir, approaching through an arched doorway, was outfitted regally in a boot-length jacket that was open in the front and a gilded belt and ceremonial sword that clattered as he walked. He locked eyes with Plousine. It was easy for her to read his mind, for it was the mirror image of her own: a profuse passion held at bay only by furious self-loathing.

Plousine staggered, and Chares, concerned, put an arm around her. "What is wrong, my love?" he asked.

"I'm not feeling well," she whispered, her eyes on the floor.

"Poor dear," her mother said. "Must be vertigo from the trip."

"Why don't you go lie down," her father suggested. "We'll call you to the chapel when it's time."

"I'll go with you," Chares said to her.

She made herself stand tall and fixed her gaze on the door and the stairs beyond. "No," she said to him, "I wish for you to stay and get to know my parents." For she had decided, right then and there, that they would be returning to Peaceful

Island in the morning at first light. This evening would be the only chance for her husband to be with her family. She would never come back to the kingdom again. She would not again take that risk, not with her own heart, or Atimir's, or the faithful Chares'.

Reluctantly he acquiesced, and she left the room and climbed the stairs to her bedchamber.

"She's a strong one, that Plousine. Don't worry," the king said, gesturing to a settee and armchairs so they might sit. But before they were able to do so a short bell rang in the outer hall, then again, and a third time.

"Oh, I'm sorry," the queen said, "but that is the call for the king and me to meet with the chaplain. Atimir, perhaps you could show Chares around the grounds?" Atimir gave a nod, and so the royal couple left the two princes alone.

The self-hatred that Atimir had brought into the room with him had, as he stood in stony silence, begun to seep out in Chares' direction. Atimir could not stop himself from imagining the intimacy between Plousine and her husband, the tortured thoughts like a beast inside him. He looked his rival up and down, regarding his feathers in a disparaging way. Then he noticed the saber.

Chares, confusing Atimir's reticence for nervousness over his impending vows, said, in his light and friendly way, "There's nothing to worry about! If I can survive a wedding night, anyone can!"

Which served only to raise the temperature of the blood coursing through Atimir's veins. He ushered Chares to the grand doors of the hall, which spilled out onto the palace gardens. But he didn't have in mind a meandering stroll through the topiary and fountains. He stayed on the central path, which led beyond the rear gates, and didn't stop until they reached the meadow.

A hand now on the hilt of his heavy sword, he said to Chares, "Plousine and I loved each other. That is why she was taken from me by a fairy." He gestured to the riverbank, then looked up to the now-twilit sky.

Chares had no reason to think this was untrue. Plousine had a history, or else Anguillette would not have escorted her to his island. He had a history, too, though he could remember none of it now. Such was the island's way. So it was empathy Chares was feeling at this moment, empathy for Atimir.

"I'm sorry," Chares said. "For all your pain. But you don't have to worry about Plousine. She is happy in my realm. I will love her for as long as we are together."

Atimir clutched the sword's hilt tighter now. He loosened the sword from the sheath. "That is not all." And what would come next, a lie, he had not planned to say, for Atimir was not diabolical. But the beast within had become so. "Plousine and I have plans to run away together. That is why she brought you here."

Chares told himself not to believe this. "I'll ask her myself," he said, and turned to go back up the hill.

But Atimir drew his sword. "Not until you fight for her and win, birdman."

Chares lifted his saber from his belt. Though he had not wielded it for anything but sport (at least not in his memory), he was exceptionally skilled in its use, and his urgent desire to get back to Plousine drove him to meet every clash of the sword, though Atimir had the greater strength of the two of them, and he fought like a man who set no value on his life.

Back in her chambers, Plousine lay on the bed of her childhood. She had been listening to the sounds outside her window, the crunching of shells under the boots of people strolling in the garden, the birds that chirped from the chinks of the palace walls. Their song made her long to be back on the island, where her heart was safe, where Chares' heart was safe. And then, suddenly, she bolted upright and ran to the window. For she'd heard it: the clash of steel.

She arrived in the meadow at the very moment Atimir and Chares dealt each other the furious blows that made them fall simultaneously onto flowers and grass red with their blood.

"Precious lives that have been sacrificed for me!" she wailed over the still bodies, touching their gaping wounds. Then she pulled Atimir's sword from her husband's chest and flung herself upon it.

The fairy Anguillette appeared then, the misery having found her. She cried out to the fates for help but was able to revive only Chares, who was still a hairbreadth from death. Anguillette healed his wound, and before he awakened she sent him back to Peaceful Island, where, by the power she had conferred on it, he would console himself for his loss until he would forget it entirely.

By the time the search party arrived with their torches, there was no trace of the tragedy that had occurred. Where the ill-fated lovers' blood had been, two trees now stood. The guardsmen looked at them curiously but then moved on. They didn't see the eel on the riverbank or its flash of color in the moonlight before it disappeared into the water.

CHARLOTTE-ROSE LA FORCE

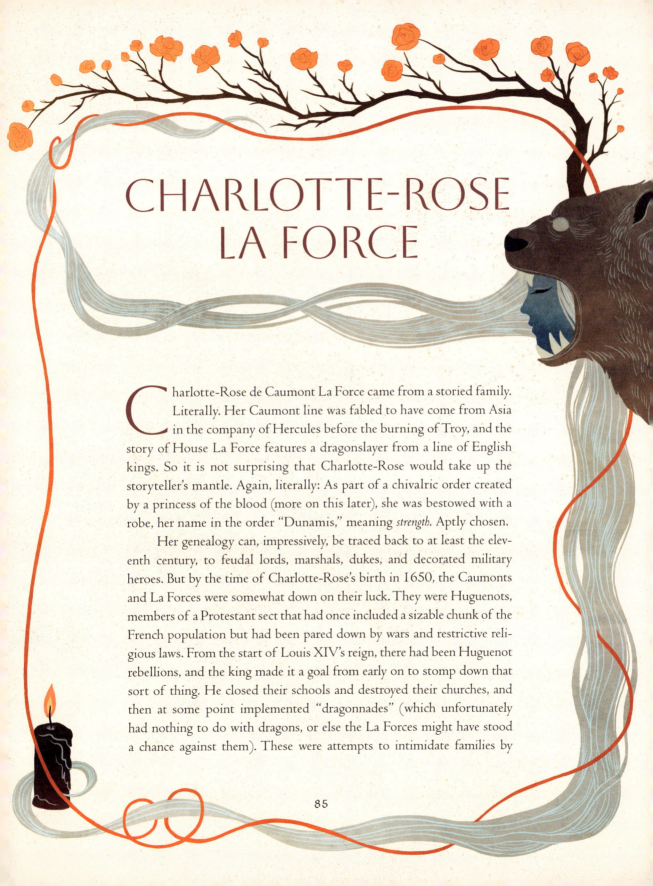

Charlotte-Rose de Caumont La Force came from a storied family. Literally. Her Caumont line was fabled to have come from Asia in the company of Hercules before the burning of Troy, and the story of House La Force features a dragonslayer from a line of English kings. So it is not surprising that Charlotte-Rose would take up the storyteller's mantle. Again, literally: As part of a chivalric order created by a princess of the blood (more on this later), she was bestowed with a robe, her name in the order "Dunamis," meaning *strength*. Aptly chosen.

Her genealogy can, impressively, be traced back to at least the eleventh century, to feudal lords, marshals, dukes, and decorated military heroes. But by the time of Charlotte-Rose's birth in 1650, the Caumonts and La Forces were somewhat down on their luck. They were Huguenots, members of a Protestant sect that had once included a sizable chunk of the French population but had been pared down by wars and restrictive religious laws. From the start of Louis XIV's reign, there had been Huguenot rebellions, and the king made it a goal from early on to stomp down that sort of thing. He closed their schools and destroyed their churches, and then at some point implemented "dragonnades" (which unfortunately had nothing to do with dragons, or else the La Forces might have stood a chance against them). These were attempts to intimidate families by lodging soldiers, called dragoons, in Huguenot households. The soldiers had to demonstrate certain behaviors before earning these positions—that is, the worst disciplined of the bunch were made dragoons. That way a key stratagem of the operation—to abuse the residents and steal their possessions—didn't need to be said aloud. As a result of all this, most Huguenots throughout the countryside fled France or converted to Catholicism. Charlotte-Rose's family did neither.

Though the Château de La Force had been the object of an intense siege earlier in the 1600s—one that lasted four days, during which hundreds of cannonballs left the place in rubble and ash—there is no record of Charlotte-Rose's own home, the ancient Château de Cazeneuve in the southwest of France, having ever been under assault. At least in a military sense. But Louis XIV and his retinue stayed there on his way to marry his first wife, Queen Maria Theresa, and maybe this didn't go so smoothly, judging by the fact that he had Charlotte-Rose's mother forcefully taken from her home not too long afterward. Her refusal to renounce her religion was obviously at the core of the abduction, but other behaviors on her part seem to have also ruffled the king's feathers. She would spend the rest of her life in a convent, and Charlotte-Rose, twelve years old at the time, would have to do without a mother after that. And without a father as well, as it appears he was dead by then.

Charlotte-Rose's next appearance documented by history was her presentation to the royal court at age sixteen, which had to have been at least a little uncomfortable. She was, from the start, known to push against what she considered the "cult of the Sun King." Nevertheless, Louis seemed to take a special interest in her—perhaps out of guilt, but that might be generous—and gave her the prestigious job of attending the queen. He must have thought the impressive connections would help get her settled with a suitable husband, given her family's relative poverty and thus her lack of a dowry.

She was, however, a believer in *tendresse*, or love based on true and natural feelings, and thus she followed her own instincts. She was an avid reader of works in the popular romance genre, so her ideals may have had roots in those, as apparently did the first scandal she was involved in at the palace: a brouhaha over her reading a "pornographic novel." (The specific book is never named in any accounts, so one can only guess at its level of raciness.) Perhaps in response to this, devout ladies of the court began visiting Charlotte-Rose's bedchamber at Versailles to pray with

her, and her room soon became the setting of a scene right out of a dramatic comedy. It starred Michel Baron, a young and popular actor she'd taken up with, who burst into her room early one morning, certainly eliciting gasps from the praying ladies. Charlotte-Rose is said to have feigned indignation and asked him why he was there. His response was to scoop up a nightcap he had left beside the bed, take a bow, and exit. The stir in the palace that followed brought the curtain down on that relationship and prompted her change of employment to a role outside the court, attending an aged noblewoman.

But Charlotte-Rose still managed to see her friends, of which she'd made many in the five or so years she'd been tending the queen, including the aforementioned Princess of Conti, at whose apartment she was known to spend a lot of time. This was a group of people who liked having fun, especially out and about. They frequented the Society of the Temple, a club associated with the House of Vendôme that was a favorite of Paris' most free and wild. Also popular were cabarets in Ménilmontant (still a hopping district today), which Charlotte-Rose came to frequent with her first serious love interest, the Marquis de Nesle. He was a young man from a well-connected family, and they were smitten with each other, going out every night of the week. The king, still watching out for Charlotte-Rose, saw the Nesle wealth plus the La Force name as a winning combo and approved.

The young marquis's father, on the other hand, didn't have such a positive outlook. Not thrilled that his son was dating a woman who had a poor reputation and was, well, poor, he began following his son around. After finding the lovers carrying on lasciviously in some hot spot, he rallied together relatives and staged an intervention. They took the young man to a remote castle outside Paris, one surrounded by a large moat, and told him he would have to stay there until he came to his senses. Some time elapsed, during which his inclinations didn't budge. And then, suddenly, everything changed. According to the family, this is what happened: One day, the young marquis decided to drown himself, so he ran down the castle steps, tearing off his clothes as he went, and, in the process, he pulled from his neck a sachet that he had been wearing nonstop for a very long time, a gift from Charlotte-Rose. And when he was separated from it, he suddenly didn't want to kill himself, and he lost all feelings for her. Naked and standing at the edge of the moat, he came to realize that the sachet had been a love potion. And so he joined the army and never went back to Paris.

WOMEN OF THE FAIRY TALE RESISTANCE

Whether you believe all that or not, the reason such a story would have seemed plausible is that this was during a chapter of the Sun King's reign called the Affair of the Poisons. After a string of noblemen's deaths, Louis became convinced that they had been poisoned (probably true at least in part: some were likely killed by desperate housewives), and so, freaking out at the idea that someone might poison *him*, he set up a special investigation unit called the Chambre Ardent, "burning chamber," because it met in a secret cellar lit by candles. There, over the course of three years, investigators worked through the cases, and, in the end, they arrested over two hundred people (mostly women) and executed thirty-six, not including some number who died while being tortured or by suicide. The linchpin of the whole affair, according to the Chambre Ardent, was one woman in particular known as La Voisin. Before she was burned alive, she had a bustling business in telling fortunes and providing powders and potions for just about any purpose. Her shop was popular with all levels of society, including, as it turned out, people living at Versailles. Even a couple of Louis' mistresses were customers. Though they were questioned, none of those women were arrested. They claimed to have purchased only aphrodisiacs, which I guess Louis didn't mind so much. And maybe that's why he gave Charlotte-Rose a pass, too, because though she was interrogated, she was not accused of any crime in conjunction with the Marquis de Nesle incident. Which would have added insult to injury—she was already devastated by the breakup.

To make matters worse, in the ensuing years Louis officially criminalized Protestantism, and thus Charlotte-Rose felt compelled to do what her mother and so many ancestors had lost their freedom or their lives refusing to do: renounce her religion. In return, the king gave her a pension of one thousand crowns a year, said to be "irregular," so obviously it was not a totally reliable income. But it was still better than nothing, and especially welcome since her bid at marriage had not worked out. And then her fate took a turn for the better—or so it must have seemed to her at the time—and she found again that elusive tendresse, no sachet involved.

His name was Charles de Briou, and the two fell madly in love and immediately wanted to get married. But he, too, had a father who wasn't keen on Charlotte-Rose. The father's name was Claude de Briou, and he was a bigwig in the law, in fact president of a *cour des aides*, a regional court system. He had only two children, a

daughter and a son, and the former had been married off to a nobleman, poisoned him, and ran away with a flute player. There are other lessons a father could have drawn from that, but the one he chose was that he needed to be ultracontrolling of his only son, who was also heir to an immense fortune. Claude de Briou was surely upset by Charlotte-Rose's reputation and her lack of a dowry, but the objection he seized on was her age. She was in her early thirties by then, and Charles was in his midtwenties. (Which may not seem like much of a gap when it was common practice for a girl barely in her teens to be married to a man three decades older, but there you go.) Claude de Briou refused to consent to their marriage, and since his son was shy of majority—at the time men were considered minors until age twenty-six—the two lovers had to bide their time.

After a year or so of seeing Charlotte-Rose on the sly, Charles finally did reach his majority. On a sunny day in April 1687, he was out on a hunt when appeared another hunting party, this one part of a ruse concocted by Charlotte-Rose, who had in her possession a marriage contract. Much to their combined delight, their union was supported by luminaries of the court, including Louis XIV himself. After the wedding, the king gifted them an apartment in Versailles, probably patting himself on the back for finally getting this troublesome charge of his settled. What a dream those days must have been for the happy couple: strolling garden paths infused with the aroma of jasmine and hyacinth, winding through mazes of orange and pomegranate trees, breathing in the cool mist of fountains, feeding the elephant in the royal menagerie (yes, the king had one). And the nights: dining on pheasant and oysters, taking in a ballet, playing piquet or billiards, and then retiring, as husband and wife, to their own home. They enjoyed this state of marital bliss for, oh, about a month.

That was when Claude de Briou managed to get a meeting with the king and somehow convinced him to let him do what he wanted to do. Which was, for starters, to take possession of his son. The newlyweds got wind of this before the capture and surrounded themselves with sword-wielding friends, but they were overpowered in the end, and Charles was forcefully taken off to his father's house and kept under guard. It's unclear what went on there and for how long, but the married couple did manage to surreptitiously exchange letters. In one, Charlotte-Rose told Charles to listen for a trumpet followed by a brass band and, when he saw dancing bears in the courtyard beneath his window, to convince his captors to take him down to see them.

The ploy that Charlotte-Rose had hatched would eventually inspire a fairy tale told in the salons, "Peau d'ourse," about a woman who is sewn into a bearskin. Because she basically was. There was a street performer in Paris who had a troupe of dancing bears, and Charlotte-Rose convinced him (a few crowns were involved, I imagine) to let her, dressed in a bear costume, join them for an afternoon so she could get inside the gates of the Briou home. Charles' guards saw no harm in his enjoying a little entertainment or even admiring up close a bear who was unusually gentle and graceful. And in this way, husband and wife at least got to have a conversation. That was probably the last pleasure they enjoyed together. Soon after, Claude de Briou had his son committed to Saint-Lazare, a Christian mission in Paris that had a boarding program for "incorrigibles," young men of prestigious families whom their parents deemed out of control. Saint-Lazare's methods, a well-kept secret, had a high success rate, and in Charles' case success was considered his denouncement of his wife. Five months in, he was still unwilling to reject her, so whatever his regimen of mistreatment was, it was ratcheted up. And soon enough he acquiesced.

Now with his son a willing witness, Claude de Briou could execute his grand scheme: to have the marriage legally voided. This should have been no easy feat given the extremely narrow rules surrounding annulments (which is why women had such a hard time ridding themselves of even the most horrid husbands), but Claude de Briou was connected and creative. And evidently also unethical, as the law he used to argue for the marriage's nullification was brand-new at the time of the case, making one wonder what judicial levers he'd been pulling behind the scenes since his son had first declared his intention to marry Charlotte-Rose. The statute was *rapt de séduction*, a form of abuse that involved coercion to marry based on, *yes*, age difference. Charlotte-Rose fought the charge in a public trial and also counterclaimed for monetary damages for the harm to her reputation. For that, she was heckled in court and lampooned in the press. The judgment, in the end, was rendered as "abuse in the celebration of marriage." She was ordered to pay one thousand francs to Briou for his claim, and he was ordered to pay her one thousand crowns (three times the value of francs) for hers. The marriage was annulled, and both Charles and Charlotte-Rose were forbidden to ever see each other again. To a

friend, she described herself as "a ship agitating the waves, without pilot, without masts, without sails."

Taking refuge in the salon scene, which by then included her younger cousin Henriette-Julie Murat, Charlotte-Rose began to write. Her first books were "secret histories," fictional accounts of prominent figures, a genre of her own invention that was immediately very popular and would endure (think historical fiction). In her narratives, she pulled women from the wings, elevating their contributions to the achievements of lionized men. She wrote four of these by the mid-1690s before turning her attention to fairy tales. Sharing and workshopping stories with her fellow conteuses, she crafted a batch of eight tales featuring independent women and star-crossed lovers. In 1697—the same year the salons were fêting Marie-Catherine d'Aulnoy for the publication of the very first full collection of fairy tales—Charlotte-Rose received royal privilege for her manuscript. The book, *Les contes des contes*, or *The Tales of Tales*, came out the following year to great fanfare. But missing from the celebrations of its launch? The author.

This was due to a poem she wrote that took some witty jabs at Louis XIV's court. It was likely included in one of those popular satirical pamphlets that were sold on the street. Unfortunately, we can't read the verses and judge the content for ourselves, as there are no extant copies, but the subject matter included Louis and that "unofficial" wife he'd married fifteen years before, after Queen Maria Theresa died. She was known as Madame de Maintenon, and everyone in France was well aware that she was functioning as the queen. But she and Louis kept up the façade that they were not married, and no jokes about their relationship were allowed, especially those that might be considered blasphemy—as, really, any criticism of Louis was, since he thought he was a divine king. So did Madame de Maintenon, who was extremely pious. In fact, she was the one everyone blamed for the over-religiosity that was, in the views of the salongoers and their ilk, making Paris a very dull and increasingly scary place to live. So when this poem by Charlotte-Rose came to light, the king called her in for a sit-down. He was already irritated because she was getting more attention from the public than he was, so when his wife became upset over the verses, he decided a punishment was necessary. Like her mother before her, Charlotte-Rose was sent to a convent, with the instruction to reform her morals. So it was that when her *Tales of Tales* hit booksellers in 1698, she was sequestered in a Benedictine abbey far from Paris. There she would stay for sixteen years.

Unlike her cousin Henriette-Julie, who was still a few years away from her own banishment, Charlotte-Rose was allowed to lead a fairly normal life while in exile. She was watched, for sure—as revealed by a note from the Count of Pontchartrain in 1700 that asked the king for permission to increase her surveillance because she was supposedly plotting an escape to England—but she was permitted to continue her literary career and kept receiving a pension from the king. Though she had to stay at the abbey, she could have visitors and could write freely to her friends and associates. That's how she was able to participate—from afar—in the previously mentioned chivalric order, which was the whimsical invention of a bored princess in the reigning House of Bourbon bloodline. All members were issued elegant robes embroidered with silver, a wig in the shape of a beehive, and a medal engraved with the name of the society: the Order of the Honeybee. Undoubtedly, given the reputation of the princess, there was a wild soirée at her château to celebrate the induction of members, but that was the kind of romp that Charlotte-Rose would never again be able to enjoy.

She penned a number of works while in the convent, some of them poetry—including verses to the Princess of Conti, who remained a friend—and one a fictional story set in a fairy tale salon of her imagining. To demonstrate her "reform" and plea for freedom, she wrote letters to Madame de Maintenon and a long essay entitled "Christian Thoughts," but to no avail, at least in the short term. When she did finally regain her liberty, she chose not to return to Paris. Speaking of herself, she wrote late in her life:

> *Court is a land I once inhabited,*
> *To my own peril I speak of it with knowledge;*
> *In these slippery places, innocence*
> *Can seldom walk in safety.*

Her tale "La bonne femme," or "The Good Woman," seems to speak of that knowledge, if in the coded language of the contes de fées. It includes a king who is capricious and cruel and who spies on his subjects. A trusted and learned fairy who makes potions and spells. Young women and men who fight external forces

that want to control whom they can love. And a woman of court who has retired to the country to tend sheep and spin yarns. Her backstory is the only one that is never explained to the reader, that remains veiled. Charlotte-Rose surely saw herself in this character and in this tale that was likely the final conte she wrote. Which is why I've titled my retelling "Dunamis."

The other retelling you'll find here is "Persinette," that grandmother text of what would become world-famous as "Rapunzel" after the Brothers Grimm published their version and misrepresented its origin tale, crediting a German man instead of the French woman who actually crafted it. I've done little more than translate the original work so you can see just how closely the well-known Rapunzel's story hews to Persinette's—which itself hews to the author's own story in the way young lovers must endure lengthy and brutal tests to be together. Perhaps the reason this tale has endured as it has—it's still popular today, more than three hundred years since its writing—is that Charlotte-Rose La Force felt a very real empathy for these characters she conceived. That would explain, too, why she gave them in the end what she herself wanted more than anything but could not have.

WOMEN OF THE FAIRY TALE RESISTANCE

DUNAMIS

DUNAMIS WAS CONTENT, and would be so for ever after. She told herself this constantly. *How fortunate to be rid of courtly life*, she'd think as she tended her sheep. Sure, it was a bit rustic, this existence, for someone as young as she. *But in this humble glen*, she'd remind herself as she spun her yarns by firelight, *I am not scorned, not told whom I must and mustn't love*. Her solitude satisfied her. She was quite certain of this.

Then the children arrived. They bounded down a hill one evening to where Dunamis, tired from the day's work, leaned on her distaff. (She preferred it to a shepherd's crook because she was able to set her spindle, like a spearhead, at an angle atop the shaft.) They were small children. Toddlers, really. But strangely agile. They helped her chase the sheep into the fold, and when night came they followed her into her small cottage and wound her yarn into tidy skeins for her.

There were three of them, two girls and a boy. Around their necks they wore ribbons, each with an odd little jewel attached: one a cherry enameled in crimson and engraved with *Lirette*; one a tiny plum carved from lapis and bearing *Mirtis*; and one, around the boy's neck, an emerald almond etched with *Finfin*. Dunamis asked whether these were the children's names, and in response they threw their little arms round her waist and her legs and told her they loved her. They were really quite endearing.

Dunamis taught them the ways of her life: how to fish with nets, hunt with bows, and grow plants for foods and fibers. Their delicate hands were well suited to cultivating flowers, and so the cottage garden, over the ensuing years, grew as tall and lovely as the children did. There was a rose tree that Lirette was especially fond of, for she thought nothing so beautiful as a rose. She had an urge one day to open a bud and try to find its heart, but in so doing she pricked her finger on a thorn. The pain was sharp, and so Finfin, ever by Lirette's side, took some rose leaves in his hands and squeezed the juice from them into her wound. The pain eased immediately.

"How did you know to do that?" Dunamis asked him, ever amazed at what these children came up with.

"A remedy can be found in the same thing that has caused suffering," he said. "It is thus with Lirette, who when she gives me a cross look causes me great distress. But when she smiles, I am filled with such warmth that I forget all else."

It's not that Finfin didn't care for Mirtis; the three were inordinately close, often found curled together like kittens. But he *really* cared for Lirette. And now that they were getting into their teens, Dunamis was becoming acutely worried about this. "What if they are brother and sister?" she would ask the blue sky when out for a walk. She knew it was her duty to talk to them, as she was the closest thing they had to a mother. "But whatever will I say?" she would ask the dust in the air of her cottage when she swept the dirt floor. One morning there came an answer: "No need to say anything, *bonne femme*."

The voice came from the window, although Dunamis could see no one there, just a plump partridge resting on the deep ledge. She recognized this bird because Mirtis had had her eye on it for some time. As the best bowhunter of the three children and the one who most appreciated a good partridge, particularly when roasted with tarragon, Mirtis had pretty much vanquished this game bird's population on the family's modest hunting ground. But this one had eluded her. Mirtis had been coming home with frustrating stories of pursuit, such as how three sharply honed arrows had passed straight through it without ruffling a feather. The stories impressed Dunamis greatly, for she valued the ability to tell a good tale and, in her wistful moments, missed her friends in the city, who had loved to stay up all night conjuring stories from their imagination. But Dunamis realized soon enough that Mirtis' trials in the hunt were not imagined when she herself witnessed a swift and true arrow not an inch from the bird's breast curl suddenly around it and then resume its course as if nothing had gotten in its path. And now here that partridge was, lifting itself onto its scarlet legs and saying, "Do stop fretting about those children." Then it winked a caramel-colored eye and flew from the ledge.

Magic, she thought. *Fairy magic. Of course. Why didn't I think of that before?* And so, when she heard Lirette's voice from the garden, expressing, as she often did, curiosity about why they had such strange little jewels around their necks, Dunamis poked her head from the window and said, "You might try making a wish."

"A wish . . .," Lirette repeated. "Now, why didn't I think of that before?" She held the enameled cherry to her lips and murmured into it, "I wish for a house of roses. No thorns, please."

At the same moment, with not even a tremor or a flash of light, as one might have expected, the little cottage was no more, and in its place was the most heavenly abode. It was not lofty but was exceedingly more spacious than the cottage. The walls were covered with braided branches, from the ceilings dangled curls of vines, and in the middle of each room was a rose tree in full flower. The floor, no longer hard under Dunamis' feet, was thick with soft pink petals whose aroma filled the air, reminding her of the bouquets she had once carried in court alongside the other ladies-in-waiting.

"Go ahead, Mirtis, it's your turn!" Lirette cried, after the three of them had run through the halls of the house of roses and now lay breathless, in the grass beneath the window, where Dunamis still stood looking out. Only now she peered through an elegant frame, the window flung open, its crystal clear panes shimmering in the sunlight.

Mirtis ran her fingertips along the ribbon at her neck until she had the lapis plum in her cupped hand. She scanned the shallow wood that abutted the yard. "My wish," she said, "is for a forest so thick that one can walk for an hour without seeing the light on the other side, a forest filled with every species of game." A rustling came from the wood, a quiet whooshing of shoots pushing upward and outward. "Heavy on the partridges!" Mirtis added, her gaze landing on the bird that had been vexing her. It sat on the branch of a chestnut tree that was still rising from the soil though it was already three stories high. The partridge tutted, and a chorus of identical tuts joined in from the darkening forest. Mirtis, a grin on her face, strode into the house to retrieve her bow.

"What about you?" Lirette asked Finfin. They were on their backs, looking up at the patch of sky over the house, a view framed more tightly now by the creeping canopy.

"I have nothing to wish for," he said, "except to be loved by you as much as you are loved by me."

"Oh," she replied, "my heart can satisfy you on that point. You needn't waste a wish."

"Well, then," he said, lifting the emerald almond from his chest, "I wish that in this new forest, there will be a handsome prince out hunting, and that our paths will cross and he will fall desperately in love with Mirtis."

Mirtis, returning just in time to hear this, took immediate umbrage. "What did I ever do to you?" She stood with hands on hips, her bow and quiver of arrows strapped to her back.

"Isn't it your desire to find love?" Finfin asked.

"Of course," Mirtis said, "but in a natural way. Not by *enchantment*. A person should have a choice in the matter, not have dictated to him whom he must or mustn't love."

Dunamis, who had been taking all this in from the window, sighed deeply.

"But he will be a prince," Finfin pointed out. "And he will be handsome."

"On the outside or the inside?" Mirtis huffed. Then she turned to Dunamis. "Do you happen to know what the princes are like around here?"

Dunamis had been out of the world for so long that she knew little of such matters. It was true that she had, when she'd first arrived in the glen, heard a story of a nearby king, one who had gained his power by cruelly putting to death the rightful sovereign of the kingdom. Maybe she had heard of sons, but with no definitive knowledge to share regarding their existence, or more importantly their character, she chose to say nothing at all to Mirtis about the whole matter. "Perhaps a wish can be taken back," she said instead, and she looked up inquiringly to the partridge, which still sat on the chestnut branch. It gave no indication of an answer, just puffed out its mottled neck feathers.

"Then I take it back," Finfin said, getting up and stretching. "But perhaps, Mirtis, you are thinking too much."

Lirette put out a hand to him and let him pull her to her feet. "Or perhaps, Finfin," she said gently, "you are thinking too little."

Mirtis, by that time, had pulled an arrow from her quiver and was running her fingers along its shaft, smoothing the fletching, tapping the sharp point of the flint. "Oh, let's just go, I'm famished," she said, tromping off to the path in the dark wood.

They had quite a day of it, catching a fat hare and cooking it up for lunch, then pursuing a roebuck all afternoon until Mirtis launched an arrow, clean and quick. It was the largest deer they'd ever carried, and that, combined with the trek being lengthier than they were used to, tuckered them out, so they decided to rest under a sprawling tree. Soon they were sound asleep, dreaming the dreams of the well fed and well exercised. Lirette dreamt of Finfin and Finfin of Lirette, and in Mirtis' visions she was at a great banquet with the most agreeable people. She shared a wild turkey leg with one of them, a young man with the kindest disposition. They both bit in at the same time, their eyes locking, then all else was gone but that mutual gaze, now in a fog, now in the wood, now under the very branches of the tree where they lay. "Love at first bite," whispered the young man, leaning over her.

"Yesss," Mirtis whispered back. But then, eyes wide, she jumped to her feet and cried, "No-no-no-no-*no!*" She gave Finfin a swift kick that woke him and Lirette from their joint reverie.

Finfin sat up against the tree and took in the young man's elegant hunting vest with its gold fleur-de-lis studs, the blue sash across his chest, his gleaming steed tied to a sapling. "Most definitely of royal stock," Finfin said with a yawn.

"And he *is* handsome," Lirette said. Then, noticing the worry in Finfin's brow, she gave his arm a squeeze. "He looks like you."

"Oh, you probably think we all look alike," Finfin said. "After all, I'm the only man you've ever seen until now."

The prince, seemingly oblivious to this exchange, continued to study Mirtis with a look of absolute helplessness. "I don't think I can spend another moment of my life without you."

Mirtis rolled her eyes to the heavens. Twilight was beginning to wash over the web of branches, she could see. "Get up, will you?" she said to Lirette and Finfin. "We have to take this roebuck home."

"Would it ease the burden if my horse were to carry it?" the prince asked.

The answers of "No!" from Mirtis and "Yes!" from Lirette and Finfin came at precisely the same moment, the latter handily drowning out the former. So Mirtis could only watch as the heavy carcass was hoisted over the saddle (it, too, studded with gold), and Lirette and Finfin took the reins of the well-mannered steed and began leading it in the direction of home.

The prince stood at a crossroads in the path. "If it is your preference that I don't go with you . . ." he started, his tone quite nearly dire.

"We have your horse," Mirtis said with a sigh, and she waved for him to come along as she followed the clopping of the animal's hooves, one of its shoes (also gold) catching an errant ray of the setting sun through the myriad trunks of the new forest. "You can stay the night in the house of roses."

"House of roses?" he repeated, skipping to catch up with her. "I'm enchanted."

In spite of her mood, she let out a laugh.

Mirtis stayed one step ahead of the prince as they walked, though she did (it was hard not to when rounding bends) shoot him ever-so-quick glances. Yes, she determined, this was the same man from her dream, the one who appreciated a good turkey leg. And yes, he was quite handsome. For what that was worth.

Meanwhile, back at the house of roses, Dunamis had been pacing nervously in the yard for some time. Darkness had almost completely fallen, and there had been no sign of the children. "What if there *is* an evil king, and he *does* have an evil son," she worried aloud, "and he's taken them off to his evil court?"

The partridge, bathing in the garden's birdbath, muttered, "Honestly," then gave itself a good shake and pointed a wing to the wood, from whence could now be heard the bubbling of Lirette's and Finfin's laughter as they neared.

"What a relief!" Dunamis said, a hand on her heart. She watched as her children materialized, followed by the steed with its load.

"Mirtis had quite the catch today," Lirette said, nodding not to the roebuck but to the prince, who appeared out of the shadows at Mirtis' heels.

Dunamis studied him suspiciously, but then her expression softened. There was not a bone of malice in this young man, this she could see from a glance. This anyone could see. He adored the house of roses and was more than comfortable in the room Dunamis chose for him. It was far from Mirtis' (one mustn't take chances), and he stayed on for days, helping with the tending of the sheep, the fishing, and the hunting. He had a knack for the culinary arts, which he put on display one night with roasted partridge so savory the entire family practically swooned. "The secret," he told them as they scraped the bones clean and licked their fingers, "is the tarragon."

"He's quite charming, you have to admit," Finfin said to Mirtis as they did the dishes after dinner. It was his turn to wash and hers to dry.

"And that is exactly the problem," Mirtis said, pulling a fork from the dishwater and drying it with such vigor that the tines bent in all directions. "He is precisely the kind of person I could fall in love with, if only our relationship had not been arranged by the wish of another."

Dunamis, hearing this from the hall, let out a long sigh.

The prince, as you might imagine, was also held in high esteem at his palace home. The queen, for one, had been beside herself with worry since his disappearance. Though she was not his natural mother, she loved him as if she were and had raised him from the time he was a baby. His mother had been beheaded by order of the king, for reasons no one could recall exactly, except to say that the king had been in "one of his moods." He was, to be sure, a capricious and cruel tyrant (just as Dunamis had heard), and his current wife, the queen, had been but part of the plunder he'd made off with when he overthrew the rightful sovereign, her brother. She had been quite young at the time but also quite clever. She quickly discovered two ways to manipulate the king. The first was flattery, which, when used effectively, could derail "one of his moods," thus helping her to avoid being hanged or beheaded or eliminated by whatever means were currently in fashion for doing away with royal wives who fell out of favor. The second had to do with a certain shrub in the hedge of the palace gardens, the odor of which the king found positively putrid. Cat urine, he likened it to (and oh, did he hate cats). She kept sprigs of the shrub in the outer hall to her boudoir, helping her to avoid, well, *him*. She thus spent a great deal of time in her quiet bedroom, most recently in the throes of her worries over the prince. "He is lost now, like the other children," she lamented, salt tears streaking the rouge on her cheeks. "Like my nieces and—"

"Shh! The walls have ears!" It was the partridge who'd issued this imperative. It had swooped in through the window and sat now on a jewel-encrusted perch on the queen's dresser. (The partridge was a fairly regular visitor who had kept the young queen company through her lonely years at court.) "The boy is safe and happy," the bird clucked. "It is best to let him be."

But what the partridge didn't know was that the king, who had been raging nonstop ("I have but one heir! It would be different if I still had two!" he'd shrieked till the turrets shook), had sent out every last one of his troops to find the prince, and one scouting party had happened to come across him in the vast woodland as he was pursuing Mirtis, who was, in turn, pursuing a portly fox. They apprehended the prince tout de suite and delivered him to the king, who, rather than calming down, much to the disappointment of the palace inhabitants, turned his fury on his son: "I have but one heir! It would be different if I still had two!"

That's for sure, the prince thought. The only pleasure he took in being the heir to his father's stolen throne was that he would one day be able to return it to its rightful people. His stepmother had filled him in on his family's awful history, though she never went so far as to tell him what exactly had happened to his older brother. She had almost gotten there once, as they sat in front of a crackling fire after reading together a tale of a maiden in a tower, but, strangely, a rotund bird had appeared in the parlor and tangled its scarlet feet in the queen's carefully coifed curls. "Shh! The walls have ears!" the bird had squawked, though the prince, still a young child at the time, figured he must have imagined that last part.

"Where have you been?" the king stormed.

The prince was not sure how to answer that. He was averse to telling lies, but he was also averse, in this case, to telling the truth. He shuddered at the thought of what his father would think of his having fallen in love with, well, *anyone*. The prince had long understood that he was to be paired with someone of his father's choosing, someone who would expand the king's riches. "I can't remember," the prince said loudly (as he was accustomed to doing in order to be heard, his father's sense of hearing having suffered considerably from years of being in such close proximity to his own shouting), and then he finished in a mumble, "being happier in my life than I was these past few days."

"You can't *remember!*" the king bellowed. "Did you hit your head?" But before the prince could answer that, the king had summoned his court physician, who was tasked with thoroughly examining the young man.

There was nothing wrong with the prince, of course. At least not then. But soon enough his longing for Mirtis did make him ill, visibly so. He was pale and listless. At meals, he moved his food around his plate but rarely lifted a morsel to his mouth. Then one evening at supper, when a platter of wild turkey legs à la tarragon was brought to table, he broke down and wept.

"The heir to my throne will not weep!" the king yelled from his high seat.

"Apparently he will," the queen said.

The king, not one to overlook a contradiction at his dining table, glared at his wife. "*What* did you say?"

"I said," the queen responded, clearing her throat, "that you parent with such skill."

"Ohh." The king snorted. "Right you are. To set a good example for a boy, he must have a strong and talented father figure."

The queen, slicing into her turkey leg, nodded in agreement. "So true. I'll be on the lookout for such a man."

The king, who had been taking a slosh of mead, sent a spray of the stuff across the table. "*What* did you say?"

"I said," the queen volleyed back, "Oh, boo, I sure lucked out when I won your hand." She flashed him a coy smile, then pulled a linen hanky from her sleeve and handed it across the table to the still-sobbing prince.

The queen knew what ailed her stepson: love. She'd never experienced it herself, but she'd read enough novels to be familiar with the symptoms. So that evening, as the royals took their after-dinner strolls around the palace grounds, she surreptitiously followed his wan frame until she found him sitting dejectedly under an arbor of climbing roses. She held a finger to her lips as she approached him (ever aware that the king's spies seemed to lurk in every shadow) and carefully extracted a branch from the hedge that lined the path. Then, kneeling next to the prince, she wrote in the tawny silt *Who has stolen your heart?* and handed the branch to him. He wrote the name *Mirtis*, and next to that drew a house, then set alongside it a rose he had pulled from the arbor. And in this silent way, the two hatched a plan to save the prince from his melancholy.

They were gone by first light the next morn, on the queen's softest-footed mares, and they arrived at the house of roses just as Mirtis was walking from the door with a pitcher of mint tea for the family's lunch in the garden. When she saw the prince emerge from the tree line, she looked as if she'd seen a ghost. "Whatever happened to you?" she cried. "You're skin and bones. Have you been lost in the wood all this time?"

"He's been lost, but not in the wood," answered the queen, materializing beside him.

It was then that Dunamis came from the house, a basket of bread in the crook of her arm. "Oh, my, we were so worried about you!" she said to the prince.

"Especially Mirtis," Lirette and Finfin added simultaneously from the table.

Mirtis gave them an annoyed look, then said airily, "Well, he *is* a good cook."

"Come, come!" Dunamis waved them to the table. "We have venison coming out of our ears."

The prince slid onto a bench with Mirtis and inhaled the savory aroma. "I couldn't eat a bite without you," he said dreamily.

"You're his mother?" Dunamis asked the queen, pulling up a chair for her.

"Stepmother," the queen said, looking proudly at the prince, who was filling his cheeks with food like a chipmunk. Then she gazed around the table, her eyes lingering first on Finfin and then settling for an even longer time on Lirette and Mirtis. "These are your children?"

"Well, it's a bit of a story—"

But Dunamis was interrupted by a clopping of hooves, then the sound of a bugle, then a loud pronouncement at the edge of the yard: "All rise for the king!"

"Oh, no," the queen mumbled. Then she got up and said cheerfully in the direction of her husband, "How clever you were to find us, dear! How did you ever figure out our little lark?"

"The hedges have eyes," he replied, and he dismounted and approached the luncheon party. "No heir of mine is going to be cavorting with people like this!" he boomed, taking in the plain tunics and sandals that Mirtis, Lirette, and Finfin had donned for the day's work in the sheep meadow. "Come now, get away from the riffraff," he said to the prince.

"How dare you?" Dunamis said.

The king turned a savage eye on her. "*What* did you say?"

"She said," the queen jumped in, taking Dunamis' hand and squeezing it in the folds of her gabardine skirt to signal that she should play along, "'How fair, you.'"

"No, she didn't," the king said. Then to his right-hand man, he spat, "Seize the witch. I shall burn her at the stake."

"What a trope," Dunamis muttered.

"*What* did you say?" the king thundered.

The queen held Dunamis' hand more closely. Unlike her own, it was calloused from country life. But there was an inner softness, an unusual warmth, the queen found herself thinking. "My king, what she said to you was—" the queen began, but Dunamis gave her an *Oh, do let me have a crack at this game* look and turned to the ruler.

"I said," Dunamis told him, quite loudly enough to be heard, "'What a dope.'" At which one of the henchmen pulled her roughly away from the others and began binding her wrists.

"Father," the prince pleaded, standing now and placing a hand on Mirtis' shoulder, "I'm in love, and I want to spend my life here."

"Are you daft?" the king said to his son. "You can't spend your life with commoners. You can't spend another *minute*. Get on your horse and let's be off." And then to his entourage he barked, "Take the whole lot to the palace and fling them into the dungeons!"

Finfin, who had been taking all this in from where he stood next to Lirette at the table, had in his fingers his emerald almond, poised at his lips. "I wish us away," he said.

"Perhaps a little more specificity would be, uh, prudent," Lirette said, and then she breathed into her own charm: "I wish us transported to a place where we will be able to live safely. A place with some roses, if it's all the same to you."

And they began to float upward, away from the grasp of the king's guard: first Dunamis, then Finfin, then Lirette, then Mirtis. Those left in the garden could only watch with expressions of awe or powerlessness or fury (in the case of the king) or relief (in the case of the queen) or, as Mirtis couldn't help but notice, abject misery in the case of the prince. "Poor guy, I wish he could escape, too," she said, and his body lifted off the earth as well.

"Touché," Finfin said to Mirtis.

"Who says I meant that to happen? I could have been using the word 'wish' figuratively. It could have been unintentional." The others nodded politely, but their eyes were on her hand, which still rested on the lapis plum at her breast. She dropped it and said defensively, "Well, it would have been cruel to send him back to his lovelorn self-starvation, which was the fault of, um, *whose* wish?" and she sent a piercing look in Finfin's direction.

"But what will happen to *her*?" Dunamis asked, peering down at the now-small blur that was the queen.

The prince, who had just reached their height, said, "If anyone knows how to handle him, it's my stepmother."

"And she has help," said a voice from the cloud that was now surrounding them. "Hold on tight, please," the partridge squawked (for that was who had spoken), and they began zipping through the air, over the vast woodland and beyond, until they landed on a knoll covered with grass and flowers that sparkled like gems. To one side of the mound on which they stood ran a shimmering river, fish leaping over its weirs as if part of a ballet. To the other side of the mound was a forest of tall trees that they could not see over.

"Welcome," the voice of the partridge said, but now it was not attached to a bird but to a rotund person with scarlet boots, a mottled shawl, and caramel-colored eyes. A fairy, to be sure. "You will be safe in this realm, so long as you stay within its bounds. You may fish and bathe in the river, but never touch its opposite shore," she said. "You may hunt in the forest, but mind the perimeter, which is marked by great oaks with roots and trunks of iron. If you cross the river or pass the iron oaks, you will not be allowed back. Know that your necklaces cannot save you any longer, as their powers expired upon your passage into the fairy lands."

"Oh, my, that's a lot to be mindful of," Dunamis said.

The fairy shrugged. "Paradise has its conditions."

She waved her hand to reveal a castle of gleaming quartz on the bank of the river. "You may set up house there. You will find all you need to amuse yourselves in a hundred different ways." She waved her other hand to reveal dewy hills of pasture. "Fairy sheep grow fibers so supple that the yarn you create will be like none you have spun before," she said to Dunamis.

And so they settled in. They tended the flock, and they fished and hunted, and they cooked fine meals for each other. It wasn't long before the prince was in the pink of health again and quite content, even while Mirtis made a point of remaining aloof to his attentions. For Dunamis' part, she certainly had no cause to complain. Her distaff and spindle were of gold, her yarns undeniably exquisite, and her accommodations were more elegant than any she had known, even during her days at court. But all the same, there was something nagging at her, a certain emptiness she hadn't felt in her life in the glen. It was not that the fairy was poor company. In fact, she reminded Dunamis of her old friends, talkative and original. But she was often away, attending to the duties of her domain.

"They pile up and pile up, the responsibilities," the fairy complained one afternoon while pulling books from a shelf in her library. "When you live as long as we citizens of the supernatural do, you end up with a whole bevy of souls in your care, and then their descendants and cousins, and while they are all multiplying freely, there is still just one of you!" She opened a book on the table in front of her, and ran a finger along the page. "And the precedents! They continue to grow, too, so it takes ever longer to find what one needs to solve the array of problems that develop on any given day. Case in point: A dairy farmer in my care is dealing with a curse on his milk that has rendered it undrinkable, and he and his family will become vagabonds if a remedy cannot be found. The *right* remedy, that is. Not one that will turn the milk chartreuse or make it the consistency of glue. When you get something like that wrong, the embarrassment can be practically debilitating. It is easy to just give up. I have a friend who exiled herself after such a humiliation. She's been living in a colony of gryphons. They do try to amuse her, but it's not the same. She can't be herself, she says."

Dunamis sighed.

"Then there's the issue of jurisdictions!" the fairy went on. "The districts are drawn so unevenly. I find myself losing hours to travel, when my charges are in such need. I could, for instance, take up permanent residence in that dastardly kingdom you've had the misfortune to intersect with, but I've hardly had time to stop there since we flew off from the house of roses. I'd better hop over there tomorrow."

"So you don't know if the queen's okay?"

"She's as okay as she can be," the fairy said, looking up from the book and studying Dunamis' face. "Is this what has you bothered? You've seemed troubled since your arrival. Or is it the children? Are they not entirely happy?"

"They are certainly happy. Though I do have my concerns about them, as you know . . ."

"Oh, yes, right, the relations thing. I promised to fill you in on that," the fairy said, putting a bookmark on her page and giving Dunamis her full attention. "Lirette is not related to Finfin. She is, however, related to Mirtis. They are twins. The queen's nieces."

"Her nieces?" Dunamis repeated. "But the queen didn't seem to recognize them."

"Oh, but she did," the fairy said. "She has tremendous self-control, that one, and there was no way she would risk the king getting even an inkling that her nieces, the children of the rightful sovereign, ever existed. This is why the queen parted with them those many years ago, to save them. You see, when their parents were murdered, the infants were with their nursemaid, who, having a smidgeon of fairy blood in her veins, was able to reach me very quickly, before the king's scouts discovered them. It was easily within my skill set to take the children and place them with a trustworthy guardian such as yourself, but I wanted them to have an extra layer of protection, something that would allow them to escape if the king did learn of their existence and seek them out."

"Ah, the necklaces," Dunamis said.

"Yes." The fairy leaned to her left and ran a finger along the spine of a book. "It was in this one," she said, "*Early Voodoo*. Charmed jewelry, the passage read, can be used to protect children whose parents have been assassinated by a usurper. But only if the usurper is made to give up a child. That is where Finfin comes into the picture."

"Finfin is the king's son?"

The fairy nodded. "His elder son."

"Did the king recognize him at the house of roses?"

"No, but he's a lamebrain," the fairy said, sticking her nose back in the book. "The bottom line is that you needn't worry about Lirette and Finfin. Let them enjoy their love."

Enjoy their love they certainly did. The two were positively gleeful living in the fairy realm. They helped each other with their morning chores to free up lazy

afternoons, which they spent in hammocks or crooks of tree limbs or napping in poppy fields. The hunt they usually left to Mirtis and the prince, whose instincts for the chase were far better than theirs, but on this day, this unlucky day, they had decided to join their friends in the forest. It was a long day of pursuit with nothing to show for it (these animals were more intelligent than those of the lay world), and fatigue most surely was a contributing factor in what was about to happen. They were near the iron oaks, and Lirette caught sight of a white fawn leaping. It was so graceful and mesmerizing that she followed it a step too far. Just a step, but she knew right away that all she could do was wait for the king's guard. She could not move. Finfin, without hesitation, ran to her. "I will perish with you!" he cried, and in a moment he too was frozen.

The prince and Mirtis rounded a bend in the path just in time to see Finfin and Lirette surrounded by spearpoints. The prince took off in their direction, but he was pulled back with but an inch to his doom by Mirtis, who had run full speed to gain on him. She had a look of utter terror on her face. (Terror of the losing-the-one-you-love variety, though she would not admit that, not yet.) "My father will abuse them," the prince cried, breathless. But Mirtis, composing herself, turned him around gently, away from the scene of the abduction. "We will be of better use to them if we stay here and get help," she said, and the two wended their way back through the forest to apprise the fairy of Lirette and Finfin's plight.

"Oh, no," the fairy said, her furrowed brow just barely visible over the stack of books that she'd accumulated in the course of her day's work. "But what did they expect? That was, after all, the clearly stated consequence of the fault they committed."

"It had to have been my father's trickery at work," the prince said.

"You can surely get them out of this mess," Mirtis pleaded. "You have powers, after all."

"See?" the fairy said, peering around the stacks at Dunamis. "Everyone thinks we do this off the tops of our heads. I can tell you that this one will need some time. You have to take into account not only the begotten son of a monarch, a usurper no less, but also the daughter of the displaced ruler. A week, minimum."

"That might be too late," the prince said gravely.

"I can help with the research," Dunamis said. "I'll stay up as long as it takes."

"But these books are in the languages of the fae," the fairy said.

"Oh, come on," Mirtis said, exasperated. "Surely you have the power to translate. Don't you have a wand or something?"

"And there's another misconception! A stereotype, I would go so far as to say. We don't *all* use wands."

"But the books," Dunamis said softly. "Can't you translate?"

And the fairy, noticing now that Dunamis was holding back tears, put a hand on hers and nodded. "All right, all right, we'll give this our best effort."

So Mirtis and the prince were sent off to the kitchens to prepare food for an all-nighter, and the fairy and Dunamis dug in, trying to find a potion or incantation that would free Lirette and Finfin from the king's bonds.

The sun had just sent its first rays of morning into the library when Dunamis let out a long breath and pushed a book across the table and under the fairy's eyes. There was silence as the fairy read, then she said simply, "No."

"Well, have *you* found anything?" Dunamis whispered, not wanting to wake Mirtis and the prince, who were sleeping in the library's armchairs.

"Not yet." The fairy yawned. "But we must be able to do better than a sacrifice."

"I am willing to do that for my children."

"We'll give it another day" was the fairy's response, and she pushed the book back to Dunamis and began scanning the page in front of her again.

Dunamis leaned closer. "I'm *doing* it," she said, and she slid the book back to the fairy.

The fairy studied the passage again. "It says that 'a female must present herself and satisfy the vengeance of the monarch,' but there is no mention of that female's race or realm. I should be the one. I've lived a lot longer than you have."

Dunamis shook her head adamantly. "We need magic in this world."

"But so, too," the fairy said, "do we need spinners of fine yarns."

Dunamis could not be swayed, however, and the two of them made their solemn plan. They kept Mirtis and the prince in the dark about the whole matter, Dunamis fearing that they would weaken her resolve if they knew. They were told that she was close to finding the answer and thus needed to be left alone in the library, and so they let the fairy take them up to her writing desk, where she asked them to fashion hopeful letters to Lirette and Finfin. The couple poured their hearts into the task, and when they'd completed the first letter, the fairy said she would attempt to deliver it right away and try to bring back a response. And that was when the fairy secretly took Dunamis off, escorting her to the forest's edge.

The fairy peeled a palmful of moss from the shady side of an iron oak and put it into Dunamis' hand. "When you are in the greatest peril that can befall you, throw this moss at the feet of the king," she said. And then the two of them stepped across the threshold together, the fairy-turned-bird flying swiftly for the palace (the letter in one claw and ink and pen in the other) and Dunamis standing tall as the king's men closed in to seize her.

They had her before the king in no time. "Ha!" he cried triumphantly from the high dais where he sat on his throne next to the queen. "I have you at last, wicked creature, and I will put you to death by the most cruel torture!"

"Please do," Dunamis said. "I have come willingly for that purpose."

The king, taken aback, said, "You could not have come *willingly*, because you were brought here *forcefully*."

"Not mutually exclusive, those two things," the queen said under her breath, but the words reverberated under the vaulted ceiling, producing a smattering of gasps from the gallery.

The king turned a venomous eye on his wife. "*What* did you say?"

She smiled sweetly at him. "I said, 'How unusually lucid, O true king.'"

"Hm," he said. "True."

"And might I be of some help to you, my sweet," the queen asked him, "in the vanquishing of Dunamis? I could pick some foxglove and have the cook stir it into her porridge in the morning."

"She's not having porridge in the morning. She won't even *be* here in the morning!" he roared, and then he ordered the troops to take Dunamis to the holding cell so the pit could be prepared. "I want it filled with snakes! No, no, better still, vipers and adders!"

"Which *are* snakes, last I checked," the queen mumbled, rolling her eyes.

Dunamis let out an amused snort, and her eyes met the queen's for just a moment before she was pushed roughly from the chamber.

"*What* did you say?" the king spat at his wife.

"I said that vipers and adders *are* snakes, you dodo." And she rose from her throne and strutted away before being dismissed.

At the same moment, in the bowels of the palace, Lirette and Finfin huddled together to keep from shivering. The partridge was perched on the stone ledge of a tiny window. She'd slid the letter through the bars, and it had provided some solace to the captives, who had heretofore thought the only grace in their final, fearsome days would be that they had been kept together. *We shall meet again, in spite of malice, and be happy*, Mirtis and the prince had written in their closing. And now Lirette and Finfin, weak in body but buoyed in spirit, wrote back:

> We have received your letter, and it has brought us more joy than we could have anticipated. In these regions of horror, our torments would be insupportable but for the sweet consolation we derive from each other's presence. Near the object of our affections, we are insensible to pain. Dear prince, dear Mirtis, encourage your mutual passion. Be always inspired by a tender fidelity. You have held out to us a hope that we now share. Adieu, Lirette and Finfin

The partridge tucked the new letter into her claw and told the captive lovers she would return soon, but they entreated her to stay and give them more news. They asked about Dunamis, how she was handling their absence, and the partridge answered in a warbling coo, "More bravely than you can imagine." And she set her caramel-colored eyes on the tower, where she knew executions took place, and took flight off the ledge.

Mirtis and the prince were relieved to get the letter upon the fairy's return, and they opened it immediately and read it eagerly together.

"What wise words," the prince said when he'd finished. He looked at Mirtis with such love in his eyes.

Her own gaze remained on the letter's script. "Encourage your mutual passion," she read aloud. "But how does one do that in good conscience when the other's heart has not been free to choose?"

"What are you prattling on about?" the fairy said, scooping up a new letter that the couple had written. "You were right there when Finfin took that wish back. Didn't you hear him?"

Mirtis stared at the fairy for a beat or two, then said, "But the prince, he, um, you know . . . fell so hard. It doesn't happen that way."

"But it did," the prince said.

She looked at him now, closely, seriously, wonderingly, as she hadn't let herself before. "The fairy could be making that up," she said to him.

"Whyever would I do that?" the fairy huffed, and she ducked out the door, leaving behind a room that was suddenly very quiet. *The quiet of tender fidelity*, she thought with satisfaction. And with a smirk, she set off on her delivery.

When she arrived back at the palace, she could hear a commotion, and so, though leaden with dread, she flew lightly as a swift up to the top of the tower and through a slit of a window. Hardly any natural light saw this room, but it was bright nonetheless, with sconces lining the rounded walls. A crowd of witnesses was being hushed now as the king and queen were installed on the viewing dais, and then Dunamis was brought in and set on the block at the edge of the pit.

"I can't hear my vipers!" the king yelled, though their hissing was more than audible.

"Perhaps they have escaped," the queen said, "because they do not wish to end the life of a good woman."

"And perhaps," the king said, "*you* are to be next on the block today." And he strode to the edge of the pit and looked down at his writhing tangle of reptilian executioners. "Oh, there you are," he cooed, his expression suddenly soft with sordid pleasure. His eyes twinkled as he looked first at Dunamis, then at his wife.

It was at that moment, when his head was turned, that Dunamis launched from her cupped hand the little bundle of moss the fairy had pulled from the iron oak. It landed behind the king's feet, so when he pivoted to return to the dais, he slipped, and precipitously so, falling directly into the snake pit. His shrieks reached such a decibel that sconces began to burst, raining glass shards onto the witnesses, who stood stunned, hands over their ears.

"Nicely done!" the partridge squawked from the window ledge. "I shall gather the children." And she shot off into the blue.

The queen alighted from the dais and, taking Dunamis' arm, said, "Let's never set foot in here again." And they headed for the exit.

"But my queen," one of the witnesses called out, "what should we do now?"

She looked around the room at all those who had gathered for the day's intended spectacle and said, before disappearing down the curling stairway, "Damned if I know."

Which was pretty much what the prince said a few hours later in the throne room, when the same question was posed to him by a member of the king's guard. "Finfin is the heir," he said (for the fairy had by this time filled them all in on their genealogies). "Ask him."

"No, no, no," Finfin said. "You're the one with the wardrobe. You take charge."

"Then I cede the reign back to its rightful family," the prince said, looking at Mirtis and Lirette. "You rule."

They gazed up at the lavish pair of thrones, whose colorful gems danced in the flickering torchlight.

"That's just not me," Mirtis said.

"Me neither," Lirette agreed. "Auntie, you stay on," she said to the queen, and hugged her warmly, as she had done no less than a dozen times since learning of their kinship.

"No thank you, my darling," she said. "I've had enough of this kingdom to last a lifetime." And she took off her mantle of ermine and put it around Lirette's shoulders, then placed her crown on Mirtis' head. "Let's see if your generation does a better job than ours did."

The guard, now to the two young women, said, "So what should we do?"

Mirtis and Lirette looked at each other, then at the throne chairs again, and then they nodded.

"First, take those away and dismantle them. Distribute the valuables to those of our kingdom with the greatest need," Mirtis said.

"And bring in a couple of comfortable sofas in their stead," Lirette said. "There will be four of us ruling." She blew Finfin a kiss.

"Okay, I shall acquiesce, so long as you never leave me," Finfin said.

"I echo my brother's sentiment," the prince said to Mirtis.

From that moment they considered themselves perfectly happy. Their marriages were celebrated throughout the land. When the splendid nuptials were over, the widowed queen and Dunamis made an announcement: "We shall be retiring to the house of roses."

And so they did, and they found happiness in their tranquility. For ever after.

PERSINETTE

ONCE THERE WAS a young couple who married after a long pursuit of their love. Their bliss was unmatched. They wanted a child, and the young wife was soon pregnant.

In their neighborhood, there also lived a fairy. She was very proud of her garden, which had a profusion of all kinds of flowers and fruits. Among the plants was parsley, rare in those regions. The fairy had brought it from India.

Whenever the young wife walked by the garden, she felt an intense desire for the parsley. These cravings increased by the day until she was in a state of distress. Her husband begged her to tell him the cause, and she finally confessed to him that she could not live without eating a bite of parsley.

(At the time, parsley must have had an excellent taste.)

The husband knew, as all in the neighborhood did, that entering the fairy's garden was taboo. Nevertheless, as nothing seems too difficult in love, he walked day and night around the garden, trying to climb the wrought iron fence. But it was of too great a height.

Then one evening he noticed that the garden gate was open, and he slipped in and hastily took a handful of parsley. How relieved he was! He brought the leaves back to his wife, who ate them avidly and instantly felt better.

This did not last long, however. Her cravings returned, worse than ever, and her condition became more dire by the day. Her husband returned to the garden over and over, until finally he again found the door open. But this time the fairy was waiting for him, and she scolded him vociferously for trespassing. The young man got down on his knees and begged her forgiveness, telling her that his pregnant wife would die if she didn't have some parsley.

"Well," said the fairy, "I'll give you as much as you like, as often as you wish, if you give me the child when your wife gives birth."

WOMEN OF THE FAIRY TALE RESISTANCE

The distraught husband could think only of how ill his beloved had become and how he would surely lose her if he did not get the parsley. That was something he couldn't bear, and so he agreed to the fairy's terms. He grabbed a large handful of parsley and ran home.

When the time for the birth came, the fairy was there to receive the child. She named her Persinette and swaddled her in spun gold. Then she sprinkled her face with precious water that had the power to make her the most beautiful creature in the world. After these ceremonies, the fairy took the baby away from her desolate parents.

Persinette was raised with the utmost care and grew to be a marvel. By her twelfth birthday, the fairy began to regret endowing her with the charms she had. She was fraught with worry over the dangers the dear child might face from men with ill intent. To save her from this destiny, the fairy conjured a silver tower in a faraway place and took Persinette there to live. The tower had spacious apartments that received daylight through the enormous gemstones that made up the walls, giving the rooms a warm and colorful glow. Everything necessary to life was found there, and splendidly so. All the meals were delicate and delicious, and the wardrobes were filled with dresses as intricately sewn as if for the queens of Asia. Her bedchamber was at the very top, where there was a window, the only one in the tower. The fairy, after seeing Persinette to her room each evening, would descend from the window to return home. Because, you see, there was no door to this tower.

Persinette knew only the fairy, so she did not recognize solitude nor want for company. She read, painted, played instruments; all her desires were satisfied. It was a pleasure for her to look out the window to the sea in one direction and the vast forest in the other. She liked to sing there, her elbows on the ledge, her voice as lovely as everything else about her. The fairy, who visited often, would stand beneath the window and listen for a while before calling out her usual request: "Persinette, let down your hair!"

The child's hair was yet another of her great beauties. It was thirty yards long (though not a bother to her, as you might imagine) and she wove ribbons of all colors into it. Whenever she heard the fairy's request, she would drop her long braid down from the window and the fairy would climb up it. This was their routine, and the two of them, like mother and daughter, were content with this arrangement. Time went by.

Then one day when Persinette was at her window, a young prince heard her singing. He was out on a hunt but had gone off his usual course following a fleeing deer. Spellbound by Persinette's voice, he looked up to see her in the window, and her appearance only charmed him further. He circled the tower, and finding no entrance, he thought he would die of longing. He was in love, he was bold, and he wanted to climb the tower.

Persinette, for her part, became speechless when she noticed him. She stared in astonishment, then withdrew from the window. She worried that he was some kind of monster. The fairy had told her to beware of monsters, that some could destroy with merely their eyes. Persinette had never seen a man before.

The prince sought out the nearest village to ask about the mysterious tower, and he was told in hushes that someone evil had built it, an ogress, some said, a witch, some said. That a girl had been locked away there. The prince, now even more determined, returned to the tower and waited. And waited.

But instead of Persinette appearing at the window, the fairy appeared beneath it. Taking cover behind a shrub, the prince watched as she called up, "Persinette, let down your hair!" How surprised he was when he saw a gleaming braid drop from the ledge and the fairy latch on and climb into the tower.

Persinette, he thought, *now I have a name for my love*. Fearing for her safety, he stayed right where he was, working out what to do next. Some hours later, when the fairy climbed down and left, he sprang into action. Standing under

the window and imitating the fairy's voice, he called out, "Persinette, let down your hair!"

Assuming the fairy had forgotten something, Persinette tossed her braid down without even a glance out the window. The prince climbed it, and when he was at the top and saw her face-to-face, he thought he would fall right there to his death, her beauty even more striking up close. But, regaining his boldness, he leapt into the room and threw himself at her feet.

Persinette was, of course, frightened, and she cried out, then trembled. The prince cried and trembled, too, and then professed his love for her in the most tender terms. Her confusion over what was occurring only served to give him hope, and the more he hoped, the more he talked, saying the most endearing things. Soon she felt her heart swelling, until it held just as much love as she had inadvertently put into the heart of the prince.

How happy they were. They saw each other every day, the prince climbing her braid to the top of the tower. They held a marriage ceremony of their own making and set about devising a plan for her escape. It could not be soon enough, they knew, because the fairy would surely be on to them. She had already expressed suspicions that something was amiss, but Persinette had always managed to assuage her worries. That is, until she became pregnant. Persinette didn't realize the cause of her symptoms, never having learned about such things. But the fairy, well, *she* knew just by looking at her.

"Oh, such unhappiness you have caused me!" the fairy cried. "You have fallen, and you will be punished for it!" She grabbed Persinette by the hair and cut off her braid. Then she ushered a cloud into the room, which enveloped Persinette and carried her away.

When the air around her cleared, Persinette found herself in a meadow, a stream of fresh water bubbling by. Ahead she saw a small hut made of branches, and when she went inside she found a bed of reeds. Next to it was a basket filled with biscuits, which she would soon discover were very good and the basket always full. It was in this place that she would give birth to a little girl and a little boy, and it was in this place that she would nourish them, and where she would mourn the loss of her lover every day.

Back at the tower, the fairy waited. There was only one way a man could have gotten in to deflower her Persinette and it was through this window, so there she sat. When she heard footfalls down below, she let the braid drop, and the prince climbed up, as he was so accustomed now to doing. When he saw the fairy there, his ardor turned to anger. He cried out for his Persinette.

"She is no longer for you," the fairy seethed. "Your crime is infinite. The punishment I have planned for you is terrible!"

But the prince, his fury and grief too strong to be constrained even by the fairy's art, threw himself to the ground. He should have died from the impact or fractured a thousand bones, but he landed in a thicket of roses. Staggering to his feet, he went in search of Persinette, moaning her name over and over.

He could not see in front of him, which he thought was because of his relentless tears, but soon he came to realize that he had been blinded by the thorns in his fall. Still, he kept going, feeling his way. When he became too tired he slept, when hunger pressed him he fed on herbs and roots, and when he was so weak that his death seemed certain he cried "Persinette! Persinette! Persinette!" and kept going. He trudged on in this way for years.

On one especially exhausting day, after walking from dawn to dusk, he stopped to lie in a patch of soft grass. He began to nod off, but he soon was jolted awake by a sound that went right to his heart. It filled him with a gentle pulse that he had forgotten he ever knew. *It is my Persinette's voice*, he thought. But then he wondered if his mind was playing tricks. *Or I am dying. This is the end of my journey.*

He was not wrong. He *had* reached the end of his journey. It *was* Persinette's voice.

She sat at the door of her hut, singing a sorrowful song of lost love. Her two children were playing a few steps from her. They moved a little farther away and discovered the place where the prince was lying. No sooner had they seen him than they both threw their little arms around his neck and cried, "You are father! You are father!"

Their mother heard their cries and ran to them in fear, for they had never seen another person in all the time they had been exiled. What danger might her children be in? But upon recognizing her dear husband, her worries turned to a joy that mere words can't express. She shed a cascade of tears. And oh wonder! Scarcely had the precious drops landed in the prince's eyes than they regained all their light. He could see as clearly as he once had, and there in front of him was his Persinette.

The family held each other so tightly that it seemed as if they would all be crushed by the force of their happiness.

But, alas, the fairy's curse was apparently not spent. When Persinette offered her famished lover a biscuit, the moment he touched one, every biscuit in the basket turned to stone. The children were soon wailing from stomach pains, and when their mother went to the stream to at least get them a drink, the instant she dipped her pitcher, all the water turned to crystals. The night seemed to last forever.

At first light, they went out to gather herbs, but before they could pull even a leaf, the plants transformed into toads. The bees that had buzzed around the flowers became venomous beasts, the birds turned to dragons and harpies. The family ran for cover in the hut, but its construction was no match for the new terrors of the sky, and the walls began falling down around them.

"So it is done, my dear Persinette," the prince said sadly. "I found you only to lose you in a more terrible way."

She kissed him tenderly, then her children. "Let's hold each other to the last, then. Our enemies will envy the sweetness of our demise."

Who would not have been touched to see this family dying in this way? *Nobody*, you must think. And you would be right. Not even the fairy could bear witnessing their suffering. Watching from above, she recalled how much she had cared for the amiable Persinette and felt remorse for the misery she'd caused. She swooped down and lifted the four innocents from the maelstrom. Then she took them to the palace of the king, the father of the prince, who had been gone so long they had mourned his loss. Later, the fairy returned with Persinette's parents, who had remained childless and forlorn but lit up again with love when they were reunited with their dear daughter. The agitations of the storms ended now for all, and nothing can compare to the happiness they all felt.

> *Tender spouses, learn from these*
> *How advantageous it is to always share love;*
> *The pain, the work, the most burning concern,*
> *Everything is finally softened*
> *When passions are mutual:*
> *We brave fortune, we overcome fate,*
> *As long as two lovers are one.*

MARIE-JEANNE L'HÉRITIER

Marie-Jeanne L'Héritier was born in 1664, her family a notable one as well. Her mother was the niece of a "keeper of the seal," a title that may conjure images of a caretaker in Versailles' menagerie, but the holder of this job safeguarded the king's gold seal and presided over its use (i.e., stamped it into sealing wax on royal papers). And though it might be difficult to imagine what could possibly distinguish one in a long line of "keepers" from another, Marie-Jeanne's ancestor was considered among the most famous. Also on her maternal side, she was related to Charles Perrault, usually referred to as her uncle, who after a long career serving Louis XIV was just beginning his retirement project of dabbling in tales about the time she was coming of age in Paris. Her paternal side also had an impressive pedigree, including her father's service as a royal historian.

Marie-Jeanne and her siblings were raised in a liberal environment in which they learned about the Greeks and Romans, about literature, philosophy, and science. Her sister became a poet, her brother a mathematician, and she a full-time writer of prose and verse. Because she was allowed to lead an independent life (read: to not marry) she didn't have access to familial wealth, but those familial courtly connections certainly helped her gain patronage for literary pursuits. In the early years, her sponsor was the uber-rich Duchess of Nemours, whose parents had been leaders on the monarchy's side of the Fronde (Louis XIV's first war, which started when he was ten years old). After the duchess died, Marie-Jeanne was given a pension from the current keeper of the seal, which was said to be modest. Although she is considered to have been her generation's most outspoken champion of women writers, she somehow managed to steer clear of scandal and remained in Paris for the entirety of her relatively long life, unlike many of her salon sisters. In comparison, by the time Marie-Jeanne passed, Murat had been dead eighteen years, La Force ten, and d'Aulnoy nearly thirty.

Like the other conteuses, though, she was the recipient of prestigious prizes, hers including academic letters from the Toulouse Academy. This was a first for a woman, and she was presented with her work in gilded notebooks in a ceremony that was described in the *Mercure galant* at the time of her death in 1734. Also from the same obituary—and also, you may already be thinking, in contrast to that same magazine's death notice on Murat's passing—we get a real peek, a sensitive and respectful one, into who she was as a person: "brilliant," "beneficent," a "solid and generous friend." It goes on to say that when she "discovered a beautiful soul, she fell in love with her, and soon the friendship was perfect." And that the loss of "loved ones or friends made her tears flow decades later with the same tenderness." She "honored her sex," it extols at the end, "by her knowledge, by her talents for poetry and by the quantity of works that she gave to the public." But missing from this lengthy and laudatory tribute is any mention of her fairy tales. The blotting out of these women's contributions to the genre was underway by that time.

This was in no small part due to the constant batterings the conteuses had taken in the public square from the time of Pierre de Villiers' *Interviews on Fairy Tales . . . a Condom Against Bad Taste*, that first attempt at quelling readers' passion for contes de fées. (Call it *contes interruptus*?) His was not a lone voice. Misogynistic writers had had a readership for decades, their works mostly going uncontested. Marie-Jeanne L'Héritier may have been one of the first women to launch a counter-attack, and that was against the infamous "Satire X" in a book by Nicolas Boileau. The piece is a one-sided rant in verse by a man who is trying to steer another away from marriage, claiming that all women are "true demons bringing hell into their households" and categorizing wives into types. Here are just a few: "the woman who contradicts her husband," "the madwoman," and "the old woman with dominant arrogance who still wants, twenty years after the sacrament, to demand from the husband the respect of a lover." Marie-Jeanne would have agreed with him on one point—that marriage was to be avoided—but it was obvious that the satire really pissed her off. At about the same time that a new edition of Boileau's book was being stocked by booksellers, a beloved Parisian poet, Antoinette Deshoulières, died, and Marie-Jeanne was tasked with writing an elegy. It would become, in part, a response to "Satire X."

Its title loosely translates as "The Recognition at Parnassus," and the elegy/riposte stages Deshoulières' installment among the Muses of Greek mythology. The reader is taken on a journey through the afterlife that passes through triumphal arches honoring women in the literary arts and ends at Mount Parnassus, home of the Muses, where Apollo conducts the inauguration ceremony. The mood of the piece is elevated, heroic, and stays so even while getting its digs in. The worst—or let's say best—insults come through Apollo. He claims that he has already punished the satirist, proof being Boileau's lack of talent, and that the "calls to scandalize" women in such a "cruel manner" are further avenged by the very act of Deshoulières' elevation to Parnassus. Apollo's final quip: "And the ladies have already taken revenge in their toilettes for the insult of this libel, by tearing it to make *papillottes*." (Sorry to have to say, but *papillottes*, an archaic French term that was hard to track down, didn't mean toilet tissue. It apparently referred to curling papers, meaning the Parisian women were ripping the pages of "Satire X" into strips to curl their hair. Still fun, but not as.) Marie-Jeanne received laurel wreaths from readers upon the publication of the elegy.

In addition to honoring a revered poet's passing, "The Recognition of Parnassus" was dedicated to a living legend of the time, Madeleine de Scudéry. She had been the most famous novelist in France for much of the seventeenth century and was especially known for her encouragement of other women taking up the pen. This had also made her a longtime target of the likes of Boileau. He made room in his "Satire X," which otherwise stuck to the theme of disparaging wives, for a hostile aside about her and her fans. He referred in the satire to "the insipid authors" who sought Scudéry's advice, using the derogatory word *précieuse* to describe her. (Basically meaning "preciousness," this term became popular as a way to belittle these women and their literary movement, most notably by the famous playwright Molière. It stuck, to the point that many historians apply this label to the female writers of the era, though they wouldn't have used it themselves. Unless, of course, there was some kind of playful appropriation going on—akin to wearing pussyhats at the 2017 Women's March—but there's no evidence to support that.) This slight was at least part of what set Marie-Jeanne on the path to Parnassus. She considered Scudéry, though old enough to be her grandmother, a very close friend.

The feeling must have been mutual, because Scudéry made Marie-Jeanne the heir of her literary salon, and this was no minor bequeathal. Scudéry's salon was part of the first wave of feminist social clubs (one of those "hotbeds of radical thought" that had rankled Louis in the early years of his reign) and was also popular in the second wave, when the conteuses were writing. Marie-Jeanne carried on her friend's tradition when she took over, opening the doors twice a week for a workshop where writers, mainly women, read their work aloud and received feedback. "One writes in order to instruct oneself and to amuse oneself," she said in one of her books, and "one also writes in order to instruct and amuse one's friends." She had this to offer about the withering criticism that female writers inevitably faced: "What does it matter if people . . . are discontented with works that were not made for them?" In these ways, she kept alive the spirit of Sappho, the nom de plume Scudéry had chosen, as a symbol of learned women writers inspiring other women. Whether Scudéry had also been drawn to this ancient poet from Lesbos for her reputed homosexuality is unknown, because she never spoke of that. Of course, she likely wouldn't have. What we do know is that Scudéry never married and that she advocated that women, whenever possible, remain single and keep control of their lives. She viewed heterosexual sex as something to avoid. From what can be gleaned, her protégé, Marie-Jeanne, was of the same mind, about marriage and about sapphic bonds.

Marie-Jeanne's relationship with Henriette-Julie Murat seems to also fit this mold. From two pieces that she published in her *Oeuvres meslées*, or *Mixed Works*, we can see the devotion to her friend and colleague. This book came out in 1696, one year before Murat would publish her first book of contes de fées, although it's apparent that she was already sharing those tales in the salons. Here are a couple of lines from the first of the two pieces, an ode to Murat: "You tell us in abundance certain naïve tales full of the prettiest tricks: Praxille, I see you bring back to France the happy time of the troubadours." (Praxille was an ancient Greek poet often associated with Sappho.) "With all your gifts will you have the power

to bring back the taste of ancient loves?" Obviously, there is much heartfelt praise and encouragement in that. The second piece was a preface to a fairy tale she dedicated to Murat, and we see now an adviser trying to warn her friend away from trouble: "If you want to preserve your heart, your mind must be occupied . . . Be wary of those brusque lovers who say they are on fire from the first moment . . . Your rest and your safety depend on your just distrust." It would appear that she was trying to replicate that mentor-mentee relationship she had had with Scudéry, though Murat was only four years younger than L'Héritier, both in their twenties at the time of these writings. Whatever their bond, we know that they would soon part forever.

Marie-Jeanne did not publicize her sexual orientation, so we can't say for sure whether any of her friendships were of a romantic nature. But no accounts of her life refer to any heterosexual relationships, and she was known to spend her time among women. Most of her poetry was written for women; in the book that included the ode to Murat, there were more than a dozen such pieces. One revealed that Marie-Jeanne, too, was friends with the Princess of Conti, for whom she wrote a sonnet. It was in a form called *bouts-rimés*, showing that it was crafted in a social setting—probably part of a salon game—because a bouts-rimés requires two people: one to make a list of words in a rhyme scheme, and one to write a poem that uses those words as end rhymes. It's fun to imagine who might have filled the first role—perhaps La Force? Murat? Or the princess herself?—but we can assume Marie-Jeanne played the latter part, since she claimed the work as hers. Offered the pair *glaçon* and *moissons*, she wrote (in English translation, which, apologies, doesn't rhyme):

What heart near you can keep its icicles?
Your beautiful eyes every day reap a thousand ample harvests.

In the poem, she also calls the princess "a zealous seducer" and tells her that even Apollo can't write beautiful enough verses "to paint all the brilliance of your various charms." Combine this kind of rapturousness with the rest of what we know about Marie-Jeanne, and it follows that she may have been gay but keeping it hush-hush. It certainly was her nature to be cautious and on the alert. Consider the advice she offered her friend Murat in the aforementioned fairy tale dedication: that a "just distrust" was necessary for self-preservation.

That tale was titled "L'adroite princesse, ou Les aventures de Finette," which has often been translated as "The Discreet Princess, or the Adventures of Finette." But "clever princess" is a more accurate translation, and it also makes a whole lot more sense, as I think you'll see in the retelling that follows. The story, like all of Marie-Jeanne's tales, highlights the importance of women's education and "virtuousness." I put that in quotation marks because it is so often the precise term used to describe not only her intended lesson for readers—that girls should strive to be virtuous—but also the main component of Marie-Jeanne's own character. Which is always, in histories of her, treated as synonymous with "moral" or "pious." It is true that she did promote the concept of virtuousness in her life and her tales, but I've come to believe that she glossed the term a little differently. Merriam-Webster gives three meanings for "virtuous," the first being about morality and righteousness, the second being "chaste," and the third being "potent." Given the Marie-Jeanne L'Héritier I've gotten to know, it's box #2 and box #3 that I'd check. She definitely believed in chasteness, at least when it came to men, and she was definitely potent, a powerful defender of her sex. And while she probably went to church, accounts of her life lack any specific references to religious activities. The same can be said of her tales, whose protagonists are "virtuous" but don't look to deities, or even fairies for that matter, to solve their problems. You'll see that in Finette, a young woman whose agency comes from her own ingenuity and industriousness, which also shines a light on Marie-Jeanne's goal of imbuing girls with survival skills. And, I'd add, a sense of humor. One way Finette resists a prince who's a demonstrated sexual predator is by playing a trick that lands him in a putrid sewer.

Another retelling you'll find here is of "The Enchantments of Eloquence," renamed "Blanche" to honor the main character, a long-suffering Cinderella type who, like Finette, earns her place in the fairy tale resistance. Her act of protest? Reading! Marie-Jeanne L'Héritier was pushing against attacks on literature in her world, but see if a scene from the tale doesn't transport you right to school board meetings in ours. Charles Perrault also published a version of this story, shorter and simpler, called "Diamonds and Toads." It came out after Marie-Jeanne's, so perhaps he was present at a salon where she read hers. She commented at times that

her "uncle" plundered her work, although it's not clear if she meant that playfully or with pique. He did have a reputation for standing up for female writers against the misogynists in the Quarrel of the Ancients and the Moderns, but his tales were, at the same time, chock-full of inert ladies rewarded with husbands for their passivity, which had to have been maddening to the salon women. He was much older than all of them, so that may account for some tolerance on their part. But I have to think that his niece (or grandniece, or whatever she was) would have taken him to task for his sexism, even if she did it indirectly. Which might possibly have an example in an unusual dedication she wrote. The norm was to dedicate literary works to members of the royal family or wealthy patrons, but Marie-Jeanne chose instead Charles Perrault's daughter as the dedicatee of one of her tales.

That tale was "Marmoisan," later retitled by the author as "L'amazone française," or "The French Amazon." This is a story on the order of d'Aulnoy's "Belle-Belle." The protagonist, Léonore, steps into the shoes—literally, plus full wardrobe—of her dead brother, Marmoisan, and goes off to become a war hero. Referring to her as an "Amazon" is not a one-off but establishes her as part of a pantheon of valiant French women of history: Joan of Arc, and Dame Saint-Balmon (whom "Marmoisan" is loosely based on), and Jeanne Hachette—so named for saving her fifteenth-century town from invasion by wielding a hatchet. These and others became associated in legend with the Amazon race of ancient Greece (those same women more recently credited with raising Wonder Woman), and it wasn't just a French thing. These stories of larger-than-life women are in bodies of lore from around the world. But we'll have to leave them for another day—or another book—and return now to the story of a life-size woman with far less power: Marie-Madeleine Perrault.

Almost every biographical reference to Charles Perrault, including his own memoirs, mentions only his sons, but his first child was a daughter. By the time of Marmoisan's tale, she was in her twenties and in a dispute with her father over her inheritance, which would only get worse; his attempts to control and isolate her are referenced in legal documents. Marie-Jeanne L'Héritier, being a cousin of some stripe and only about ten years older, would surely have been aware of all this, and so it raises the question of whether her offering the tale of a French Amazon to Marie-Madeleine was a way of (a) giving her a role model for fighting against paternalistic forces and/or (b) subtly shaming Charles Perrault for mistreating his daughter. The prefatory dedication doesn't shed light on her intent, but she ended the tale with a moral that includes these (roughly translated) lines:

> *One who makes a point of pursuing reason and glory*
> *Knows how to vanquish fate*
> *And triumphs with virtue.*

Marie-Madeleine did, in fact, triumph over her father, winning the battle for an inheritance equal to that of her brothers, remarkable for the era. (Sad footnote: She never enjoyed the spoils, dying in childbirth at age twenty-seven.) We can't discern the specific role Marie-Jeanne L'Héritier may have played in this life, but it can be said that all the protagonists of her tales, including the ones you will meet here, were standard-bearers for how to take what power a young woman could and vanquish fate.

MARIE-JEANNE L'HÉRITIER

FINETTE

IN A TIME long ago, there was a king who became widowed and soon after resolved to start a war in another land. He put his kingdom into the hands of an able minister, so he felt easy on that account, but the care of his three daughters was another matter. They were of marriageable age, and he planned to begin making matches for them upon his return. In the meantime, he worried they could fall prey to the passions of ambitious young men.

To be more precise, his concerns were about two of his daughters. The oldest, Drona, was lazy. She didn't wake till afternoon and took such little care of herself that she often spent the rest of the day in mismatched slippers. The second daughter, Pratilia, was just as idle, though she had nervous energy to spare. She never stopped talking. Neither of them were thinkers.

The youngest, Finette, was quite the opposite. She was a pleasure to be around and was exceedingly clever. In fact, she regularly volunteered to help the king in his duties and even caught mistakes and came up with ways to turn the tables on cheats. If the king had to leave Finette alone at the palace, he knew she would be fine. But he believed in treating his daughters equally so as not to sow resentment between them. What applied to two, applied to three.

And so he went to visit a fairy who had long been a help to the monarch and his family, and he asked her to create three distaffs of glass that would break if the holder did anything contrary to her honor. The fairy was skeptical of the idea and suggested that he consult his youngest daughter, whom she well knew for her adroitness. But he responded impatiently, asking her who ruled the kingdom, and complaining that the war wasn't going to fight itself, and on and on, until she complied and sent him off with his charmed implements.

He then took the princesses to one of his castles in the countryside and installed them in a tower. There he gave them their distaffs, explained the enchantment, then kissed them goodbye, locking the only door to the outside and taking

the key. Though they were not allowed to bring any attendants with them, he had arranged for his daughters to have all they needed. There was a pulley installed in one window of the tower, and with that they could let a basket down on a rope each day to receive fresh food and delicacies, plus volumes of lively stories and letters that contained the news of the day. Their apartments were comfortable and the common areas stocked with entertainments of all kinds. There was even a garden terrace where they could find some peace in nature.

Thus, Finette found plenty to keep her mind and her hands occupied. She used her glass distaff when she felt like spinning, played the lute when she wished to hear music, watched the birds, and read all that came her way. But her sisters were extremely bored and also deathly afraid of accidentally breaking their distaffs, so they barely moved. They spent their days parked at one of the windows, looking out.

Which is why they were the ones who took notice of a poor old woman in rags who was wailing miserably outside, just beneath the window. She begged to be let in, saying she would serve them with the utmost fidelity. The two sisters, who had just been complaining to each other about the hardship of not having even a maid in their service, decided that their father wouldn't mind an old woman being there with them. What threat could such a person possibly pose to their chastity? And so they let the basket down and pulled her up in it.

As you might suspect, this was no old woman. Indeed, it was a prince, and not a good one but one renowned for his artifice and cunning. His name was Richcraft, and he was the eldest son of a king known widely as "The Gentle" because he had such a kind nature. The king had another son as well, named Belavoir, who was as like his father as Richcraft was unlike him. Still, the family was close, the bond between the brothers as strong as any.

But Drona and Pratilia knew nothing of this as they watched an old woman climb over the window ledge and into the tower room. When Finette discovered they had company, she was disappointed in her sisters, but there was nothing to be done. Richcraft, worried that the princesses' cries might attract attention from passersby, waited until nightfall to shed his costume, and then he stood before them in his gold and jewels, feigning gallantry by bowing low to each of them. They, of course, turned and ran for the safety of their apartments. Finette and Pratilia easily made it behind locked doors, but unbeknownst to them, the slow-moving

Drona was not as fortunate. Richcraft overtook her and threw himself at her feet, praising her beauty and fine bearing (though she was in her usual state of disarray), saying he was there to offer his faith and vows to her if she would receive him as a husband. It didn't take long before her distaff broke into a thousand pieces.

In the morning, Richcraft snuck from Drona's bedchamber while she slept and pushed a heavy sideboard against the door to keep her in. He roamed the tower until he heard Pratilia's voice behind a door, and, listening at the keyhole, he realized she was alone and fretting aloud. In a flattering tone, he told her what a mellifluous voice she had and offered her, too, his vows. She was not as quick to relent, so he listed all the advantages she would have as his wife, how she would be queen and what a tender and faithful lover he would be. At last he heard the lock open, and she accepted the prince for her husband without a thought for the distaff until it shattered.

Come evening, Pratilia told the prince that she wanted to share the news of her betrothal with her sisters, and she ducked into her closet to find a suitable gown for the occasion. While she was busy in there, he crept from the apartment and rolled a carpet up against the door. He prowled about until he found what could only be Finette's apartment and began his spiel. He was at the height of his false professions when she interrupted him from inside and said that she'd be happy to give him audience, but only if her sisters were present. She was worried about what might have happened to them, and even more so when he declined the request. She said she would not open the door, in that case, so he found a rake in the garden that he could use as a billet and rammed Finette's door until he broke in. She was standing in the middle of the room, armed with a large hammer, and said to him, "If you approach me I will cleave your head."

"Does the love I have for you inspire such cruel hatred?" he asked, preaching anew but now with a stirring of actual passion that had been lit by the sight of her: that angry blush in her cheeks, the sweat on her brow, both her hands firm and steady on the hammer's handle. "I beg you to have me as your husband," he said. He took a step forward but stopped when she raised the hammer a notch, and he continued his monologue from the far side of the room, describing to her the royal life she would have as his queen, etc., etc.

Finally, her arms too tired to continue holding the heavy tool much longer, she told him she would consent but that she was convinced that marriages made at night were always unhappy and therefore their union must occur in the morning. She asked that he retreat to the garden so she could say her prayers in peace and told him she would soon come to take him to a comfortable chamber to spend the night. Richcraft, not overly courageous and still nervous about the hammer she gripped, agreed to the conditions and left. No sooner had he gone than she zipped into the kitchen, off of which was a room with a hole in the floor: a chute through which they tossed the tower's waste into a deep cesspool. She found some weak boards in the pantry to lay over the hole and made up a handsome-looking bed with sacks of flour and a tapestry tablecloth. Then she escorted Richcraft there and returned to her apartment.

He was remarkably tired, he realized, and threw himself onto the bed, which, of course, collapsed into the hole. Not able to stop himself from doing the same, he bump-bump-bumped his way after it, his fall making such a great clattering that Finette could hear it from her room and knew she had been successful. The echoes of angry mutterings that followed were an entertainment she could have enjoyed for hours, but her concerns for her sisters pulled her off to find them. Soon she had them freed from their apartments, but their relief was quickly replaced by devastation when they realized the full extent of what had happened, that the two sisters had been deceived and violated. All three sisters cried for hours.

As for Richcraft, he passed the night groping through dark, disgusting tunnels until, at last, he managed to slither on his belly out of a drain that ran into a river a considerable distance from the castle. He found the means to make himself heard by some men who were fishing, and they carried him home. The horror and disgrace of it all stirred in him now a passion for Finette that could only be described as loathing. As he lay recovering, he thought of nothing but revenge.

Back in the tower, the three sisters were safe again, but Drona and Pratilia lived in fear of their father's return and the expected reprisals. They began paying attention to the news that came up in the basket each day, in case it carried the status of the war, so they would know when to expect their fate. When word came that the battles were dragging on, they were relieved, but not for long. Because it soon became apparent that they had even bigger problems: Both were pregnant. On top of that, rumors of their condition were spreading because the shameless prince had made no secret of his conquests, and now Drona and Pratilia were requesting in their daily basket the most unusual foods to satisfy their cravings, which tipped

off the servants who were preparing their meals. And when that piece of gossip made its way through the grapevine to Richcraft's ears, he saw a way to get back at Finette.

After an extensive search, he found sources for a variety of fruits from the most exotic trees, and he had his men haul great tubs of them to the tower and march in a loop around the perimeter. Because Drona and Pratilia still had the habit of sitting by the window, they became more and more desperate to sample the fruits with each pass of the parade. But their daily basket had already been delivered, and no matter how much they pleaded, the men with the fruits ignored them and would not fill it. So violent was their desire for these treats that the two sisters felt they had no other option but for one to lower the other in the basket to retrieve some. Finette, who had been diligently caring for her sisters, knew that they had grown too large for that to be a viable option, but her pleas to talk them out of it were for naught. So she herself got in the basket, seeing that as the only way to keep them from harming themselves, even though she had a bad feeling about it. And rightly so. As soon as Drona and Pratilia lowered Finette in the basket, she was ambushed by Richcraft's guards and carried off.

She was transported to a mountain where the prince was standing at the top, on the edge of its steepest incline. While she stood stoically, chin in the air, Richcraft proclaimed that she was to die on this day to avenge the harms she'd done him. Then he turned to his men and said, "Bring me the instrument of my vengeance!" And while they obeyed and brought forward a large barrel, it was clear from their expressions that they'd had no idea who the victim was going to be when they'd pounded penknives, razors, and hooked nails into the sides of it. The looks of sympathy Richcraft's men directed at the princess did not go unnoticed by the prince, who began to wonder if they had even done their job. He leaned over the barrel to make sure it was, in fact, riddled with his murdering weapons, and in that moment Finette gave him a dexterous push that landed him in the barrel and set it rolling down the mountain. Richcraft's officers made no attempt to detain the princess, racing instead after the barrel and trying in vain to stop it. When it came to a halt in the valley below, they extracted the prince, who, though covered in the most grave wounds, was still plotting his next attempt to destroy his nemesis.

Richcraft's dire condition threw his father, the kindly king, into the depths of grief. The equally compassionate Belavoir tried all means to have his brother cured, but the wounds seemed every week to grow worse, and the prognosticators had to tell the family that the heir to the throne would soon be dead. Belavoir was pierced with the most profound sorrow, which Richcraft, perfidious to his last moment, seized on as a way to achieve a final aim. "You profess to love me," he said to his younger brother, "but if you truly mean it, you will grant one thing I ask of you." Belavoir swore that he would do whatever his brother desired. "Then this is what you must do," Richcraft said. "Immediately upon my death, ask for Princess Finette's hand in marriage, and on your first night as husband and wife, plunge your dagger into her heart." Belavoir shuddered at these words, repenting the rashness of his promise. But he held tightly to his brother's hand, reassuring him to the last. The kingdom went into mourning. The people, however, at least among themselves, celebrated that the succession of the crown was now out of Richcraft's evil hands and in those of Belavoir, who was dear to all.

By the time this news reached the sisters in the tower, Finette had delivered two babies into the world. To the relief of all, the infants were healthy and seemingly unlike the man who had sired them. They were both girls and cut from the same cloth as their mothers: Drona's child slept all day, and Pratilia's was always either crying or cooing. Soon after, the king, their father, returned from his war. Finette greeted him at the tower door, her distaff at her side, fully intact, of course. He hugged her warmly and asked where her sisters were, but the answer came in the form of wailing from Pratilia's hungry infant. The king, livid, stomped up the tower stairs and, finding not just one babe but two, pronounced that he would be sending his debauched daughters that very day to a life of hard labor under the strict eye of a sorcerer known for his cruelty. His words rang throughout the tower: "You will perish there, never again seeing any family or friends!" The mothers and babies cried now in unison, a chorus of misery.

Finette, who had quite had it by then, set her distaff against the wall and let go a tirade against her father. "And who do you think is going to take care of these children? You haven't the least idea of the dangers you have exposed us to with this ill-conceived—" But she was drowned out at that moment by trumpets at the castle gates, and looking out the window, they saw a procession of white horses, the standard-bearers holding flags with the crest of the neighboring king, "The Gentle." They all descended the tower stairs to receive the entourage, which, they learned, had been sent to request Finette's hand in marriage to Prince Belavoir. And while the custom was, of course, to marry off the eldest daughters first, their father, glancing at Drona and Pratilia with their babes in arms, didn't raise the point.

Finette agreed to the match so long as her sisters were not punished, even though she had much trepidation about the marriage. Not only because she had never even met this prince, but also because she was worried that the hatred she knew Richcraft had felt for her might have also infected Belavoir, even with his reputation for being tenderhearted. She decided to ask the advice of that fairy who had long served her family and had helped her at times throughout childhood. But when Finette described her fears and asked the fairy if she would protect her, the answer was thus: "You are sage and prudent, dear Finette, and you know well that distrust is the mother of security. Continue to keep in mind this maxim and you will come to be happy without the assistance of my art." Finette left with her agitation little relieved.

The wedding took place the following Sunday with an ambassador as proxy, as was common practice, and then Finette was taken in a magnificent carriage to meet her spouse in his father's kingdom. The people greeted her warmly, but Prince Belavoir wore an expression of such desolation on his face that her concerns were only deepened. He was, in fact, struck immediately by her beauty and eloquence, but he made his compliments in such a strange manner that the two courts, both of which knew how much wit and gallantry this prince was master of, were initially silenced by surprise. But blaming the force of love for his lost presence of mind, they pushed aside all worry, and joyfully celebrated the union with concerts and fireworks, and then an extravagant dinner before preparations were made for conducting the couple to their bedchamber.

Finette, who had kept the fairy's maxim in mind, had gained access ahead of time to one of the women charged with attending her. She had given her orders to place into a cabinet in the royal apartment some straw, a bladder of sheep's blood, and the guts of some of the animals that had been dressed for supper. Then Finette, on some pretense, retreated to the royal apartment alone for a short spell amid the celebrations, during which she made a life-size doll from the straw, inserted the guts and blood into it, and dressed it in a nightgown. Later, after she and the prince had separately been made ready for the consummation of their marriage and all the attendants had taken the torches and left them alone in the dark, she slipped her creation under the covers of the bed and hid herself in a corner of the room.

Belavoir, having sighed three or four times very loudly on his way to the bed, drew his dagger and plunged it into the body of the effigy. Then he cried out in misery, "What have I done? After having so much weighed with myself whether I should keep my vow at the expense of committing a crime, I have taken the life of someone I was born to love! Her charms ravished me the moment I saw her, and yet I didn't have the power to free myself from the oath my brother, possessed with fury, exacted from me by an unworthy surprise. Well, Richcraft, I have satisfied your unjust vengeance, but now I will avenge her death with my own. By my dagger—"

"But I am not dead," Finette said, coming out of her hiding place. "Do not end your life. Your reputation for faith and goodness made me guess this would happen, and that you would repent as you have."

Belavoir, transported to tears, professed his infinite obligations to her. And she, in her turn, silently thanked the fairy.

For if Finette had not been persuaded that distrust is the mother of security, she would have been killed and her death would have been the cause of Belavoir's. It was cleverness and presence of mind that preserved this charming pair, who would pass through a long succession of happy days with so much felicity and glory that it is impossible for the most able pen or tongue to describe.

WOMEN OF THE FAIRY TALE RESISTANCE

BLANCHE

AT A TIME in France when there were still fairies, ogres, and other spirits (a time that is difficult to mark), there was a man, a marquis, who loved his wife passionately (which also makes it hard to imagine what time we are speaking of). The marquise loved him no less. They therefore lived quite happily for sixteen years, until the marquise died, leaving behind a grieving husband and their only child, a daughter named Blanche.

While the family had once been prosperous, their means had been depleted over the years by the marquis's poor business decisions, so it wasn't long before he decided he had to remarry for money. Blanche was of marriageable age, and though she showed no interest in marrying, he wanted to be able to provide her with a dowry. When he met a wealthy widow with one daughter herself, he thought this would be a good fit. The woman was enthusiastic about the arrangement, as he was titled and she had been looking to move up in the social world.

The new marquise and her daughter, Alix, quickly proved to be vain and mean-spirited, and the marquis just as quickly realized his mistake. But with no way to remedy the situation, he decided he could live with his new wife's many and tiring faults, so long as he never contradicted her and left her absolute master in all things. He consoled himself with the riches she brought, and when her shouting became too much, he retired to his study to read. Thus it is only his amiable daughter who should be entirely pitied.

Blanche's stepmother had nothing but contempt for her and planned from the start to send her away to a convent for a cloistered life. Which would have happened had not Alix talked her mother into letting Blanche stay so she could play with her. That is, make her the victim of her whims. Alix's first project was to dress her in horrible, ill-fitting attire and then take her out to promenade with the goal of encouraging ridicule. This backfired, however, as Blanche received only kind attention from passersby and Alix only sneers. After that, it was decided that

Blanche would be hidden away in the house all day and put to work. Not only was she given a thousand chores, but she was left in a state of neglect that would have amounted to squalor if not for her ability to turn anything she touched into something artful. Even the faded and patched dresses she wore had a way of augmenting her natural grace.

This is not to say that she was happy. She was quite bitter about her ill treatment and fantasized often about leaving in loud protest. But her natural disinclination toward conflict and her affection for her father gave her the patience to endure. For his part, he assured his daughter that her goodness would land her in a better place one day, which was all the comfort he could muster. Well, that and books. Novels, to be specific, which he passed along to her surreptitiously, since her stepmother didn't allow her any diversions. This need to be secretive meant she could read only at night after her chores were complete. However, sometimes Blanche found herself so caught up in a story, so transported to the world invented by the writer, that her day became but a quest for stolen moments to sneak off to her room and her only joy in life.

On one such day, her stepmother, taking umbrage at the serenity she saw in Blanche's expression as she went about her labors, stealthily followed her to her room and discovered the source. The marquise tore the book from her hands, threw it across the room, and shrieked at the top of her lungs, "Dirt! Filth! Obscenity!" She beckoned her husband to come immediately, at which point she turned her ire on him: "I just caught your daughter in the lustful act of reading a novel!" Pointing to the book splayed open on the floor, she added, seething, "The word 'love' is in the title! Any man who lets his daughter read such a thing is training her in the ways of a *slut!*"

This accusation seemed to awaken in the marquis something akin to courage, for he strode across the room, picked up the book, brushed off its cover, handed it back to his daughter, and looked his wife square in the eyes. "Blanche does well to be entertained by novels. They take on worldly matters and model the sweetness of language. Her habit of reading them is the very reason she speaks so eloquently, something you and your daughter might realize, and learn from, if you would just listen." Under his breath he added "For once," and then he turned and left. The marquise stood speechless for some seconds and then bolted after him, taking up where she'd left off in her spewing of invectives.

Summer was upon them, though, which involved a season away from the city. So the marquise turned to packing and, it seems, to plotting brand-new torments for her stepdaughter. Once at their country house, Blanche was informed that her main job would be to fetch all water for the household's needs. Without a cart. And though there was a water source right there in the village, she was forbidden to use that one and instead had to travel to a far distant well. The marquise had gotten the idea that constant exposure to the sun would turn Blanche's skin tough and wrinkled, thus making her ugly, and then all the attentions of the provincial men would be directed toward Alix. Quite the opposite happened, though. The solar rays seemed only to brighten what was already appealing in Blanche's features, making her more attractive than ever. Men and women alike vied for her attentions constantly, though she had no time or energy for such associations, what with the ceaseless and laden trekking over hill and dale.

The well was next to a wood that had a reputation for hungry wolves (I suspect this was an unspoken part of the marquise's malevolent planning), but Blanche never ran into any of those predators. However, one day when she was drawing water from the well, a wild boar raced toward her. She dropped her pitcher and ran to the forest with the idea of climbing a tree. But just as she was stepping into the shade, a burning pain shot through her shoulder and she fell to the ground. The wild boar raced past her and into the wood, and the next moment the hunter who had obviously been pursuing the animal was standing over her. He cried out and fell to his knees, then tore his scarf from his neck, ripped it into strips, and swiftly tended the wound.

Blanche, it is said, in turn caused a wound to the hunter. After he had stanched the bleeding and looked into her eyes, he found himself instantly smitten with this young woman he had so clumsily harmed with his normally steady spear. "My happiness and my unhappiness are extreme today!" he wailed. "What bliss to have met such a charming person! What agony to be the cause of your pain!"

Blanche was nearly as stunned by how this stranger was looking at her as she'd been by the stab of the spearpoint. "You are innocent of malice," she said, weakly but stoically. She had noticed that he was not an average hunter. His jacket was made of brocade, and from cuffs of ruffled lace, now stained with her blood, extended manicured hands. "This misfortune does not deserve to disturb your tranquility."

MARIE-JEANNE L'HÉRITIER

❋

"I could have killed you," he moaned, his head bowed. He seemed on the verge of tears.

(I'll point out here that this behavior was not in character for this young man. He had a reputation for being cold and callous.)

"If you had killed me, then it would have been your destiny to do so." Blanche was now studying a medallion on his vest, a coat of arms. "For my part," she added, "it would well have been a paradisiacal escape."

It was then that he noticed something that, curiously, he had not before: that she was dressed in the rags of the impoverished. *How is it*, he wondered, *that she is so silver-tongued when she obviously comes from a wretched place?* "Let me take you to clean quarters and a doctor," he said to her, "to ensure there's no infection." He spotted his squire, who had fallen far behind him on the hunt but could now be seen cresting an adjacent hill. "You shall have my horse."

But Blanche said, "You push your generosity too far. I insist you leave me in peace. I will walk home anon, when I have recovered sufficiently."

And though he pleaded with her to the contrary, in the end he respected her wishes.

Night had fallen by the time she got home. Her stepmother seemed at first disappointed at her return (wolves on her mind, perhaps) and then angry that she had no water in tow. Her father put her to bed himself, resolving not to rely on his wife for his daughter's convalescence.

And now that Blanche is in good hands, let us return to the prince. For that, of course, is what he was. His name was Phelan, and he was the great-nephew of Merlin and a distant descendant of Melusine. It is not clear what country he was future sovereign of, as the location of the fountain where Blanche fetched water appears on no historical maps. We can assume that there was magic involved in Phelan's encounter with the wild boar (a stock character of myth, as it is) and most certainly in his piercing of a young woman's shoulder and in consequence his own heart (if not hers). Perhaps one of his ancestors had had enough of his brutish manners and decided it was time for an adjustment. But whatever the reason, Prince Phelan went home to his palace a changed man, one with an ardent infatuation and a pervasive melancholy due to the injury he had caused.

Plagued with the acute concern that Blanche might not be getting adequate care and could ultimately succumb to her wound, he charged his squire with the task of finding her and assessing her condition. The squire skillfully carried out his commission and returned with not only a report on her present state but also an account of her birth, inclinations, and misfortunes. Phelan was relieved to learn that she was the daughter of a marquis, but not for the reason that might have held sway before, that her noble birth made her worthy of a prince's attentions, but because it meant that her family had the resources to provide medical care. Still, he wanted to be absolutely certain that she healed, so he took steps of his own.

Although he carried the genes of those learned in magic, he himself had no such skill. But he did have a godmother who was of the fairy realm. Her name was Dulcicula, and he went to see her to tell of the accident and his desire to help. He did not admit that he had fallen for Blanche, but he spoke of her with such fervor that any woman of the world, fairy or not, would have easily guessed that he was in love. And therefore did Dulcicula. She had always had a soft spot for Phelan, even with the faults he had hitherto demonstrated, and so she was delighted to be entrusted with healing the person who had stirred such compassion in her godson.

Dulcicula set about preparing a balm that could heal all manner of maladies, even mortal wounds, in a matter of minutes. Then she changed her form (she was an elegant fairy known for her flowing gown of sage) into that of an old peasant woman, and in this guise she transported herself to the marquis's door. The first person she met there was Alix, whom she told, using the village vernacular, that she had a gift for the marquis's daughter from a secret admirer.

"What is this crazy bag saying?" Alix asked, seemingly to the ether. "She looks like a dog ready for a bump in the cemetery! And mad, like the rest of the vermin who are obsessed with my monkey of a stepsister!"

Dulcicula was surprised to see a young lady all covered in gold and jewels speaking such strange and offensive jargon. She did not know how to respond, but that was no matter, since Alix stormed off, leaving Dulcicula alone in the foyer. She poked around until she found the kitchen, where a kindly nurse who had been hired by the marquis to take care of Blanche was preparing a tea tray. Dulcicula explained her mission (leaving out the matters of magic) and was invited to follow her to the bedchamber.

Blanche was resting in bed, but in an awkward position so as to keep a book open with one hand. She set it down on the coverlet when the two women entered the room. The nurse introduced Dulcicula as a well-wisher, set the tea between them, and left the room. It was apparent that Blanche's shoulder still pained her greatly by the way she held it so close to her side. She used her other arm to greet her guest and again to awkwardly lift her teacup, as it was obvious her dominant hand belonged to the injured side. Dulcicula wasted no time in telling her that she had a balm that would free her of discomfort in practically an instant.

Blanche had observed in her time in the country that many dubious remedies circulated, most of little to no effect. But she did not want to hurt the old woman's feelings. "You are abundantly generous to leave your own affairs and come to please me," she said. "But I am in the able hands of surgeons and so it is best I do not change protocol. I will speak about you to my father, and I know that he will take your goodwill into account and offer charity, since we cannot purchase your wares."

"But this is free," Dulcicula said, holding the charmed crock in her palm and scooping a dab onto a fingertip. "See here: I will rub this on my cheek, and just watch as the age spots disappear." And so she did, and in but moments her skin was as smooth and clear as if she were in the bloom of youth.

"Oh, my," said Blanche. "I suppose, then, there's no harm in trying." And she let Dulcicula apply the balm to the ugly gash. Then they watched together as it closed, leaving no scar at all, and Blanche lifted her arm and moved it about without the least bit of pain. "What a marvelous effect!" she cried happily. (And it has to be said that it had been quite some time since that poor young woman had felt anything close to happiness.) "I must compensate you for this."

But Dulcicula told her it had been paid for already. "By Prince Phelan."

"By whom?" Blanche asked, but even before she finished the question she knew the answer. She pictured the fine jacket, the coat of arms. "The hunter."

Dulcicula nodded. "My godson." She waved a hand over her head and was again her elegant, sage-gowned self.

"What good fortune for him," Blanche said, "to have a fairy godmother." And while this was uttered with graciousness (for she was, indeed, grateful for the healing), there was an unmistakable undercurrent of resentment in her tone. She couldn't help but think that the only reason she was getting attention now was because of her brush with a prince, when she'd long been suffering abuse and could have used a rescue.

"Alas, such is the way," Dulcicula sighed, as she could tell what was on Blanche's mind. "You are right that fairies tend to be partial to royalty, but it is from them that we draw our comforts and entertainments. And so, dear, may you! The prince is desperate in his desire for you. Come with me, and your life of luxury can begin."

"Thank you, but no," Blanche said. "I do not reciprocate his feelings."

"But he has a genealogy that you may find very intriguing," the fairy said. "Let me tell you about it."

Blanche merely shook her head. "I am not in love with the prince."

Dulcicula took notice now of the books scattered about the room. "Ah, you want *that* kind of love. Tendresse."

Blanche nodded.

"What is that one about?" the fairy asked, pointing to the novel that Blanche had been reading when she arrived.

"Oh, it's an entrancing story," she said, with a dreamy look. "It calls to mind Tristan and Isolde."

"They're the ones who fall irretrievably in love because of a potion, right?"

"Yes, but that's not part of *this* story," Blanche said. Then she added with a side-eye, "I hope you're not getting ideas."

"Who, *moi*? I wouldn't think of it," Dulcicula said. "So who are they and how do they fall in love?"

"Claire and Tallis are their names. They become inseparable when she sets eyes on his birthmark."

"His birthmark," the fairy repeated.

"Yes, it is in the shape of a leaf, just under his ear. His great-grandmother was a dryad, and some in her line inherited the mark. He learned early on to keep his hair over it because the attention annoyed him and he had no interest in love. Until he meets Claire, that is. He falls for her at first sight."

"Let me guess," Dulcicula said. "He decides it's a good time to get a lace and pull his hair back."

"No, he wants Claire to fall in love with him naturally, so his plan is to court her. But on their very first outing together, which is a stroll in the Tuileries, a strong wind whips up and blows his hair back."

"So magic *does* bring them together," the fairy says.

"Well, yes, technically. But I think she would have fallen in love with him anyway. They're perfect for each other. But of course they can't be together. That's the central conflict. Claire's parents have promised her to someone else, someone she abhors. She delays the wedding for long enough to plot an escape, and she and Tallis leave the country altogether and get married by an abbot in a monastery."

"And they live happily ever after," Dulcicula said in a singsong tone.

Blanche picked up the book. "Not yet, but I'm hopeful." She showed the fairy where the ribbon marked her place. There was a good third she had yet to read.

"I'll leave you to it, then," Dulcicula said, and she vanished.

By day's end, the marquise had figured out that Blanche was fully recovered, and early the next morning the pitiless woman sent her stepdaughter back out to resume her chores. As Blanche approached the well with an empty urn in her arms, she heard on the breeze a cheerful "Bonjour, chère!" and there was Dulcicula, lounging in the grass.

"Good morning to you, too," Blanche said, wasting no time letting the wooden bucket descend into the well.

"Phelan was relieved to hear of your recovery."

"That is very kind," Blanche replied, yanking hard on the thick rope of the pulley. "You thanked him for me, I hope."

"Of course. But he was devastated to learn that you have no interest in him. He can't eat or sleep."

"Can't you make a balm or something to fix that?" Blanche asked, speedily filling the urn now and dropping the bucket into the well again.

"He asked me not to. But Phelan does want me to keep helping you. He asked me to lighten your load."

Blanche heaved the full bucket up again. "How so?"

But the fairy just watched as Blanche tipped the bucket over the urn, topped it off, and then squatted to lift it.

"Oh, you meant literally!" Blanche cried, for the usually heavy urn was as light as a feather. She turned immediately to the path and bounded off, calling over her shoulder, "Thank the prince for me!"

"Will do," Dulcicula said. Then she waved a hand at Blanche's retreating figure, murmuring, "And *that* one's from me."

WOMEN OF THE FAIRY TALE RESISTANCE

✷

The reason Blanche had been in such a hurry to begin with was that she was eager to return to her book, which she had not been able to finish before being pressed back into service by her stepmother that morning. And now, she thought, she'd be able to grab even more time, what with this newfound ability to move unencumbered. As she ran, she thought of the two lovers and where she'd left them: They'd been captured by a search party, and Claire had been taken to prepare for her nuptials while Tallis was set to be hanged. Blanche was in utter suspense over how, or if, they would find their way back to each other. The anticipation filled her so completely that when she reached the house she didn't even notice the marquise lounging in a chair on the porch.

"What took you so long?" the woman asked sourly.

Blanche groaned. "You can't mean—" But she stopped there, because something dropped from her mouth. She looked down, and there was a gleaming gemstone by her foot.

The marquise got up and snatched it from the floorboards, then studied it. "It's a *diamond*. Where did you get this?"

"Hm," Blanche said. "I guess it's possible the lady at the well—" But she stopped again, for something else had dropped from her mouth.

The marquise grabbed this, too, and a smile began to spread across her face. "A ruby! Say something else! Who was this lady at the well?"

"A fairy," Blanche said, and out popped another stone, this one an emerald.

By now her father, who had been listening through the open window of his study, joined them on the porch. "What is going on, Blanche?" he asked.

"A spell, it would seem," she said. And, yes, another precious stone fell from her lips.

"What does this 'lady at the well' look like?" her stepmother asked.

"She wears a sage gown," Blanche told her, two stones popping out this time, right into her father's hand, which he had put under her chin.

"Let's go to my study, dear girl," the marquis said, guiding her into the house. "We'll have a long chat."

"Wait just a minute!" the marquise called after them.

"Blanche is *my* daughter," he said, beaming.

(The marquis's joy in the situation cannot adequately be described, which is why I will say no more about that.)

MARIE-JEANNE L'HÉRITIER

The next day, the marquise sent Alix to the well to find the fairy and show her every courtesy so she might show her the same favor that she had Blanche. With the singular intent of impressing the fairy and no inkling of the actual effort involved in the trek, Alix dressed as if going to a ball and took with her a golden vase, the most valuable in the house. In this pompous display, she got to the fountain exhausted and in even more of a pique than usual. To make matters worse, she found at the well not an elegant woman in a sage gown, as had been described to her, but the old peasant woman who had been at their house just days before. (Dulcicula had returned to the well that morning in hopes of finding Blanche to bestow more gifts, but upon seeing Alix approaching in her finery, she had decided to change into something more appropriate for the occasion.)

"Mademoiselle," she said to Alix, "I beg you to allow me to use your vase to draw water, because I am so very thirsty."

"*Really!*" Alix spat. "You need a vase of *gold* to put your muzzle on? Go on, you twisted beast! If you are thirsty, go back and drink from the trough of our oxen."

"I have done you no harm, so why do you treat me so?"

Alix shouted with all her might: "I advise you not to warm my ears any longer, or I will beat you to death with blows when you next pass our door! Now, *go!* I am waiting for a lady."

"As you wish," the old peasant said, offering a generous wave as she lumbered off.

Alix waited in vain for the remainder of the day, and then she returned home. Her mother was burning with impatience to see her. "What happened?" she asked. But when Alix tried to answer, her words were unintelligible because her mouth was crowded with snakes, toads, and mice, which teemed from her lips with every attempt at speaking. It was the most disgusting sight, so we'll leave them there and turn to other matters.

To the despairing prince, specifically. Having tired of his court's constant attempts to cheer him up, he had ventured out to the woods alone and now lay prostrate under a chestnut tree. This is where Dulcicula found him after her encounter with Alix at the well. She described the scene to him, complete with theatrical gestures, hoping it would cheer up her godson, but to no avail. He would not even utter a word.

"Let me tell you, then, about the spell I cast on her," the fairy said. "This is sure to bring a chuckle: Every time she opens her mouth, her usual vulgarities are replaced by vermin."

"That sounds unnecessarily mean," he said.

Dulcicula clapped her hands. "Glory day! You're not catatonic!"

"Please undo it."

She sighed. "If I must. I can pay a visit tomorrow, perhaps. But I'm so enjoying the mental image of what is occurring in that house: While diamonds drop from the mouth of fair Blanche, toads drop from her rude stepsister's."

Prince Phelan sat bolt upright now. "*What* drops from Blanche's mouth?"

"I forgot to tell you about that. In addition to the thoughtful gift of yours yesterday, I gave her a bonus. Every time she speaks, she emits a priceless jewel that matches her eloquence."

"She must loathe that!" Phelan was on his feet now. "Go now and fix things!"

Dulcicula let out a long, defeated breath. Then a thought came to mind. "If you come with me."

"She won't like that."

"But it's the only way I'll go. So let's fix you up a bit. Just look at your curls, all matted with dirt and leaves." She pulled a brush and a lace from her pocket and held them out to him.

"All right," he said, resigned. "But let's hurry. She must be miserable. If it were me, I would refuse to even open my lips."

And, indeed, this is what Blanche had done, vexed by not only her father's greed but also the attentions of the villagers, the news of her endowment having spread like wildfire. They were determined to witness the spectacle by any means they could, including climbing up trellises and on window ledges and even using spyglasses. She was, at this moment, hiding in the kitchen pantry. She'd taken her book and a candle in with her and was now reading the final paragraph. And, yes, the lovers make it back to each other safely, all threats vanquished. *The end*, Blanche read to herself, and closed the book. And though she could hear the caterwauling of her stepsister and stepmother from somewhere in the house, she felt totally at peace. *Ahhh*, she thought, and closed her eyes.

"Blanche," whispered a voice at her ear. She recognized it as Dulcicula's, but she had no interest in opening her eyes. Or her mouth. "I'm sorry," the fairy said.

"I thought it would be fun, a clever metaphor. And also useful. You know, to give you wealth of your own. But I didn't think it through, obviously. It took Phelan here to point out my error."

At this, Blanche did open her eyes, and she saw that the two of them were crouched in the small space beside her. The prince's eyes were locked on hers, as they had been the day of the hunt. But instead of turning away, as she had before, she looked back into them. They were really quite beautiful, she couldn't help but think. Somehow mesmerizing in the candlelight. And didn't he have a nice chin? And neck? And what was that under his *ear*? Something inside her stirred.

"You can speak now," Dulcicula said. "I undid it."

"Thank you," Blanche said. But her gaze hadn't shifted from Phelan's neck. What *was* that? A fish tail?

"A mermaid tail," Dulcicula said. "As I have attempted to tell you, he's descended from Melusine."

Blanche picked up her book again. "You mean, like—" But she was interrupted by a racket just outside the pantry door.

"*Alix!*" the marquise was screaming. "*Close. Your. Mouth!*"

Phelan gave his godmother a nudge.

"Yes, yes," she said, popping into the kitchen with a reluctant sigh.

Blanche was still holding the book, a stunned look on her face.

"Good story?" Phelan asked.

She nodded.

"What's it about?"

"Uh, two people who fall in love with each other but have to go through trials before they can have a life together."

"How do they fall in love?"

"They find each other charming." It was the returning Dulcicula who answered the question, all quiet now in the kitchen.

"I'd like to read it," Phelan said to Blanche.

She held out the book, and their fingers touched as he took it from her. Their flushed cheeks were noticeable even in the dim light.

"Did you do this?" they both asked Dulcicula at the same time.

She shrugged. "Maybe, maybe not," she said. "But don't fairies have as much right to work wonders as the gods of myth and fable?"

CATHERINE BERNARD

Catherine Bernard is hailed as the conteuse who established the guiding principle for writing a fairy tale of the vogue: A character's feelings should be natural and realistic, but the plot should be fantastical. And though she published only two fairy tales (one can assume she wrote more, given that she was an active force in the salons where the contes de fées were crafted), those two stories were among the most reproduced in collections over the ensuing century.

Catherine was born in 1663 in Rouen, a city known at the time for its bourgeoisie and its artsy vibe. She represented both, being a child of merchants and determined from a young age to be a writer. In the 1680s, she made her way to Paris only to find that in the capital she would need more than determination to be a literary success and, well, eat. She didn't have any aristocratic connections, and on top of that she was a Protestant. So she renounced her religion, something she managed to do publicly, which gained her the attentions of Louis XIV and his coterie. An announcement in the *Mercure galant* proclaimed that (somewhat loosely translated) "after a serious and long search for truth, Catherine Bernard recounted the errors her birth committed to her." Her family back home disowned her, but this did launch her into a living—if modest—by her pen.

Writing for the stage seems to have been her first love and something that she was clearly good at. The world of drama was dominated by men at every level, and yet her very first play was accepted by the

Comédie-Française, Paris' premier theater. It was a tragedy in five acts of verse and a smash hit. Theater records show she was not only the playwright but was actively involved in the production. She was known to be outspoken when decisions were made that she didn't agree with, as evidenced by letters of complaint she lodged with the theater's management. Apparently this didn't put them off, though, as they went on to produce her next tragedy, *Brutus*. It was an even bigger success, running for months. "Ladies today are capable of anything," a reviewer marveled. The world-famous Voltaire, forty years later, would also compliment the work, but by plagiarizing it in a play he claimed as his own. More on that in a moment. But for now, let it be said that though Catherine Bernard was a lady capable of quite a lot, she wasn't capable of lodging a complaint from the grave.

Before and during the runs of these shows, Catherine was working on novels and applying, successfully, for royal privilege to have them published. She was still a teenager when her first book came out, and she went on to create a series she called Malheurs de l'amour, or Misfortunes of Love. She explained her theme in this way: "I see so much chaos in even the most reasonable love that I thought it would be better to present . . . misfortunes coming from passion than to show . . . lovers happy at the end of a book." The first book in that series proved to be very popular in and beyond Paris. There was even a counterfeit copy published, which wouldn't have resulted in any profits for her, but authors welcomed the attention from these causes célèbres. Reviews of the novel lauded her concise prose style, "so fine," according to the *Mercure galant*, "that it is apparent that much more time was spent in shortening it than in making it." This recognition of her skill at revision—arguably the most important part of writing a book—had to have been gratifying, especially when you consider just how arduous the revision process would have been at a desk sans computer or typewriter or even eraser. She was either a gifted writer or had a magic wand.

More novels followed in the subsequent years, and at the same time she was writing poetry and submitting it to literary contests. Her first prize was from the Académie Française for a poem she'd written about King Louis, which flattered him so much he gave her two hundred crowns. This award was followed later by Toulouse's Floral Games prize, three times, and a couple of more awards from the Académie Française. Her crowning achievement, though, was joining several of her salon sisters as members of the Accademia dei Ricovrati in Padua, where she was

CATHERINE BERNARD

dubbed "Calliope" after the Olympian Muse of epic poetry. That she was recognized as a significant author in her time is more than evident from her inclusion in the pantheon of "Illustrious Women of the Century of Louis the Great," as published (with royal privilege) in the 1698 *La nouvelle Pandore*, or *The New Pandora*. In this book, Bernard's literary prowess is compared to that of the most famous writers of the era, and her awards are listed as well as the titles of her novels and plays, including the acclaimed *Brutus*.

All these laurels would have been celebrated in the salons, of course. Catherine was especially known for being a fixture at Marie-Jeanne L'Héritier's, which was perhaps the most serious salon in terms of operating as a writing workshop. She often showed up with Catherine Durand, whom you'll soon meet, and probably her friend and fellow émigré from Rouen, Bernard de Fontenelle. He, too, was a successful writer of dramatic works, among works in other genres, and supported women writers; he was on the side of the "Moderns" in the Quarrel. Many of the histories that mention Catherine Bernard (scant though they are) suggest that Fontenelle had a hand in her work, that he wrote some of her oeuvre, but this is demonstrably false. Catherine was a success before he was, his first play in Paris bombing to such a degree that he burned the script, and he was repeatedly rejected for prizes that she won. Logic aside, there was not ever a claim during her heyday, indeed her lifetime, that Fontenelle was her ghostwriter. It was later that this rumor started to churn, the lie first coming from the lips of Voltaire, who was probably embarrassed after opening night of his *Brutus* (yes, he even gave his play the same title as Catherine's) when someone in the media pointed out that he'd followed her outline exactly and full passages were identical. He swore that wasn't true until a publisher reprinted her play, and then he switched the narrative, claiming that Fontenelle was the actual writer of Catherine's work. Though this would hardly seem to excuse Voltaire's plagiarism, somehow it did in the eyes of his devotees. And later, when he was officially chronicling the literary history of Louis XIV's reign, a volume that would be relied on by historians, he listed Catherine Bernard as the sole author of . . . nothing. (*What* a guy.)

Both of her published fairy tales were embedded in one of her novels, *Inez of Cordoba*, which has at its center a Frenchwoman who is the queen of Spain. She is young and bored, so she brings interesting people together for intellectual conversation—basically, a salon. One day, when they are discussing a new trend for gallant tales, she decides to hold a contest to see who can write the best one. Her rules: that the characters' feelings should be natural and realistic but the plots fantastical. Yes, the very standard that Catherine Bernard was said to have set for the conteuses in *their* salons. It's not clear whether life imitated art or art imitated life here, but no matter. In the novel, two women take up the challenge, and they go off to write for a day, and then they return with their notebooks and tell their tales. Which, by the way, is how L'Héritier ran her salons: The prompt was given out, a day or so was allowed for crafting, then the writers returned and shared. One of the tales in *Inez of Cordoba* was "Ricquet with the Tuft," which we'll come back to with Catherine Durand because she, too, wrote a version of this story. So did Charles Perrault. Which probably means that the three of them were at the same salon where a prompt was given out and wrote these variations in response, then returned and shared their stories. But let's untangle ourselves from the meta and move on to the other fairy tale in the novel.

"Le prince rosier," or "Prince Rosebush," features a couple of motifs that we saw in Henriette-Julie Murat's "Anguillette"—a human-to-plant metamorphosis and a lovelorn character who is compelled to go to an island. These are actually not uncommon tropes in the tales of the conteuses, though each spins them in unique ways. For instance, in "L'oranger et l'abeille," or "The Bee and the Orange Tree," Marie-Catherine d'Aulnoy traps a prince in a botanical form as Bernard does, but the circumstances are as different as those that Murat's Plousine and Atimir experience. As for magical islands, they were part of the cartography of the contes de fées from the very beginning. One was at the center of the very first fairy tale published in France, d'Aulnoy's "L'île de la félicité," or "The Island of Happiness." In this story, a prince hears about a beautiful princess on an enchanted island and is obsessed with getting there. When he does—with the aid of an invisibility cloak—he finds exactly what the island promises: happiness. He stays for what feels like months to him but turns out to be three hundred years, a realization that makes him panic and insist on returning to his kingdom for a visit. But, like Plousine's leaving Peaceful Island in "Anguillette," that choice spells doom. Like Bernard, d'Aulnoy embedded her island story in a novel. But there are few other similarities, as you'll see in the story of Prince Rosebush, retold here as "Florinde."

There are no existing stories of Catherine Bernard's own loves, misfortunate or otherwise. Unsurprisingly, given her stated view on the chaotic nature of love, she never married. She clearly felt comfortable with both sexes as friends and colleagues, but there are no references to romantic relationships with anyone, unless you count some insinuations about Fontenelle that are as unfounded as the ghostwriter claim. An emerging conversation among scholars who have been putting her life and writings under an LGBTQIA+ lens raises the idea that she may have been asexual or aromantic, orientations that have generally been overlooked by history. The work of these researchers includes, among other analyses, a focus on spots in her fiction where the voice of the author comes through—that is, narrative intrusions that use the first-person "I" or otherwise express a comment—thereby revealing, or at least hinting at, her inner life. Even if it's impossible to prove Catherine's sexual identity given the paucity of information available, it's nice to see her getting attention, and respectful attention at that. The research record has tended to not only dismiss her as a "minor" literary figure (at least post-Voltaire) but also use the insulting label "old maid" to describe her, along with Scudéry and L'Héritier and other literary women who chose not to marry.

One could say that Catherine Bernard's writing career started with a literary tragedy and ended with a prolonged personal one. Her financial situation was always an issue no matter how popular her published or produced works, so she was always in need of other sources of income. Her poetry got the most attention from Louis XIV's circle, who increasingly looked down their noses at dramatic works and fiction, including fairy tales—those fairies seeming a vestige of pagan idolatry to the likes of the pious acting queen, Madame de Maintenon. A friend of Maintenon's, equally devout, offered Catherine a modest pension, which must have had some strings attached because it marked her pivot away from genres she had up till then put such energy and spirit into. This patron was the Countess of Pontchartrain. Yes, wife to the same Count of Pontchartrain who was, at pretty much the same time, facilitating Murat's separation from her world. Catherine was still in her late thirties when she apparently retreated from social life and began writing nothing but religious poetry, none of which she published. Even with the patronage, she was said to have lived in poverty, and she died before age fifty. Maybe we can take some solace in knowing that, unlike some of her salon sisters, she made her own choices. But with so much of her story erased, it's impossible to say for sure.

WOMEN OF THE FAIRY TALE RESISTANCE

FLORINDE

IN A KINGDOM that does not appear on any map, there lived a widowed queen who missed her husband dearly. A daughter, the only fruit of their marriage, reduced her sorrows, but Florinde (the name of the princess) was to cause her some in her turn.

One morning, when the queen was alone in her room, there appeared a small ivory chariot drawn by six butterflies whose wings were painted in a rainbow of colors. It circled several times before a diminutive person reached an arm out of the chariot and let drop a letter. The queen picked it up and read:

Florinde was born with many appeals,
But her misfortune will be extreme
If she ever falls in love with
A man she cannot see.

The fairy, for that's what she was, had disappeared by the time the queen looked up from the page, so she was left to ponder the message on her own. It certainly seemed ominous, and she did feel troubled by it, but at the same time, she reasoned that all she needed to do was let Florinde meet potential lovers and then make her own choice. She would hold a jousting tournament, she decided, to which every prince in all the neighboring kingdoms would be invited. Surely Florinde would be drawn to someone, given so many men to choose from.

That actually turned out to be the problem. Florinde, even more anxious over the prospect of misfortune than her mother, attended the tournament with an open mind, and she did esteem many of the jousters, even tried to imagine herself falling in love with one or another. But in the end, it was pity for all that prevented her from deciding in favor of any; to choose one would have made too many others unhappy. The queen tried to ease her daughter's (and her own) anxiety by pointing

out to Florinde that she was young and might yet change her mind about one of the princes. "And haven't we effectively defeated the prophecy?" the queen asked her. "For you have now laid eyes on every eligible man in the country."

But of the princes in the neighboring kingdoms, there was one who hadn't been at the tournament. The king, his father, had years before lost a wife who was so beautiful that she had caused him to suffer horrors of jealousy. And therefore he had chosen for a second wife someone who was ill-suited to inspire jealousy, only to find that she was prone to *being* jealous. She carried the whims of her passion so far that the king had to wonder which of the afflictions, jealousy or being the target of jealousy, was the greater. In his uncertainty, he concluded that marriage was a dreadful bond, and he resolved to keep the only son he had away from all women. He had him raised in a remote but magnificent castle, where he was given all the amusements of his age and taught all the subjects a prince should know about, including the sciences. Only one thing was left out: love.

Then it happened one day that this prince, his name Rosier, found at his feet a miniature portrait of Florinde. He looked at it first with surprise, and then admiration followed closely, accompanied by a disturbance unknown to a young man accustomed to exercises that had nothing in common with these emotions. Judging that something important had been kept from him, he made it his intention to leave this place that had always seemed pleasant to him but that he now regarded as a prison. He slipped out of the castle at the first opportunity to elude his supervisors, but he had barely taken a few steps when he was met by the fairy of whom we have already spoken. "Prince Rosier, you are heading toward that which they were trying to save you from," she said. "You see? You cannot escape destiny."

Meanwhile, Florinde, still filled with ennui that no words from her mother could assuage, obtained permission to retire to a country house. There she took long, pensive walks alone in the gardens, brooding to such an extent that she often didn't even notice the flowers that surrounded her. Then one day she felt a brush of leaves against her bare arm, and looking up, she saw a rosebush, more vivid in hues of green and red than any she had seen before. Though there was not even a wisp of a breeze, its slender branches were bending toward her as if inviting her to come close. Finding this eerie, she scurried away from it, but her curiosity made her circle back, again and again, and each time the rosebush bent as she passed. Finally she stopped in front of it and, reaching for a rose, was pricked by a thorn.

The sting was so severe and lasting that she found it hard to sleep that night. When she did drift off, she dreamt of the fairy her mother had described, a woman no bigger than her thumb in a gown trimmed in royal purple, her chariot pulled by butterflies. *Or were they bees?* she woke up wondering. The next time she drifted off, she saw the face of a man in a rosebush, which startled her so that she got out of bed and waited at the window for dawn. She decided she would spend the day indoors. After breakfast, she roamed the library in pursuit of a book, but her gaze kept drifting out the windows to the garden. Soon she found herself on the paths again, and then in front of the rosebush again.

As she watched, blossoms opened before her eyes, and the branches swayed and bowed with an eagerness that touched the princess and made her forget the sting the thorn had caused her. Thinking now that this rosebush could be a miracle and she should thus witness it, she stayed in front of the shrub, mesmerized by the energy it seemed to hold within it. And then, all of a sudden, she realized that she was entangled in its branches. She had to struggle to pull herself free, at which point she heard, as if from the leaves, a sound like sighing. "A *sighing* rosebush?" she marveled.

"And so much more, madam," a voice said. "I will tell you my sad story: I am a prince from whom the most precious thing in the world was hidden. I fell in love with your portrait and took a journey to find you, but a fairy interrupted my quest and changed me into this form, saying that I will stay this way until the day you tell me you love me. Now that I see you in person it is clear you are reserved for the gods. And so I am fated to always be a rosebush." He sighed again.

The sense of calm that had just enveloped Florinde was pierced now by a sense of umbrage at his boldness in entangling her in his branches and speaking so openly of his love for her. "What did this fairy look like?" she asked him, taking a large step away from the bush.

"She was small," he said. "Obviously powerful, her gown trimmed in king's purple."

"Hm," Florinde said. She was agitated with confusion. The truth was that she, too, felt stirrings that she suspected were love, and she worried that these feelings might trigger the fairy's prognostication. She could not see this prince, after all. *But,* she wondered, *are these feelings of love for a man or a plant?* She convinced herself that it was the latter. Pity was what she felt for the prince, that was all. It

was the rosebush she was so strongly drawn to, not the man, and she could forgive a shrub its brazenness.

She had a marble bench placed close to it and sat there each day for long hours, reading poetry from magazines and writing her own verses in a notebook, then hiding the words behind drawings of leaves and roses. The prince piped up with his expressions of love, which she discouraged, but she always spoke kind words to console him about his unfortunate metamorphosis. Little by little, though, she let him speak his feelings, and they were so tender and genuine that she was moved. The human face she had seen in her dreams was there in her mind's eye all the time now. She could no longer push it away with thoughts of the rosebush.

Back at the palace, the queen was sorely missing the company of her daughter, so she sent word that she must return home. Florinde went to the garden as soon as she heard. Taking a rose into her palm, she sadly said goodbye.

"But I love you," Rosier told her. Drops of dew fell from his leaves like tears.

"And I you," she said. And she began crying in such a torrent that she couldn't see the transformation occurring before her: The flower that she held was turning into a human hand, and a man, the same one from her imaginings, was standing awkwardly before her as if still part of the shrub that had hidden him.

When she came to realize what had happened, her feelings of passion were replaced by panic. Not only because she found herself unchaperoned with a lover, but more importantly because she had to admit now that her feelings of love were, in fact, for a man, and one she had fallen for before seeing him in the flesh. "We are doomed!" she wailed, running from the garden.

Since she had not spoken of her own encounter with the fairy in the presence of the rosebush, Prince Rosier was utterly confused by her reaction to his appearance. Though his limbs were stiff from being planted in one place for so long, he hurried after Florinde and caught up with her on a terrace where she sat sorrowfully with her lady-in-waiting.

"I am sorry to have surprised you so," he said to Florinde. "I was surprised, too. I didn't know until that moment that you do love me." His cheeks became as red as the roses that had been so recently a part of him. "That made me happier than I have ever been in my life. Why does it make you so unhappy?"

She asked her lady-in-waiting to return to packing for their departure, and then she told Prince Rosier about the fairy's visit and all that had transpired since, all the efforts she and her mother had made to try to avert the cursed prediction. "Alas, unsuccessfully," she said in conclusion. "I am doomed to misfortune for having fallen in love with you. But nothing in the prophecy says *you* must share that misfortune. Save yourself by leaving me."

"But that would be doom itself for me," he said, and they were quiet for some time, watching the songbirds gather seeds and swoop after each other as if in a game of chase.

"What if," the prince said finally, "the fairy is just playing with us?"

"What do you mean?"

"We have done nothing to induce her wrath," he said. "Perhaps she was just bored one day and decided to pass the time by inventing a new game of Cupid."

"Perhaps. But how does that change our fate?"

"Maybe she will get bored again and forget all about us!"

Florinde pondered this. It was possible. "Or," she said, "maybe she will be struck by guilt and end the torment in an act of remorse."

"Or that," Prince Rosier said, and he gallantly, if stiffly, lowered himself to one knee. "Will you marry me?"

Though Florinde was not entirely convinced by the arguments they had conjured, she figured that it was he who was taking the greatest risk, and since he seemed unfazed, they resolved to go back together and ask for her mother's permission.

Once they explained their strange adventure to the queen and asked her not to worry about the fairy any longer, she ordered the court to begin celebrations for the upcoming nuptials. There were fêtes for the couple on a daily basis: elaborate dinners, plays, gondola rides, masked balls, and games of pall-mall on the lawn. At first the couple enjoyed this merriment, but soon it began to wear on them: on Florinde because, no matter how she tried, she couldn't keep her imagination from concocting love-related misfortunes she might encounter; and on Rosier because he simply wasn't accustomed to courtly pomp. He found himself wistfully thinking of the bark that had protected his limbs, which at times seemed less constraining than the decorums that were demanded of him now. He pressed his fiancée to speed up the process of preparing for the wedding.

But Florinde was leaning quite the other way. She'd become fixated on the fact that until she came along, Rosier had never met a woman or even knew what love was. What would happen, she worried, when the novelty of their romance wore off? Sending him away to test his fidelity seemed to her the only course of action, and so she implored her mother to help her. Though the queen thought her daughter might be overthinking the matter, she had learned through the grapevine that the prince's own parents had had a fraught relationship, so she figured it was better to be safe than sorry and agreed to take care of the details. She knew of just the place: the Isle of Youth. Florinde, distraught at the prospect of parting from her betrothed, let her mother carry the message to the prince. He would be taken to the island immediately and was not to return until he was called back.

Living far away from Florinde seemed so terrible to Rosier that he believed he would die. Indeed, in the weeks it took to travel over the sea, he became so ill that the ship's captain, before leaving him on the island, asked some children playing on the shore to call a doctor. But the request was met with curious stares because residents of an island with such a name know nothing of doctors. Laughter and music were enough to keep them all in the pink of health, and Rosier had no interest in either. So he was taken, on the wings of a black-crowned crane, to the palace of Jeunesse, their queen, to see what she might recommend to bolster his spirits. The palace attendants who received him, full of naïveté and joy, were too beautiful to describe. Queen Jeunesse, more charming and graceful than the rest, sat on a throne of daisies, a thousand cupids flitting around her, sprinkling orange blossoms.

Queen Jeunesse pointed to a chaise longue and suggested Rosier rest from his journey. Her ladies- and men-in-waiting tended to his needs, some giggling behind their hands or asking him for news of past centuries. They thought this a good joke because the prince, who was in his twenties, seemed old to them. But Jeunesse shushed them all, scolding them for their rudeness. She looked upon him favorably and forgot nothing in her attempts to engage him: charming looks, flattering words, playful attentions. But he did not engage beyond showing simple gratitude, so she explained her intentions more openly. She wanted him to be her lover; she could offer him all the pleasures he could ever desire or imagine. These advances went on day after day, and though he did not let on, Jeunesse could tell that he was beginning to desire her. And he was, it was true.

As for Florinde, she had barely gone a day without seeing Rosier before feeling the horror of living without the one she loved. She knew she had made a terrible mistake, and so she wrote him a letter in which she apologized profusely for the cruelest of orders. "Come back now!" she pleaded. "I am sorry!" The arrival of her note could not have been more timely. Rosier, who had been struggling mightily against his yearning for the young queen, was on the precipice of giving in to her. Florinde had been fading from his memory, which he suspected was the effect of a dark magic that existed in this place, but no one would admit to such. When he saw the writing on the page in his beloved's own hand, her image again filled his mind, and on the long journey back to her he remembered her voice, her touch, and how he couldn't wait to be her husband.

Florinde was so glad for his return that she didn't even ask about his experience on the Isle of Youth. They married, and soon the prince became king when his father died, and so they moved to his lands. Perhaps the misery in marriage that his father had experienced was an inherited condition, or maybe it was just the final act of a curse by a trickster fairy, but soon all their pleasures in life ended.

The prince, out of idleness one day, told Florinde that he had had a weakness for the queen of the Isle of Youth. She reproached him with an anger that shocked him, refusing his affections and suggesting he instead take company with the ladies of the court. Not realizing she was being sarcastic, he went to console himself there, only to be found by his wife, who overwhelmed him with insults. He felt so persecuted by the furies that he made a wish to become a rosebush again, and the wish came true.

For her part, Florinde could never again smell the scent of a rose without remembering her lost love. And that is why roses have made people swoon ever since.

CATHERINE DURAND

Like Catherine Bernard, Catherine Durand was not an aristocrat. Aside from that, we know her birth year was 1670. Those are all the facts we have about her life prior to the start of her literary career in 1699. Some sources append the name Bédacier to her, as in "Catherine Bédacier née Durand" or "Catherine Durand née Bédacier," which would point to her having a husband, but whether his name was Bédacier or Durand is a coin toss. That she used "Madame" as an author may strengthen the argument for her married status, though it's a mystery what exactly drove decisions about the names women used on the covers of their books during the era. While men generally had full names attached to their works, women writers were represented with abbreviations. Sort of. In the case of Catherine Durand, the shorthand used over the course of her career included "M. D.," "M. D***," "Madame ***," and "Madame D***." It wasn't until thirty years after she started writing that "Durand" began appearing on reissues of her books.

Soon after her death in 1736, a collection of her works was published in Paris by a prominent publishing house, Chez Prault. *Oeuvres de Madame Durand*, still held at France's national library, is a six-volume set that includes plays, nonfiction, fiction, fairy tales, and poetry, demonstrating her range as a writer. The fact that a publisher would invest in such an anthology reveals her popularity over a lengthy career and the professional regard she'd earned. So it follows that Voltaire, in that cataloging of writers from Louis XIV's reign, would of course have treated her more fairly and respectfully than her friend Catherine Bernard. Voltaire had not, after all, plagiarized Durand's work, so there was no reason for him to feel threatened by her inclusion. And especially having been reminded of the woman's contributions so recently with the publication of her *Oeuvres*, he could devote serious ink to her memory. He could list her works and even recognize a poetry prize from the Académie Française for verses she wrote for the king himself. But did he? No. Her entry was . . . nonexistent. The name Catherine Durand does not appear at all in that seminal history of people of letters.

By those who do remember her, she is considered the inventor of a niche dramatic genre, "comedies in proverbs." These were, in fact, her first published pieces, appended to the end of a novel written by her salon sister Henriette-Julie Murat, who was already a success and thus provided the newbie Durand with a launchpad. These short works became immediately popular, both on the page and in private performance. They were basically humorous skits, and the reader or viewer had to guess at the end which well-known proverb was being acted out. Some examples from that first published batch: "You can't judge a book by its cover," "Like master like man," "Tit for tat," and my favorite, "Washing a donkey's head is a waste of soap." Though this concept was later adopted by other writers, Durand's works were considered groundbreaking, as well as unique in their bluntness regarding sexual matters and their depictions of women as sharp-witted and men as comically clueless. One person of eminence who was apparently—and surprisingly—inspired by this work of Durand's was Madame de Maintenon, who did some writing herself. The record on Durand being so bare, we can't know whether the two of them really knew each other, but since Maintenon has at least tangentially intersected with some of our other conteuses' stories, it's worth a little explore into this seemingly paradoxical commonality between these two women.

What hasn't been said yet about Maintenon is how she rose to power, which is a paradox in and of itself. Briefly: She was born in a prison, the child of a Huguenot poet, spent much of her childhood in a convent, and then ended up the governess to a batch of Louis XIV's illegitimate offspring. He'd had these children with a mistress he'd long favored, but as soon as the governess arrived on the scene, he shifted his gaze to her. She rejected him repeatedly, something he certainly wasn't used to and may actually have found to be a turn-on, judging by his unrelenting obsession with her. When the queen died they married secretly, Maintenon's influence immediately felt throughout the kingdom. He remained faithful to her for the rest of his life, and they did everything together.

One of those things was to open a school for girls from noble families that had fallen on hard times, and that's where Maintenon's interest in writing comedies in proverbs came into play. Hers were intended to be acted out in classrooms. They had a moralistic tenor and encouraged lives of domesticity, in contrast to Durand's bawdy dialogues and promotion of a worldly life for women. You could say they both had the same goal—to help women find contentment in a society that privileged men—but the authors' views on how to accomplish that differed. Perhaps they respected each other's approaches. We'll never know.

Durand, of course, brought this art form into the literary salons. In addition to being good entertainment, her proverbs became popular as writing prompts. L'Héritier's "Finette," for instance, was surely conceived as an illustration of "Distrust is the mother of security," as she elucidates in the final line. You see a similar move in "Florinde" when Bernard ends with a pourquoi-style adage, the tale meant to explain the phenomenon of roses making people fall in love. And the tale alluded to in the earlier discussion of Bernard, "Ricquet with the Tuft," may have also been based on an axiom (perhaps "Beauty is in the eye of the beholder"?), but the three versions that were obviously spun from the same writing challenge go in different directions message-wise, so perhaps the assignment was more about proving which is of greater importance, beauty or intelligence. As mentioned before, Perrault wrote one of those three versions, and his started with the same premise as Bernard's: A beautiful but mindless young woman agrees to marry an ugly gnome if he grants her wish to become smart, and then she balks once she has her wits about her. Perrault then has her realize that she can be happy with a clever but monstrous husband. The End. In Bernard's version, the woman falls in love with a worthy man after gaining her intelligence and thus refuses the gnome, who gets revenge by turning her *lover* into a gnome, thereby leaving the woman forever unable to tell one from the other. Durand's take, "Le prodige d'amour" or "The Prodigy of Love," flips the gender dynamic by making the male character the stupid but gorgeous one. As for her message regarding intelligence and beauty . . . I'm not sure. See what you think as you read the retelling, "Brillante."

That tale was first published as an embedded story in a book called *Les petits soupers*, or *The Little Suppers*. As the title suggests, this was a foodie novel, about some women and men who meet regularly for meals and then entertain themselves. There are a lot of stories in this novel, but only two are fairy tales, the second one being "The Origin of Fairies," which is retold here as "Ogilire." It is an interesting piece, very different from prior tales written by the conteuses and seemingly mirroring a shift in how the fairy tale was being viewed by certain factions of society. It was 1702 when this came out, and though readers were still buying contes de fées at a clip, Madame de Maintenon and her followers had already begun wrinkling their noses at fairy tales and the "modern fairies" who were writing them. To put things in context, this was the same year as Murat's arrest, and La Force had been in exile for four years. Neither was writing fairy tales by this time, and they never would again. D'Aulnoy hadn't published any new tales since her liberation from detainment in a convent, choosing to work instead on a novel. L'Héritier was also in a lull (her future tales, while magical, would feature no fairies), and Bernard, as we know, was writing religious poetry for the Countess of Pontchartrain. So something was clearly amiss in fairyland. "Ogilire," you'll see, is not just a story of the origin of fairies but also, sadly, an extinction tale.

Another indication that Durand may have been channeling a disturbance in the realm is that fairies function as antagonists in all of her tales. Unlike the fairies in the bulk of the conteuses' tales that preceded Durand's, hers offer no comfort or service to the young protagonists but thwart their efforts to gain control over their own lives. In "Brillante," the fairy Coquette's envy and anger drive the plot. The same goes for "The Fairy Lubantine," not retold here, which takes the fairy-as-femme-fatale motif to an even further extreme. Lubantine, characterized as a debauchee, is cruel to the point of actually maiming and killing her rival. With the exception of a couple of pieces—including a fairy-free verse tale called "The Cat in Love," which ends in a bloodbath for a depraved tomcat who seduces a young feline—the level of brutishness demonstrated by the fairies in Durand's tales is unusual even among her own works. Those famed comedies in proverbs, for instance, had not even a hint of darkness or violence.

CATHERINE DURAND

Catherine Durand reveals in an undated poem in her *Oeuvres* the difficulty of trying to make ends meet with her pen. "I give to Parnassus a good," she writes (referring to that mythological home of the Muses), but in return she is "so poorly paid, so poorly maintained." If she received the same offer that her fellow bourgeois friend Bernard did in the same situation—the strings-attached pension—we have no record of that. But given that her books had all been published with royal privilege, that she had dedicated works to the royal family (including Louis' sister-in-law, that highest-ranking woman in France), and that she'd received the same prestigious poetry award Bernard had—in the same year, in fact—it makes sense that she could have been invited into Maintenon's fold. There is a curious gap in the list of her published works, about ten years between *The Little Suppers* and her next book. That, an historical fiction, not fairy tales, came out just after Bernard's death. So maybe the two friends were together during that time, living, if austerely, under the protection of the court. Maybe. Given all the missing pages in the stories of these women, we've got little to go on but maybes.

WOMEN OF THE FAIRY TALE RESISTANCE

BRILLANTE

THERE WAS ONCE an island called Galante, where the inhabitants were expected, from the moment of reason, to live by the following proverb: *If change is not a virtue, it is at least such a pleasure that it would be a shame to deprive oneself of it.* The sovereign king took this very seriously, especially when it came to matters of love. By the time of this tale, he had changed lovers so often that he'd cycled through the entire population of women on the island and had started taking another turn through. He wasn't selfish in this regard, by any means, holding lavish and lascivious festivals constantly for all to attend. The people of the kingdom were more than willing to abide by his expectations.

But his own household was another matter. His youngest daughter, Brillante, from *her* moment of reason, had it in mind that she wanted one lover for life. She had begun to feel stirrings for the occasional person she met, but she always stopped herself from engaging in any way, realizing that no one would ever be as faithful to her as to the proverb. So by the time of this tale, she had stopped going to any social events and instead was passing her days in solitary pursuits, often taking walks in the palace's preserve. She found solace in nature but also sorrow, for she couldn't help but notice the creatures who were paired up, especially the cranes and the swans, who she knew would stay together always.

"Why can't I be so lucky?" she said to herself with a sigh one day after a long stroll. As if in answer, a nightingale sang, the words distinct:

> *On the wings of the aerial spirit, flee*
> *And follow your heart to a place where he*
> *Will cast his gaze and set himself free,*
> *The one who can give you that fate so sweet.*

And then, seemingly out of nowhere, a mist enveloped Brillante, with an intoxicating aroma of jasmine. She felt herself rising, then in motion for she couldn't tell how long. Then there was soft earth under her feet, and the jasmine mist swirled off and was gone. Surrounding Brillante now were lush green hills, and a small village stood at a crossroads. She didn't know where she was, but she did know she was *not* on the island of Galante. Her heart pattered wildly, and she held a hand against it until it stilled. Then, with intention, she plucked the jewels from her gown and walked into the village to trade them in for a new life.

The next day, wearing boots and holding a shepherd's crook, she climbed a hillside with a small flock of sheep in her care. When she reached a meadow with a stream weaving through it, she stopped so her charges could drink. She looked out over a steep but narrow valley, and there on the opposite ridge she saw someone, a man. He was gazing across the gap at her, directly at her, for a long while. *Could this be . . . ?* she wondered, thinking of the nightingale's song. Finally he called out to her, but it was just to say "Come here," his tone as if he were beckoning a dog. She turned away, confused, and led her sheep to another pasture, though every step was a struggle, a sudden wind pushing against her so hard that it sometimes spun her round.

The next morning she chose a different route to take with her flock, one that ran along a river. It was a cloudless day, the air fragrant with honeysuckle, the fields a carpet of wildflowers. Brillante couldn't help but sing, and as songs have a way of bringing back memories, she thought of life on Galante, of childhood games. But she didn't feel any pangs of homesickness. *I'm content to follow my heart*, she thought, and sang only louder. Until she realized there was someone else singing along. Someone who knew the same song but sang it most horribly. She looked across the river to see, sitting on a rock on the opposite shore, the same man she had seen the day before. He was looking right at her again. And, strangely, as he sang, his voice changed. Before long he was in complete harmony with her. At the end of the song, he stood and bowed. *Perhaps he is the one after all*, she thought, *my sweet fate*. But then a woman appeared on the bank. She was extraordinarily elegant, Brillante couldn't help but notice, literally dazzling in the sun's rays. She took the man's arm and kissed his cheek, and then she glared across the river at Brillante. Flustered, Brillante turned to her sheep, or else she would have seen the man's beseeching look over his shoulder as the woman led him away.

WOMEN OF THE FAIRY TALE RESISTANCE

✵

On the next day, determined not to make the same mistake again, she consulted her heart long and hard before heading into the hills. But she had no sooner found a pasture than she saw a hunting party in the distance, and there the man was again. He sat astride a graceful horse, a bow across his lap, and he was looking steadily in her direction. She ducked behind a tree, only to startle at the *thwack* of an arrow hitting the trunk. Her heart racing, she waited there until the sounds of the hunt passed. When she peeked around the trunk, she saw that the arrow was lodged high up and dangling from it was a note. She could just reach it on tiptoes. It read:

> Dear shepherdess, please come back to this place tomorrow. Seeing you from afar has already saved me from so many of life's torments. If I can only be with you, I will be the happiest of all men. Palidamour

Brillante considered the odd, even boorish behavior she'd witnessed and wondered how this man, this Palidamour, could write a letter with such ardor and eloquence. Her common sense told her that she should not meet him. But her heart—which was still racing, though not out of fear, she now recognized—told her otherwise.

She was back on the path with her sheep just after dawn the next morning. When she reached the pasture, she first saw Palidamour's horse munching grass, and then she saw him leaning against the tree, waiting for her. She could see now just how beautiful he was, unnaturally so, as if he were Cupid himself. When she was near enough he took her hand and gazed deeply into her eyes. "I am free," he whispered. "Be always with me, *please*. What is your name?"

She was sure now that he was the one who would bring that sweet fate, and her heart seemed as if it might burst. She looked to the sky, half expecting the nightingale to be overhead. "Brillante," she said. "But I don't understand. From what have you become free?"

"An inability to feel, to know," he said. "I am the youngest son of a king, my mother lost to my birth. I was born mute and with a mind that could not react to the world or absorb any of the lessons of the many tutors my father engaged. Finally, giving up, he made a deal with the fairy Coquette. She told him that only her love could make me intelligent and eloquent, and that she would return me to the kingdom when the work was done. I have been her captive a long while, all her attempts at seduction for naught. Then when I saw you, my confusion immediately began to untangle, I began to speak and think. The fairy at first was pleased, since she thought it her doing, finally. Until she, too, saw you and realized what had happened: that love had indeed freed my mind, but it was not *her* love. She has been in a rage since."

"We must get out of here, then," Brillante said urgently. Although no fairy had ever visited the island of Galante, she had learned of them and feared their powers.

"She will find us wherever we go," he said. "The only way to gain freedom is to convince my father to dissolve the agreement. As much as I loathe the idea of seeing him, now that I understand how he sent me away rather than accept me as I was, there is no other way. I have begged the fairy to let me go, but she will not agree."

"Then I will go," Brillante said. "Tell me where—"

But she was interrupted by a violent and sudden storm, and a black cloud descended onto the grass and formed itself into a cave. Two furies in the form of serpents swooped out and grabbed Brillante, then pushed her into the black fog and took up posts as guards.

Palidamour charged at them, but the fairy Coquette, who had been hiding behind a bush the whole time, stepped out now, quaking with anger at all she had heard. "If you bring harm to my guards or to me," she warned, "your beloved will face a torture you can't imagine." And she called to her side a winged tiger and instructed him to take Palidamour back to her palace.

In the days that followed, she kept him close at all times. Now that he wasn't just a vacuous beauty, she wanted him more than ever, and her rage seemed only to fuel this desire. But he continued to repel her advances and retreated until he was silent again, unresponsive to anything or anyone. This upset her even more because it seemed to be proof that it was, in fact, Brillante who had awakened him. But still, she couldn't bear the idea of his returning to his former state, and so she devised an experiment: She would allow him a supervised visit with Brillante to see if that would change him again.

She called for the flying tiger and explained the mission. "Take him now," she said, "and remember to return him to me as soon as he regains his wits."

Palidamour, staring blankly, watched the tiger approach him and then stand over him. He braced himself to be roughly handled by the animal, but he didn't show it. In truth, Palidamour's mental acuity had not regressed. It was a desperate melancholy that had caused him to withdraw, and then when he realized the fairy's fears, he exaggerated his condition in hopes of somehow leveraging the situation to get away. He closed his eyes and vowed not to react when the tiger's sharp claws gripped his body. But it was only gentleness he felt, soft paws scooping him up and carrying him off.

When they arrived at the lair, the furies refused to let them in, the fairy having been forceful in her instruction to allow no one to enter or exit. The tiger explained the change of plans, but they wouldn't budge. (Furies are known to be as stubborn as they are ill-tempered.) While this negotiation was going on, Palidamour, still limp in the grasp of the tiger, peered between the writhing furies and could just barely see into the darkness to a heap at the far corner of the cave. He leapt from the tiger's grasp and ran to Brillante, who was lying in a pile of leaves and muck in a wretched state of neglect.

The furies now slunk toward Palidamour, their tails ready to strangle the life out of him. But the tiger put himself between them and the lovers. "The fairy wants him alive. *I* am tasked to take care of him, and *you* are to guard the entrance. Do you want me to tell Coquette you defied her?" They looked at each other nervously (furies are notoriously afraid of fairies) and then returned to their posts, leaving in their wake a vapor more foul than their usual stench. The tiger nodded at Palidamour and curled up nearby.

"They have been treating you cruelly," Palidamour said to Brillante, tender tears rolling down his cheeks.

"We will be all right," she said. "As the nightingale foretold."

"What do you mean?" he asked.

And she told him about Galante, about her life there, about the proverb, about her wish to leave and the nightingale's song. "Then the aerial spirit it sang of carried me here," she said weakly, worn out from telling the story. "I followed my heart after that."

"And I was set free by gazing upon you," he said, holding her in his arms.

"You are my fate so sweet," she whispered.

CATHERINE DURAND

"But how can we ever—" he started, then realized the tiger was standing over them. "*No*," Palidamour cried, "just a little more time!"

The tiger didn't reach out for him, though. He smiled (as much as a tiger can smile) and began to dissipate into a mist. The putrid odors of the lair were replaced by a fragrant scent.

"Jasmine," Brillante said dreamily, "like the aerial spirit."

"That is I, princess," the fading tiger said. "After transporting you to this fair countryside, I decided to stay. The ethos of Galante had worn on me as well, landing me more than once in the most indiscreet situations. On my first day here, the fairy offered me a position, and she acted well the part of a dignified lady, so I agreed to be in her employ. I'd never been a flying tiger before, so the new experience was a draw. It was not long before her true colors showed and I rued the decision, and thus I prepared to leave her service. Unlike the furies, aerial spirits have no fear of fairies and are consequently safe from their whims. Before I left, however, I became aware that the charge I had brought from Galante was the particular subject of her wrath, and it is against the creed of the aerial spirits to abandon one who has been in our care."

"You see?" Brillante said to Palidamour. "It is all as the nightingale said."

"But how?" he asked. "How can we stay safe from the fairy?"

The tiger, barely discernible now, said, "Prince, we will go to your father. He will deal with Coquette, and you two can live in his kingdom in prosperity."

Palidamour shook his head. "You go alone. I care not to live there."

"Neither do I," said Brillante.

"Then where shall I take you?" the aerial spirit asked the lovers.

They looked at each other so intently that it seemed their eyes were having a conversation. *Far away*, they were saying.

And the aerial spirit surrounded them and lifted them off to a place above, where their marriage would be blessed by immortals, a place with green hills and shade trees, cranes and swans, and sheep grazing in meadows of wildflowers.

There they are still living happily.

CATHERINE DURAND

OGILIRE

IT WAS NOT long ago that a woman who had fallen asleep reading fairy tales heard the strains of an instrument that seemed to transport her. She found herself in a pleasant grove with a stream flowing through it, its waters dazzling like diamonds. There was a man on the bank playing the lyre so melodically that she knew he must be the god of verse. He dipped a hand into the water and placed a drop on the woman's lips. "Go back to the mortals," he said to her, "and since they are unjust enough to treat the fairies like beings of the imagination, like chimeras, I give you the power to undeceive them. You will no sooner pick up your pen than the origin of the fairies will be revealed." She woke up surprised to be in her bed but so filled with what had just happened that she immediately began to compose the story that follows.

A couple of centuries after Jupiter sorted out the chaos of the universe, he took a passion for a mortal woman whose beauty surpassed that of the most exquisite flowers. Her laughter was so graceful, her spirit so sublime, that it was not possible to resist her charms. Nature undoubtedly, Jupiter thought, had made this masterpiece as reward for his labors. Her name was Ogilire.

Jupiter had had several lovers by this time, all of whom had succumbed to his first seduction. But Ogilire revolted against his usual means, his propensity for force: his taking the shape of a bull or an eagle, and especially his habit of announcing his arrival with a lightning bolt. She had an innate calm that served to repress his audacity but not his attraction to her.

One day when he had failed yet again to win her attention and was left alone in a meadow where she had been walking, he heard giggling that seemed to come from within a myrtle tree. It was the god Amor, who had been watching Jupiter's futile attempts.

"Lend me your help!" Jupiter cried. "Do not be so cruel!"

"Until now," replied Amor, "you have only had desires, which you satisfied without delicacy, and without that sensitive pleasure that one derives in the pursuit of a heart. Learn what feelings are and serve a mortal as if you were mortal." He set an arrow in his bow and shot the master of the gods.

Jupiter immediately felt a sweet languor, and he realized he was no longer possessed of his usual burning desire to conquer. Instead he felt tender love and wanted to please Ogilire. He stayed in the meadow until she returned again for fresh air. It was sunset when he spied her there. She was lying on the grass at the edge of a fountain, and he threw himself at her feet and told her those things that we only think when we love. She listened to him, not without emotion, but let escape her lips only what was necessary to nourish his hope, and then she excused herself. Far from being frustrated, Jupiter saw this as progress, and he returned to the heavens confident in his fate.

He left the universe at rest during his pursuit of Ogilire. Instead of the usual occupations to dominate or prove his mettle, he was only capable of sweet ideas, of cheerful designs. Every day he assured her of eternal fidelity. She often resorted to flight so as not to give in to the inclination that was already strong within her. He had been a perfect admirer for many months without having been able to obtain the slightest favor.

One day when she was with him and they were talking with that touching pleasure only known to a union of hearts, Jupiter shared with her the secrets of nature, and they found themselves in a kind of cave of clouds. It exhaled the most delicious aromas, and they saw small lines traced in the mist, which formed into words: *Enjoy the moment. It is time. Amor commands it.*

"Will you refuse," cried Jupiter, "such a sacred order?"

Ogilire first cast her eyes down as if she had not seen the message, but then she held out her hand and let him kiss her fingers.

"Until you, I had only had a false idea of perfect pleasure," Jupiter said. "What can I do to reward such a great good deed?"

"Love me for all my years," Ogilire said.

"I can make you immortal," he told her.

She shook her head. "I don't want to compete with the whimsies and jealousies of the gods. An earthbound life, unknown to immortals, is what I want."

Though convinced that he could change her mind one day about joining the gods, he complied with her wishes and created for them a hidden place in a valley cleaved into lush mountains. Their rapture was such that everything felt it on Earth and in the heavens, but no inhabitant of the celestial vault was able to discover the mysterious cause.

Soon Ogilire became pregnant and bore a divine daughter. Jupiter deemed her a "fairy," the first of her kind. "All your daughters, dear Ogilire, will carry the title, as will their daughters and *their* daughters, and on and on, using their vast knowledge and talents of enchantment in service of mortals. They will live for a period of three hundred years, after which they will become spirits of the air or the sea."

This pleased Ogilire, and she raised her daughter with great joy and attention, and had six more. Though Jupiter tried mightily to get his lover to change her mind about her own mortality, it was to no avail. Upon her death, torrents of cold rain poured for a year, after which time Jupiter assuaged his grief by building for his many daughters and granddaughters a castle where they could come together from the four corners of the world and hold a fairy council.

He built it in the middle of a low plain where a large river flowed over mother-of-pearl cataracts. The banks were shaded by fruit trees that travelers could pick from freely, for more fruits were revealed as they were taken away. The river could be crossed on different bridges that all led to the gates through which one entered the castle. Each gate was guarded by animals: one by elephants, one by unicorns, one by wild boars, and one by lions. Honest guests were easily allowed to pass, but anyone who might be dangerous to the fairies was subjected to treatment by the beasts that, while not lethal, was formidable enough that few exposed themselves to the roughness. Such was Jupiter's determination to keep his progeny safe.

The splendors to be seen inside the castle gates were unmatched by any king's palace. There were a hundred pavilions, all built of gold, and the windows were a crystal more transparent than glass and unbreakable. The arches under which one walked were alternately of turquoise, rubies, emeralds, amethysts, topazes, and sapphires. There was an enormous garden sanctuary where the fairies could relax and engage in conversation or entertain themselves. The youthful played games and the older ones rested in apartments overlooking the grounds. Above the castle, the sky was always clear, and at night the stars were brighter than anywhere else, casting a glow so it was never fully dark.

Several centuries passed, during which the fairies did much good all over the world. Ogilire's gentleness and enlightenment shone brightly in their ranks and guided the work of these eminent women. In the darkness of the crudest eras, their knowledge and creativity was a beacon. But everything has a peak, and much as empires fall into degradation, so did the council of the fairies. Some of the leaders used their power for ill, engaging in avarice or vengeance and exercising such horrible cruelties that it astonished the trembling universe of fairies and mortals who lived under their auspices. It was concluded that there was no other way to stem the course of so many horrors than by destroying the council.

Jupiter was begged to strike it down with a terrible thunderbolt, which he agreed to do without protest, no longer influenced by the peaceful nature of his long-gone Ogilire. The lightning strike was so powerful that not even the slightest trace can be found of this castle of antiquity. Such was the end of the council of the fairies, but those whose virtue did not belie their origin lived tranquilly on their own or with others of their kind. Some took spouses, with mixed results, as was the case with the learned and famous Melusine. She possessed the beauty, the grace, the spirit of the amiable Ogilire.

Over time, fewer and fewer fairies remained, until there was little regard for them at all, whether fear or admiration. Names that had once made crowned heads tremble were only uttered by the mouths of children, to whom governesses related the facts imperfectly. Such tales were even narrated with this childishness, the only language of such a tender age. But a day did come when illustrious women rescued from oblivion these fairies worthy of eternal memory and renewed the stories of their deeds with great spirit and art. Without them, the fairies' memory would still be enveloped in the darkness of ignorance.

The woman heard again the strums of the lyre, the god of verse singing now of endings. And she put down her pen.

LOUISE D'AUNEUIL

A book that is seen as marking the end of the conteuses' prominence is *La tiranie des fées détruite*, or *The Tyranny of the Fairies Destroyed*, published in 1702. The titular story lives up to its name, being about the demise of the fairy realm on the order of the tale you just read by Catherine Durand, which came out the same year. So it follows that the authors were responding to the same prompt—be that a literal prompt from a salon gathering or a prompting from the previously described social pressures. This work is widely considered to be the first of several books by Louise de Bossigny, Marquise d'Auneuil. But in my ongoing quest to rescue these writers from fairy tale oblivion, I've come to seriously doubt that she was the person who wrote this book—or anything else attributed to her. I have some theories about who did, but in the absence of actual facts, I'm leaving the name "Louise d'Auneuil" in the seventh salon sister slot. As you'll see, if there has been misidentification, no fault lies with the woman who bore that name.

All we know about Louise de Bossigny is that she may have been born in 1670 and that she was certainly a member of the aristocracy, given the circumstances of her marriage. As her married name indicates, her husband was the Marquis d'Auneuil: Louis-Claude Barjot, a military hero and widower who was thirty years her senior. His family was of high nobility, and he inherited considerable wealth and property. That he carried the title he did shows his standing; during this era in France, a marquis was just one rung below a duke, which was just one rung below a prince. The Marquis and Marquise d'Auneuil may not have been married too awfully long. They never had children, and according to a notice in the *Mercure galant*, they both died in the same twenty-four-hour period in January 1700. (A contagious disease was the likely culprit, probably measles, which was rampant back then.) Connecting the chronological dots, you can see that Louise d'Auneuil had been dead two years when *The Tyranny of the Fairies Destroyed* was published.

This was the first red flag for me regarding the claim of her authorship. I weighed the possibility that the book could have been issued posthumously, but there is no indication of that in the royal privilege notice, which was printed in the first edition. It refers to the author as if she was living. And even if posthumous publication was the case for *The Tyranny*, what about the rest of the works she supposedly wrote, which came out over a span of years after 1702? Taking into account that she was probably not even out of her twenties when she died, it's unlikely that she left behind a pile of manuscripts that someone then had the wherewithal to bring to the attention of publishers. Add to that the lack of any contemporaneous evidence that she was friends with the other conteuses or even attended the salons. Or, for that matter, that she even lived in Paris. The only geographical markers we have for her are that she was from central France and was buried with her husband in their parish in the province of Berry, more than a hundred miles from the center of salon life and the French publishing world.

So how, then, did this woman become associated with these works? The first time we see any reference to Louise de Bossigny as a writer is in the 1780s, when a man named Charles-Joseph Mayer decided to publish a comprehensive collection of French fairy tales, many of which had lain fallow since the turn of the century. He called it *Le cabinet des fées*, or *The Fairy Cabinet*, and it ended up being forty-one volumes long and instrumental in revitalizing interest in the fairy tale across Europe. (For instance, the Brothers Grimm would mine *The Fairy Cabinet* when compiling their own collection some decades later. Ignoring, of course, all the tales written by the salon women.) This epic literary effort included not only fairy tales but short biographies of each of the writers. Therein lay the challenge. If you recall, women writers were usually represented by abbreviations on the covers of their works. In the case of the books in question, Mayer had the following pseudonyms to work with: Madame la Comtesse D. L. and Madame la Comtesse D**. There was another clue in *The Tyranny*, that royal privilege notice, which referred to the author as "Comtesse d'Auneuil." Mayer at first dismissed this name because there was no mention of it in anything written about literary women of that century. Pointing to claims by other historians, he suggested that maybe it was a corruption of Marie-Catherine d'Aulnoy's name, which had been subject to a wide range of variants, even by her own hand, such as "Aunois," "Alnoy," and "Anois." But then Mayer issued a correction, reason unexplained, in which he attached the works to "Louise de Bossigny, Comtesse d'Auneuil." My guess is he discovered a real person had the name "Auneuil" and, up to his ears in an ambitious project, moved on. Clearly he missed the death date, and that Louise d'Auneuil was not a comtesse. She was a marquise, a rung up that ladder. Representing herself publicly as a member of a lesser rank would have been an unusual choice on her part.

But there *was* someone who did use "Comtesse D . . ." in her work: Marie-Catherine d'Aulnoy. So it may be that Mayer got it right the first time and the simplest and most obvious explanation was correct—an Occam's razor kind of situation. While I don't see d'Aulnoy's fingerprints on all the works that have been tagged with Louise d'Auneuil's name, there are some that certainly seem born of her pen. One example: a pamphlet published in Paris in 1703, *Le galant nouvelliste*, a supposedly fictional story told through a series of letters to a Frenchwoman living in Madrid. Aside from the obvious—that d'Aulnoy would have, in fact, written many letters to Frenchwomen living in Madrid, including her mother and a daughter who remained there—the overall content of *Le galant nouvelliste* demonstrates the kinds of international and life experiences that d'Aulnoy had had by that time. She was in her fifties when it was published, and her oeuvre included many works based on her travels outside of France, including (supposedly fictional) memoirs in the form of letters. It is far less probable that Louise d'Auneuil was a world traveler, given her marriage to a provincial marquis and her untimely death, much less that she was the author of completed stories inspired by such.

Another "Louise d'Auneuil" work that cries out d'Aulnoy to me is the fairy tale "La Princesse Patiente dans la Forêt d'Erimente," or "Princess Patiente in the Forest of Erimente," which is retold here, so I won't give away too much now.

WOMEN OF THE FAIRY TALE RESISTANCE

In this story, you'll meet an ogre who pretends to be a comely prince in order to charm a mother into letting him marry her daughter, then takes the princess to his lair where he reveals his abominable nature (including a tongue that kills) and proceeds to extract riches from her. You can certainly read that as an allegory of Marie-Catherine's marriage plight, although the greedy ogre does get his comeuppance at the end, unlike the real greedy ogre in her life. Some of the names in the story jumped out at me as well. *Patientine* means "patience," which is something Marie-Catherine surely needed in order to endure, say, her years in the convent, where she wrote a lot of her tales. Erimente was a real Christian monastery, so the forest's name might have been alluding to that same confinement. And then there's the ogre's name, Insacio. Of all the character and place names in the story (and there are quite a few), this is the only one that does not have a clear meaning or correlative, so I wondered if there might have been some wordplay going on. Anagrams were very popular in France during that period, so I put the Baron d'Aulnoy's name, FRANÇOIS, next to INSACIO, and *voilà!* It's not a perfect anagram, so maybe it's a coincidence, but you can definitely spell the name of the ogre with the letters from the name of the . . . other ogre. Though this tale was published in 1709, four years after Marie-Catherine died, if there was any writer who *did* leave behind a pile of manuscripts, it was she. She wrote the lion's share of fairy tales during the vogue, along with many novels and nonfiction books, and she was publishing works right up until her death. She also had people in her orbit with the wherewithal to bring left-behind manuscripts to the attention of publishers: her daughters.

You have already met one of these daughters, Marie-Anne, who was that babe in Marie-Catherine's arms when she was arrested and taken to the Conciergerie. By the time of the fairy tale salons, Marie-Anne was all grown up and moving in the same circles as her mother. She went by the name Madame de Héere. The previously mentioned chronicle from 1698, *The New Pandora*, or *Illustrious Women of the Century of Louis the Great*, devoted as much space to her as it did the conteuses (with the exception of Louise d'Auneuil, who was not mentioned at all). "This lady writes pleasantly in prose and verse," starts the biographical piece on de Héere, and it goes on to list several of her works, including one titled "La tulipe," or "The Tulip," and another called "Reine des fleurs," or "Queen of Flowers." These sounded to me like they could be fairy tales, so I set out to find them. A search

of the catalog of France's national library, the Bibliothèque Nationale, yielded no hits at all for an author named de Héere, but when I searched for "La tulipe," one of her mother's tales popped up. It was not a tale by that title, but the main fairy in the story is named Tulipe. Interesting, but not exactly fruitful. Then I searched for "Reine des fleurs," and what came up was a book called *Les illustres fées*, or *The Illustrious Fairies*, a collection published in 1710 that includes eleven fairy tales, one titled "Reine de l'isle des fleurs," or "Queen of the Isle of Flowers." Even with the addition of an "isle" in this title, I deemed it close enough to be a possibility, knowing too well how rife with errors the records of the contes de fées are. Nowhere in the book is an author name listed, or even an abbreviation, but more digging turned up some authorial names that had been attached to it at one time or another, including (dramatic pause) Louise d'Auneuil. Now I had a new question in my head: Might Madame de Héere have been this phantom seventh salon sister?

A review of *The Tyranny of the Fairies Destroyed* published in the *Mercure galant* upon its debut would support the view that it was written by someone like Madame de Héere—an "illustrious" young aristocrat. The reviewer glowingly predicts that if this up-and-coming author "wants to try her pen on more serious subjects, there is no doubt that she will do so with great success." The review goes on to refer to other works by her that were read "every day," probably alluding to a monthly serial sold on the streets of Paris. These were fictions in the guise of news, all light and amusing, appealing to the chic crowd. The reviewer would have surely known the identity of this "Madame la Comtesse d'Auneüil [*sic*]," but the *Mercure* was notorious for stoking mystique, feeding the fairy tale craze by providing only cryptic clues about the writers. So it would have been entirely in keeping with their style to perpetuate a nom de plume, if that's what was happening here, i.e., a pseudonym being used by the famous Marie-Catherine d'Aulnoy's daughter. Or daughters—Marie-Anne was not the only one known to be part of the salon scene. Her younger sister, Thérèse-Aimée, born during their mother's banishment from France (so clearly not a child of Baron d'Aulnoy's), was well-traveled and known for having inherited traits from her mother. Oh, and she married a nobleman from (another dramatic pause) the province of Berry, where the flesh-and-blood Louise d'Auneuil was buried.

Before we end this romp, here's one last question: If the "Comtesse d'Auneuil" was a fiction created by one or more of the salongoers, doesn't that make other plotlines possible, too? Consider Henriette-Julie Murat. Scholars have compared the structure and style of *The Tyranny* to her work, some concluding that she and Louise d'Auneuil had to have been close. But what if Murat actually *wrote* that book? It was published not long after her arrest, and prior to that she was in the prime of her life as a fairy tale writer. If she had been working on that collection before her freedom and her pen were so abruptly taken from her (and, interestingly, *The Tyranny* includes some unfinished stories), maybe her friends decided to publish it for her. They wouldn't have even tried getting her name past the censor, knowing how the royals felt about her. Similarly, others could have had reason to hide *their* names—say, the Princess of Conti, who was known to be active in the salons but whose high rank in the court would have made it impossible for her to sign any work; or Catherine Bernard, who lived under the constraints of a pension that meant she couldn't continue to publish the fiction she so obviously enjoyed. The faux Comtesse d'Auneuil could have come to their rescue, and such an act of creation would be consistent with what we do know for sure about all these women: that they were imaginative, collaborative, and rebellious.

The final tale in this book is "Queen of Flowers," a retelling of "Reine de l'isle des fleurs." After I stumbled across this conte, I did a quick translation, and what a sweet story I found. Regardless of its uncertain provenance, it feels as if it must have been written by one of our salon writers. At its core are young people who go through trials (including exile to a remote and scary place), who believe in tendresse, who make choices, who rule in the end. It features a compassionate fairy, if some abuse of the fairy arts. And also a little dog, which brought to my mind Marie-Catherine d'Aulnoy's "The White Cat," which, you may remember, had a few charming canines in its plot. My "Queen of Flowers" stays very true to the tale it is based on, although I did add a couple of character names. The original used only titles—queen, princess, prince—but since there are two sisters who figure prominently, I wanted names to help distinguish them. You'll recognize the ones I chose. Call it an homage to tangled roots, to the next generation of women of the fairy tale resistance.

LOUISE D'AUNEUIL

PATIENTINE

THERE WAS ONCE an ogre named Insacio who lived in the Forest of Erimente, in a den where the rays of the sun had never reached. The furies who had presided over his birth had spilled the foam of Cerberus on his tongue, and thus any he touched with it lost their lives. This is how he kept those around him in fear. He had no interest at all in love or friendship, his heart occupied only with a fierce passion for possessing riches.

The ogre often went to take lessons from the goddess Avarice. Consulting her one day about his destiny, he was told that if he could have within his power a princess named Patientine, daughter of the widowed queen of Lydie, he would be the richest of all ogres. Wasting no time, he took the form of a well-made young man with good manners, and he transformed the two monsters he kept in his stable into fine horses. Then he traveled to the court of Lydie and presented himself as the Prince of Thrace. He performed so well that he won in a short time the affection of the princess and her mother.

Patientine had a companion named Espritée. They had long held first place in each other's hearts. The princess confided to her about her budding fondness for this visitor, and though Espritée had a bad feeling about the match, she did not let on, seeing how excited the queen and the princess were. So Patientine, whose beauty and virtue had made all the men of the kingdom sigh, was wed to the false prince. As soon as the festivities concluded, Insacio insisted on leaving. He wanted to take his wife away with him alone, but Espritée refused to leave Patientine's side, no matter the ogre's opposition.

After a few days of travel, they arrived in Erimente, and a short time later they reached his dark lair. It is impossible to describe the shock of the princess when she found herself in such a terrible place, and she thought she would die of pain when the ogre resumed his ordinary form and cruel mien. Entirely insensitive to pity, he was not the least moved by his wife's tears. Espritée tried to win the friendship of the ogre in order to reduce Patientine's sorrow, but nothing reached his heart.

Insacio made the two young women rise before daybreak and go into the forest to gather a certain herb, which they then had to bring back to the cave and boil in a large cauldron to draw out its juice. Feeding this brew to the ravenous monsters in the stable was the next step. Patientine and Espritée were at first paralyzed with fear at the beasts' sharp teeth and piercing brays, but they soon recognized a look in the monsters' eyes that mirrored their own state of captivity, lessening their trepidation.

After completing this chore, they were sent to the mountainside to pull up madder plants and then extract from the roots a pigment that was prized for dyeing the robes of kings. With distaffs they had been given by the ogre, they had to spin fine yarn, which they then dyed so the ogre could sell the skeins at exorbitant prices to royal weavers. They worked on this project ceaselessly, Insacio's hunger for more wealth never satisfied no matter their output.

They were fed little more than acorn bread, and so they became, with each passing day, weaker and weaker. The only way they could keep going was to take short naps when they were out of Insacio's view. One such time, when Patientine and Espritée were asleep under a tree together, holding each other for comfort, they were awakened by what they thought was a storm but turned out to be the angry ogre stomping toward them. He had come to check on their progress, and when he saw them in their repose he became furious and began spewing insults. He threatened to send Espritée away, and he would have done it if he had not feared that she would go right to the queen and tell her of her daughter's misfortunes. Patientine, without saying a single word to her barbarous husband, wiped away her tears and went back to stripping the land of the roots he found so precious.

Insacio had also a crew of men he mistreated, diggers employed in a search for buried treasure that Avarice had told the ogre was hidden in a valley near his lair. He made this crew work night and day, and when he found any men idle he unfurled his noxious tongue and killed them on the spot. Patientine and Espritée were now given the job of watching over these diggers. They had to take their distaffs with them and spin while the men worked. There was no shade in this valley because all the trees had been felled, so the two women were either burned by a fiery sun or pelted with wind and rain.

One day when they were at their posts, a man rode through the valley on horseback, a prince by the name of Courageux. He immediately recognized Patientine, whom he'd met at the court of Lydie. He had since that time had an infatuation for her that he had not been able to overcome even after learning of her marriage. Surprised now by such an unexpected encounter, he dismounted and eagerly approached her. But soon his expression turned to alarm as he noticed her state of distress, and he asked how he might help her. Patientine, afraid that she would be discovered with him and incur Insacio's rage, explained that her husband was not far from them, and she begged the prince to leave.

He reluctantly obeyed, but when he was but steps away, a lion came out of nowhere and made straight for Patientine. The prince drew his sword and with a threatening cry dealt a blow to the lion, making the animal turn its rage against him. Courageux defended himself, but not without receiving a large wound on his stomach from the lion's claws. The diggers rushed to his aid, or else he would have been killed. They pummeled the lion with their shovels until it fell dead at Patientine's feet.

Insacio, attracted by the cries, arrived at the scene just as the prince was falling onto the grass, his wound having weakened him to the point of fainting. The ogre, touched by pity for the first time in his life, had the prince carried to his lair and ordered Patientine and Espritée to attend to his wounds. They were so grateful to Courageux that they gladly cared for him. They gathered healing herbs for a poultice that would bring down his fever, and soon he began regaining his strength. He was immensely appreciative of the kindness the women showed and felt lucky to spend time with Patientine, but he also was filled with worry for her, knowing now whom she had been wed to and the abuse she had endured. His kind words consoled her, and she willingly engaged in conversation when her husband was not home.

One day, though, Insacio caught them speaking fondly to each other, and he flew into a rage. His greed being now joined with jealousy, he forbade Patientine to go near the prince again. She, without Espritée by her side this time, was sent back to her painful work. Courageux was beside himself at having caused her treatment to worsen, and so he resolved to leave the forest and organize her rescue as soon as he was recovered enough to mount his horse.

When that day came, after Patientine was escorted by the ogre to her abysmal tasks, the prince told Espritée that he would be going to Lydie to tell the queen of their misfortune. She shook her head, saying that Patientine's mother had no power to break her daughter's marital chains and that the only one who might be able to help was a relative of the queen's who was a fairy. Her name was Clementine. She lived in a palace, Espritée explained, that would be impossible for him to find without her help, so she would go, too. They left right away, fearful that the ogre would catch on and stop them if they waited. Courageux lamented leaving without a word to the suffering princess, but Espritée assured him that she would know they were on a quest to get help. That there was nothing else in the world that would take Patientine's dear friend away from her.

And this was true. Patientine, finding them gone when she returned from her labors, was filled with hope even while her heart ached for Espritée, whom she could not remember being separated from for even a day in her whole life. The prince, too, had become special to her, and she would miss their conversation. But she kept her thoughts to herself, careful not to let on to the ogre what she suspected, that they were on their way to see the fairy. He had the same inkling, though, aware that her family was under the protection of the compassionate and powerful Clementine, whom he had always made a point to avoid. Certain the fairy would soon be looking for Patientine, he surrounded Erimente with an impenetrable cloud.

The gods favored Espritée and Courageux, and it took not a day for them to reach Clementine's palace, where the fairy herself greeted them warmly. She wore a gown of silver gauze and a crown of orange feathers on her head. After listening intently to their story, Clementine said, "Poor Patientine is enduring horrors shackled to this ogre. I believe I can rescue her with my art, but I will need a little time to study and prepare, during which you will be well taken care of." Reading the anxious expressions on their faces, she added, "Do not dwell on the princess's woes, as that will not hasten the process. Let yourselves engage with the pleasures here."

The fairy dispatched them to a comfortable apartment attended by nymphs, where they fell into sleep without intending to. When they awoke, there were trays of fruits and jams, which filled them with an energy they had forgotten. They were then led to the gardens, where they took a long walk on a path lined with

pomegranate trees. At the end was a pavilion surrounded by myrtles, and they stopped to sit, birds filling the branches all around them and chirping melodically as if in a choir. It wasn't long, though, before they were talking about Patientine and their fears for her well-being.

"No, no, no," they heard, and they looked down to see a bird with a crown of orange feathers. It changed before their eyes into the fairy herself. "My charms are ready, so we shall go," she said, and a chariot appeared before them, decorated with golden suns and drawn by eagles. They got in and took to the air. "Insacio has used the art of the Underworld to hide Patientine," the fairy told them, "but I will render his power useless." She handed Espritée a bottle and said to listen for her instructions. Then she told Courageux, "Entrust to me the task of severing the bonds that hold Patientine. Do not use your arms, as they will fail."

They were above Erimente now, though they could see nothing through the thick fog beneath them. Clementine told Espritée to sprinkle drops from the bottle, and as soon as she did, the cloud began to dissipate. In moments, they were able to make out the clear-cut valley and the forest, and then they were alighting near the entrance to the lair, where the ogre's two monsters were standing guard. "Remember who has the power here," Clementine said to Courageux, seeing that he was gripping the hilt of his sword. Ashamed that he had disobeyed her, he presented his hand instead to the fairy to help her disembark from the chariot.

Clementine taking the lead, they approached the monsters, whom she touched lightly with a wand she'd pulled from the folds of her gown. They immediately transformed into ogresses. "You are free now," she said to them, waving them away. Sneering at her, they scurried off into the forest. Clementine, turning to Espritée and Courageux, said, "Insacio's sisters. Not the kindest of creatures, but they did one day suggest he temper his cruelty. You can see what happened to them."

She led them into the ogre's cave, her presence chasing away the darkness. And there they saw Patientine hoisting the cauldron of herbs over the fire. Dazzled by the brilliance of the fairy, she dropped the heavy pot, and the murky water streamed out, turning to gold as it settled into the earthen floor. Stunned, Patientine looked now to Clementine, who nodded knowingly toward the door, where stood the ogre, having heard the commotion. The vexed expression he wore became euphoric upon seeing his abode paved in precious metal. He scooped up a handful of gold, but his touch made it turn back to what it had been. All he held was muddy water.

"Tremble, unhappy Insacio," Clementine said to him, "and recognize the justice of the gods by the torments to which they condemn you. You are going to lose this unfortunate princess by the evils that your greed has caused her to suffer. I will take her back to her kingdom, where she will receive a reward for her virtues. You will continue seeking your riches, only to see them disappear as soon as you touch them."

At this pronouncement, the ogre filled with such rage that he unfurled his tongue and set his wild eyes on his wife. But then he saw that what had oozed from his hands had turned again to gold when it hit the floor, and he reached again for it, only to see it change again. Forgetting the prophesied torment with each glint of the riches, he repeated this action over and over. And he would do so forever after, his hunger for riches never sated, the cure ever just out of reach.

The queen of Lydie was surprised to see the chariot's arrival and then appalled to learn of the princess's tortures. She kissed her daughter a thousand times and then fervently thanked the fairy for delivering Patientine from Insacio's yoke. She overwhelmed Espritée with caresses and assured the prince of her eternal esteem. Clementine, after showering the princess with gifts to keep her forever safe and blissful, returned to her palace.

Courageux stayed on in the kingdom, controlling his passion for the virtuous Patientine and adoring her only in secret. The princess shared the fairy's gifts with Espritée, and from that day forward she knew no greater happiness than to be loved by Clementine and by her dear princess.

WOMEN OF THE FAIRY TALE RESISTANCE

QUEEN OF FLOWERS

IN THE ISLAND kingdom of Flowers, there was a queen who had lost her husband while still quite young. He had loved her dearly and she him, and their reciprocal tenderness had resulted in two daughters of the kindest dispositions, the princesses Marie-Anne and Thérèse-Aimée. The queen raised them herself, so she had the pleasure of seeing their charms increase every day. One of those charms was transcendent beauty, which caused their mother concern, because she knew that the high queen of the dominion would be jealous.

This high queen, believing herself to be the most beautiful woman in the world, demanded that all kingdoms send their princesses of the blood as soon as they reached the age of fifteen so they could pay respect to her beauty. The queen of Flowers knew of this obligation and took it upon herself to bring her eldest daughter, Marie-Anne, to the throne when she reached that age. The beauty of the princess had already caused a stir throughout the lands, so the high queen awaited her arrival with an anxiety that presaged the envy she was seized with afterward. She was dazzled by the princess, as was every person of the court, which caused such great displeasure to the high queen that she lost all composure and withdrew to her chambers, ordering that the princess and her mother return to their kingdom.

The queen of Flowers had once spent time at this court and had made friends with the high queen's lady-of-honor, so she went to her for advice before departing. The lady-of-honor, knowing well the ways of the queen she served, warned her friend to leave in haste and advised her to keep the princess inside her palace for a period of six months, not letting her out for any cause or occasion. Being well aware of the extent of the power that the fairies had long ago given the high queen, the princess's mother took her friend's counsel seriously. When they returned to the kingdom of Flowers, she told her daughter that she was threatened with great danger if she left the palace. To alleviate Marie-Anne's boredom, her mother entertained her as best she could, and so did her sister, Thérèse-Aimée.

On the last day before the time of confinement was to expire, a feast of celebration was planned in the meadow on the palace's grounds. The princess watched the preparations from the window of her room, hardly containing her anticipation. She begged her sister and her mother to let her go out. Thinking the danger must have passed by then, the queen agreed, though she insisted on going with her and having the whole court follow. How delighted they all were to see the princess after her detention, the cause of which the queen had never explained.

Princess Marie-Anne, joyful at walking along a path full of flowers after having been deprived of them for so long, leaped gaily ahead of her mother and sister, only to have the earth open up beneath her feet and swallow her. The court cried out in misery at the cruel spectacle, and the queen of Flowers fell unconscious from the shock. The royal council had the meadow pierced to the depths, but there were no signs of the princess, no vestiges of her passage.

Where Marie-Anne found herself was on a boulder-strewn landscape that bore not the slightest trace of human existence. She sat in shock for some time, and then out of nowhere there appeared a little dog. He seemed as astonished as she at her fate. She picked him up and held him for a long while, taking comfort in his warmth and affection. When she finally put him down, he began walking away, though he stopped and turned his head every few moments, as if inviting her to follow him.

So she let herself be led, and before long they were in a grove filled with trees whose branches were heavy with an abundant variety of fruits she had never seen before. Amid the trees was a fountain with soft grass all around it. She sat at its edge and drank. The water was clear and sparkling. And though she had been quietly weeping since her arrival, she now took heart in the luck of having at least a remedy for hunger and thirst.

She spent the day in this verdant spot, distracted by the fascinating shapes and colors of the fruits, by their unusually delicious flavors. But when night began to fall she started worrying about the beasts that might lurk in such a strange place, and her anguish returned. As if sensing this, the little dog, which had not left her side, tugged at her dress. She again let herself be led, this time to the base of a boulder, where she saw a large opening into a cave that was so bright it seemed lit by the sun. But it was the stone it was made from that created the brilliance. In a corner was a small bed covered with moss, and as soon as she rested her head there, sleep came over her.

WOMEN OF THE FAIRY TALE RESISTANCE

 The next day, she was awakened by the song of birds in the trees surrounding the cave. In any other situation she would have been enchanted by this, because never before had she heard birdsong this melodious. But she was immediately reminded of her plight, which distressed her so that she did not want to rise from her mossy bed. The little dog, who had slept at her feet all night, stretched now and began his coaxing again until she followed him outside the cave. She breathed in the dawn air, so sweet, and they returned to the grove, where again she ate the fruits and drank the clear water.

 This is how she spent several months. Seeing no enemy about, her fear gradually eased and her solitude became more bearable. It was the little dog's companionship that she credited with her survival, his wagging tail and happy demeanor always redirecting her at the worst moments. He slept at her feet every night, which was her greatest comfort. But then a day came when he did not wag his tail, did not cheerfully follow her about. Fearing he was ill, she took him to a place where she had seen him eat an herb she hoped would heal him, but nothing helped. His despondency lasted all the day, and though he curled at her feet as usual when she retired, he whimpered throughout the night.

When the princess awoke the next morning, the little dog was not in the cave with her. She rushed out to look for him, but he was nowhere. In the distance, she saw what looked like an old man, but then he seemed to vanish. Sure that he had taken her little dog, she fell into despair. She wandered around the grove, lost in dark thoughts and forgetting to eat or drink, her eyes cast downward in the hope she would see her faithful companion. Hours and hours passed, until she realized she was again on that boulder-strewn plain where she had arrived. As night came on, so did a mist that grew thicker and thicker, pressing into her sides and lifting her. She made no resistance, not caring where she was bound. And then, suddenly, she was standing in front of the palace in the kingdom of Flowers.

It was a somber spectacle that greeted her as she entered, all the court dressed in mourning. But then a shout of surprise could be heard, and there was her sister racing toward her, then embracing her. They cried on each other's shoulders. Thérèse-Aimée lifted from her own head the crown their mother had worn and put it in the hands of her older sister, explaining that their mother had succumbed to the shock just days after the disappearance. Marie-Anne, feeling at fault and overwhelmed by the loss, begged her sister to keep the crown. But Thérèse-Aimée refused, for it had been, in the short time she'd had it, a burden of sorrow, a symbol of losing the two people she loved most in the world. She now wanted only to celebrate the return of her sister, the rightful queen. Marie-Anne agreed to take the crown so long as her sister took the seat at her side on the royal council. And then the new queen of Flowers set to work with all the grace and dedication of her mother.

She was so busy at first that she had little time to dwell on her recent experience, but when matters settled, she found that her mind was always on that little dog who had rescued her from the loneliness of exile. She worried that he was wandering lost and sad, as he had been that last day he was with her, and so she formed a search party of her best hunters, telling them to look for him across the lands and return him safely to her. When they did not find even the least clue of his existence, she became even more distraught, and then she offered half of the kingdom as a reward to anyone in her court who could deliver the little dog to her hands. Princess Thérèse-Aimée was surprised by her sister's obsession, but out of sympathy for what she had been through, she held back her objections.

All the lords of the court wanted the extravagant reward, so they went their separate ways in pursuit of the prize. But eventually each one returned, dispirited and with no good news. Absolutely desperate now, the queen called an assembly of her council and announced that she would be issuing an edict to the public that she would marry any person who brought to her the little dog. This alarmed Thérèse-Aimée to such an extent that she felt she had to speak up. She asked for privacy with her sister, and after the council retreated to the outside chamber, she told the queen how disturbed she was by the declaration. It was one thing, the princess said, to give away the kingdom's lands but entirely another to sacrifice herself. What if, she argued, the person who succeeded in the quest was a hideous man? She would be bound to the ruffian long after the life of any dog. But Marie-Anne's heart was set, and so they argued as they never had before in their lives.

They were still engaged in this fraught conversation when the council, en masse, burst back into the room in alarm. An army was approaching the port of Flowers in full sail, they told the queen and princess, who quickly took to a balcony to witness the scene. The sea was indeed covered with ships, the fleet adorned with flags and streamers in all shades of green. But there was one small ship in the lead, which, to the relief of all, bore white ensigns, a sign of peace. They were soon informed that the prince of Emeraudes was asking for permission to land and for an audience with the queen, so she sent her principal officers to assure him he was welcome. The two sisters walked together to the throne room, though the tension was still palpable between them, since they had not come to any resolution before the interruption.

The prince's gallant manners had a calming effect, however, immediately easing their discomforts. He told them this story:

> My kingdom lies on a peninsula that is very close to where the high queen of the dominion resides, there being just a small passage between. One day while hunting, I followed a stag into one of her forests, where I encountered her. Never having laid eyes on the high queen before, I did not recognize her, and thus I did not stop to give her the courtesy she

expected. And because she is vindictive, she told me I would be punished for exactly three months for the infraction. Then the earth opened beneath my feet and I dropped through. When I landed, I was not as you see me now. She had turned me into a little dog.

Marie-Anne was staring at him now, and Thérèse-Aimée at her. He continued:

You, dear queen, arrived the next day, and the months that followed were the happiest of my life. I kept track of time, and on my last day with you, I was saddened because I would be leaving and had no way to know who you were and how to find you. When the high queen realized I'd been in your company, she became so incensed with jealousy that instead of changing me back to myself, she turned me into an old man and pushed me deeper into the earth. I was there until a few days ago, when I stumbled upon a fairy who took pity on me. I described to her the evil deeds we had been subject to, and she assured me that the fairy realm did not approve of such abuse of their arts and would rescind the high queen's powers so our kingdoms would no longer be subject to her dishonorable whims. Then the fairy told me who you were and returned me to Emeraudes. And now I am here.

Tears of joy had begun to stream from his eyes, and he threw himself at the queen's feet. The sisters looked at each other warmly and clasped hands.

It wasn't long before the queen and the prince agreed to bind themselves in an eternal knot, and this resolution, having been made public, was received with universal applause. And not without reason, for never have subjects lived under such a free and easy rule, which they enjoyed for almost a century, the queen, the prince, and the princess living in perfect felicity until extreme old age.

FIN

ACKNOWLEDGMENTS

I WISH I could conjure fairy gifts for everyone who supported me in the writing of this book, but unless/until I come into some magic, I'll have to stick with thank-yous. The first go to W&L University librarians Elizabeth Teaff, Emily Cook, and Laura Hewett, who gathered dozens and dozens of texts from far and wide, without which I could not have faithfully brought these women's lives to the page around history's erasures. I'm also grateful to my colleagues in the W&L English department, especially Lesley Wheeler and Holly Pickett, whose flexibility allowed me to carve out time for this project. *Huge* thank-yous go to my literary agent, Mark Gottlieb (who I suspect may be a wizard), and my editor, Lisa Tenaglia, who was as instantly captivated by the conteuses as I was when I first glimpsed them in the shadows of the fairy tale canon. Thanks, too, to Khoa Le, for reviving long-forgotten characters with her gorgeous art, and to Katie Benezra, Melanie Gold, Kate Karol, and Lillian Sun at Black Dog and Leventhal, who, like the enchanted hands of the white cat's castle, worked their spells in seeming secret to make this beautiful book possible.

And then there are those who make *everything* possible. Top of list is my gentle-hearted husband, Jonathan Shapiro, constant as the stars. Then our three daughters, ever an inspiration to me, their young lives the models for my first stories and their adult lives examples of how to be our truest selves: Meghan, legal defender of the powerless and guardian of our family's next generation; Emma, warrior against censorship and creator of safe spaces for marginalized artists; Lou, exquisite crafter of yarns and words, her translation skills coming to the rescue more than once as I wrote this book. And Fiona, cherished canine curled at my feet through a myriad of writing projects, this one her last. (She was a black dog. Of *course*.) Finally, a clarion blast of thank-yous to my siblings, cousins, nieces, nephews, and friends who have been so encouraging over the years. You buy my books, write generous reviews, host book club meetings, get copies onto shelves of stores and libraries. You've been mentors, confidantes, champions. But more than that, you've been keepers of the light, helping me navigate life's trials when mere escapes into fictional worlds aren't enough. You know who you are, and I love you.

BIBLIOGRAPHY

Beasley, Faith E. *Salons, History, and the Creation of Seventeenth-Century France.* Burlington, VT: Ashgate, 2006.

Bernard, Catherine. *Inès de Cordoue: Nouvelle Espagnole.* Geneva: Slatkine Reprints, 1979.

Bernard, Catherine. *Oeuvres. Vol. 1, Romans et nouvelles,* edited by Franco Piva. Paris: Schena, 1993.

Boileau Despréaux, Nicolas. *Les satires.* Paris: Académie des Bibliophiles, 1868.

Bottigheimer, Ruth B., ed. *Fairy Tales Framed: Early Forewords, Afterwords, and Critical Words.* Albany, NY: SUNY Press, 2012.

Boulay de la Meurthe, Alfred. "Les prisonniers du roi à loches sous Louis XIV." In *Mélanges.* Vol. 49 of *Bulletin et mémoires de la Société Archéologique de Touraine.* Tours: Péricat, 1910.

Brocklebank, Lisa. "Rebellious Voices: The Unofficial Discourse of Cross-dressing in d'Aulnoy, de Murat, and Perrault." *Children's Literature Association Quarterly* 25, no. 3 (2000): 127–136.

Canepa, Nancy L., ed. *Out of the Woods: The Origins of the Literary Fairy Tale in Italy and France.* Detroit, MI: Wayne State University Press, 1998.

Charton, Édouard, ed. "Madame d'Aulnoy." *Le magasin pittoresque,* January 1870, 66–68.

Clermidy-Patard, Geneviève. *Madame de Murat et la "Défense des dames": Un discours au féminin à la fin du règne de Louis XIV.* Paris: Classiques Garnier, 2012.

Conroy, Derval. "Catherine Bernard." SIEFAR (website). http://siefar.org/dictionnaire/fr/Catherine_Bernard.

d'Argenson, René. *Rapports inédits du lieutenant de police René D'Argenson (1697–1715).* Introduction by Paul Cottin. Edited by Paul Cottin. Paris: E. Plon, Nourrit, 1891.

d'Aulnoy, Marie-Catherine, et al. *A Collection of Novels and Tales of the Fairies.* Dublin: J. Potts, 1770.

BIBLIOGRAPHY

d'Aulnoy, Marie-Catherine. *Le comte de Warwick*. Vol. 2. Paris: La Compagnie des Libraires Affociez, 1703.

d'Aulnoy, Marie-Catherine. *Contes nouveaux, ou Les fées à la mode*. 2 vols. Paris: Girard, 1698.

d'Aulnoy, Marie-Catherine. *Fairy Tales*. Translated by J. R. Planché. London: Routledge, 1855.

d'Aulnoy, Marie-Catherine. *The Ingenious and Diverting Letters of the Lady *** Travels into Spain*. 2nd ed. New York: G. P. Putnam's Sons, 1899. Project Gutenberg. https://www.gutenberg.org/cache/epub/52667/pg52667-images.html.

d'Aulnoy, Marie-Catherine. *The Island of Happiness: Tales of Madame d'Aulnoy*. Translated by Jack Zipes. Princeton, NJ: Princeton University Press, 2021.

d'Aulnoy, Marie-Catherine. *Memoirs of the Court of England in 1675*. Edited by George David Gilbert. Translated by Mrs. William Henry Arthur. London: Routledge, 1927.

d'Aulnoy, Marie-Catherine. *Memoirs of the Court of France, and City of Paris*. London: Tonson and Strahan, 1702. Eighteenth Century Collections Online, University of Michigan Library. http://quod.lib.umich.edu/cgi/t/text/text-idx?c=ecco;idno=004877886.0001.000.

d'Aulnoy, Marie-Catherine. "La Princesse Patiente dans la Forêt d'Erimente." In *Le cabinet des fées, ou Collection choisie des contes des fées, et autres contes merveilleux*, 416–438. Tome Sixième, edited by Charles-Joseph Mayer, et al. Geneva: Barde, Manget, 1785.

d'Auneuil, Louise de Bossigny. *Les chevaliers errans, et le genie familier*. Paris: Ribou, 1709.

d'Auneuil, Louise de Bossigny. "Le galante nouvelliste." In *Mélanges: Serieux, comiques et d'erudition*, 3–58. Paris: Ribou, 1704.

d'Auneuil, Louise de Bossigny. *L'origine du lansquenet, nouvelles du tems*. Paris: Ribou, 1703.

d'Auneuil, Louise de Bossigny. *La tiranie des fées détruite: Nouveaux contes*. Paris: Chevillon, 1702.

Defrance, Anne. "1700–1703: L'éclipse du conte de fées." In *L'Année 1700: Actes du colloque international du Centre de recherches sur le XVIIe siècle européen (1600–1700)*, Université Michel de Montaigne-Bordeaux III, 30–31 janvier 2003, edited by Aurélia Gaillard, 204–221. Biblio 17. Tübingen, Germany: Gunter Narr, 2004.

BIBLIOGRAPHY

DeJean, Joan. Introduction to *The Story of the Marquise-Marquis de Banneville*, by François-Timoléon de Choisy, Marie-Jeanne L'Héritier, and Charles Perrault, vii–xxvii. New York: Modern Language Association of America, 2004.

DeJean, Joan. *Tender Geographies: Women and the Origins of the Novel in France*. New York: Columbia University Press, 1991.

Depping, Georges-Bernard. *Correspondance administrative sous le règne de Louis XIV entre le cabinet du roi, les secrétaires d'état, le chancelier de France [. . .]*. 4 vols. Paris: Imprimerie Nationale, 1850–1855.

Duggan, Anne E. *The Lost Princess: Women Writers and the History of Classic Fairy Tales*. London: Reaktion, 2023.

Duggan, Anne E. *Salonnières, Furies, and Fairies: The Politics of Gender and Cultural Change in Absolutist France*. Newark: University of Delaware Press, 2005.

Duramy, Benedetta Faedi. "Women and Poisons in 17th Century France." *Chicago-Kent Law Review* 87, no. 2 (2012): 347–370.

Durand, Catherine. *Oeuvres meslées de Madame Durand*. Paris: Prault, 1737.

Ekstein, Nina. "Appropriation and Gender: The Case of Catherine Bernard and Bernard de Fontenelle." *Eighteenth-Century Studies* 30, no. 1 (1996): 59–80. http://www.jstor.org/stable/30053854.

"Eloge de Mademoiselle L'Héritier." In *Le journal des sçavans pour l'année MDCCXXXIV*, December 1734, 832–836. Paris: Chaubert, 1734.

Engerand, Roland. *Les rendez-vous de loches*. Tours: Arrault, 1946.

Feat, Anne-Marie. "Playing the Game of Frivolity: Seventeenth-Century 'Conteuses' and the Transformation of Female Identity." *Journal of the Midwest Modern Language Association* 45, no. 2 (2012): 217–242. http://www.jstor.org/stable/43150852.

Forsyth, Kate. *Bitter Greens*. New York: Thomas Dunne, 2012.

Gethner, Perry. "Catherine Durand: Proverbes dramatiques." In *Writings by Pre-Revolutionary French Women*, edited by Anne R. Larson and Colette H. Winn, 377–402. 2000; New York: Routledge, 2017.

Gethner, Perry. *Femmes dramaturges en France (1650–1750)*. 2 vols. Biblio 17. Paris: Papers on French Seventeenth Century Literature, 1993.

Gethner, Perry. "Murat, Durand and the Novel About Leisure." In *Creation, Re-creation, and Entertainment: Early Modernity and Postmodernity*, edited by Charlotte

BIBLIOGRAPHY

Trinquet du Lys and Benjamin Balak, 25–36. Biblio 17 219. Tübingen, Germany: Narr Francke Attempo Verlag, 2019.

Gethner, Perry. "Playful Wit in Salon Games: The Comedy Proverbs of Catherine Durand." In *L'esprit en France au XVIIe Siècle: Actes due 28e congrès annuel de la North American Society for Seventeenth Century French Literature, the University of Texas at Austin, 11–13 avril 1996*, edited by François Lagarde, 225–230. Biblio 17 101. Paris: Papers on Seventeenth Century French Literature, 1997.

Gibson, Wendy. *Women in Seventeenth-Century France*. New York: St. Martin's Press, 1989.

Goldsmith, Elizabeth C., and Dena Goodman, eds. *Going Public: Women and Publishing in Early Modern France*. Ithaca, NY: Cornell University Press, 1995.

Hannon, Patricia. *Fabulous Identities: Women's Fairy Tales in Seventeenth-Century France*. Amsterdam: Rodopi, 1998.

Harries, Elizabeth Wanning. "Simulating Oralities: French Fairy Tales of the 1690s." *College Literature* 23, no. 2 (June 1996): 100–115. EBSCO.

Harries, Elizabeth Wanning. *Twice Upon a Time: Women Writers and the History of the Fairy Tale*. Princeton, NJ: Princeton University Press, 2001.

Hessels, Femke. "La vie et l'oeuvre de Charlotte-Rose de Caumont de La Force." Master's thesis. Radboud Universiteit, 2016.

Hofmann, Melissa A. "The Fairy as Hero(ine) and Author: Representations of Female Power in Murat's 'Le Turbot.'" *Marvels and Tales* 28, no. 2 (2014): 252–277. http://muse.jhu.edu/article/555483.

Jones, Christine A., and Jennifer Schacker, eds. *Marvelous Transformations: An Anthology of Fairy Tales and Contemporary Perspectives*. Peterborough, Ontario: Broadview, 2013.

Kennedy, Theresa. "Gender Performance in Seventeenth-Century Dramatic Dialogue: From the Salon to the Classroom." *Early Modern France* 15, no. 1 (2013): 1–18. https://earlymodernfrance.org/journal/2013-volume-xv-1/gender-performance-seventeenth-century-dramatic-dialogue-salon-classroom.

Kulesza, Monika. "Au carrefour des formes, au carrefour des sens: Comédies en proverbes de Catherine Durand." *Orbis Linguarum* 50 (2018): 285–293. DOI: 10.23817/olin.50-22.

La Force, Mademoiselle. "Persinette, Conte." In *Le cabinet des fées, ou Collection choisies des contes des fées, et autres contes merveilleux*, 6:43–57. Geneva: Barde, Manget, 1787.

BIBLIOGRAPHY

La Porte, Joseph de. *Histoire littéraire des femmes françoises, ou Lettres historiques et critiques.* Vols. 2 and 3. Paris: Lacombe, 1769.

Lescure, Mme de. "Mme d'Aulnoy et les contes de fées au XVII siécle." In *Les contes des fées, ou Les fées a la mode*, by Mme d'Aulnoy, 1:i–xxiii. 2 vols. Paris: Librairie des Bibliophiles, 1881.

L'Héritier, Marie-Jeanne. *Bigarures ingenieuses,: ou, Recüeil de diverses pieces galantes en prose et en vers.* Paris: Guignard, 1696.

L'Héritier, Marie-Jeanne. "The Discreet Princess, or The Adventures of Finetta." In *The Histories of Passed Times, or The Tales of Mother Goose, with Morals*, edited by M. Perrault, 2:61–169. London: Franco, 1785.

L'Héritier, Marie-Jeanne. *Oeuvres Meslées.* Paris: Guignard, 1696.

Majer, Michele. "1700–1709." Fashion History Timeline (website), Fashion Institute of Technology, October 10, 2020. https://fashionhistory.fitnyc.edu/1700-1709/.

Mayer, Charles-Joseph, et al., eds. "Avertissement de l'éditeur." In *Le cabinet des fées, ou Collection choisie des contes des fées, et autres contes merveilleux*, 33: v–xi. Amsterdam: Serpente, 1786.

Mayer, Charles-Joseph, et al., eds. "Notice des auteurs, qui ont écrit dans le genre des contes de fées." In *Le cabinet des fées, ou Collection choisie des contes des fées, et autres contes merveilleux*, 37:48–412. Geneva: Barde, 1786.

Mercure de France. Obituary of Marie-Jeanne L'Héritier. March 1734, 539–541.

Mercure galant. Notice of publication of *La tyrannie des fées détruite.* February 1703, 386–389.

Mercure galant. Obituary of Louis-Claude Barjot, Marquis d'Auneüil. January 1700, 242–246.

Mercure galant. Obituary of Marie-Catherine d'Aulnoy. January 1705, 244–249.

Munier-Jolain, Julien. "Charlotte-Rose de Caumont." In *Procès de femmes: Charlotte de Caumont; Marie-Anne de Chateauneuf-Duclos; Hortense Mancini, duchesse de Mazarin; Émile de Mascranny, marquise de Gesvres; Madame Kornmann*, 3–53. Paris: Lévy, 1898.

Murat, Henriette-Julie de Castelnau. *Contes.* Edited by Genevieve Clermidy-Patard. Paris: Honore Champion, 2006.

Murat, Henriette-Julie de Castelnau. *Histoires sublimes et allégoriques.* Paris: Florentin and Delauine, 1699.

Murat, Henriette-Julie de Castelnau. *Journal pour Mademoiselle de Menou.* Edited by Genevieve Clermidy-Patard. Paris: Classiques Garnier, 2014.

Murat, Henriette-Julie de Castelnau. *Memoirs of the Countess D'Anois: Written by Herself Before Her Retirement.* 2 vols. London: Noble, 1778.

Murat, Henriette-Julie de Castelnau. *Les nouveaux contes des fées.* Paris: Barbin, 1698.

Murat, Henriette-Julie de Castelnau. *A Trip to the Country.* Edited and translated by Perry Gethner and Allison Stedman. Detroit: Wayne State University Press, 2011.

Nouveau mercure galant. Obituary of Henriette-Julie de Castelnau Murat. October 1716, 228–236.

Peterson, Nora Martin, ed. *Miracles of Love: French Fairy Tales by Women.* Translated by Jordan Stump. New York: Modern Language Association of America, 2021.

Pilon, Edmond. *Muses et bourgeoises de jadis.* Paris: Société du Mercure de France, 1908.

Planché, J. R., transl. *Four and Twenty Fairy Tales.* London: Routledge, 1858.

Plusquellec, Catherine. "Qui était Catherine Bernard?" *Revue d'histoire littéraire de la France* 85, no. 4 (1985): 667–669. http://www.jstor.org/stable/40528200.

Quérard, J. M. "Aulnoy." In *La France littéraire, ou Dictionnaire bibliographique,* 1:132–133, 251. Paris: Firmin Didot, 1827.

Quérard, J. M. "Héere (Mme de), femme auteur du XVIII siécle." In *La France littéraire, ou Dictionnaire bibliographique,* 4:53. Paris: Firmin Didot, 1830.

Quérard, J. M. "Caumont de la Force." In *La France littéraire, ou Dictionnaire bibliographique,* 2:87. Paris: Firmin Didot, 1828.

Raynard, Sophie. "Ancients vs. Moderns: The Women's Riposte." *Marvels and Tales* 33, no. 1 (2019): 116–139. https://doi.org/10.13110/marvelstales.33.1.0116.

Raynard, Sophie. *La seconde préciosité: Floraison des conteuses de 1690 à 1756.* Tübingen, Germany: Gunter Narr Verlag, 2002.

Raynard, Sophie. "Sexuality and the Women Fairy Tale Writers of the 1690s." In *Marvelous Transformations,* edited by Christine A. Jones and Jennifer Schacker, 551–554. Peterborough, Ontario: Broadview, 2013.

Raynard, Sophie, ed. *The Teller's Tale: Lives of the Classic Fairy Tale Writers.* Albany, NY: SUNY Press, 2012.

BIBLIOGRAPHY

Raynard-Leroy, Sophie, and Charlotte Trinquet du Lys. "Gender Fluidity: From Euphemism to Pride; an Editorial with Comprehensive Bibliography on Gender Fluidity in Children's Literature and Fairy Tales." *Open Cultural Studies* 5, no. 1 (2021): 295–311. https://doi.org/10.1515/culture-2020-0140.

Reddan, Bronwyn. *Love, Power, and Gender in Seventeenth-Century French Fairy Tales*. Lincoln: University of Nebraska Press, 2020.

Reddan, Bronwyn. "Scripting Love in Fairy Tales by Seventeenth Century French Women Writers." *French History and Civilization* 7 (2017): 93–107. https://h-france.net/rude/wp-content/uploads/2017/08/vol7_Reddan.pdf.

Reid, Martine, ed. *Femmes et littérature: Une histoire culturelle*. Vol. I, *Moyen Âge-XVIIIe siècle*. Paris: Gallimard, 2020.

"La Reine de l'Isle des Fleurs." In *Les illustres fées: Contes galans*, 168–197. Paris: Brunet, 1698.

Ritchie, Anne Thackeray, ed. Introduction to *The Fairy Tales of Madame D'Aulnoy*. Honolulu: University Press of the Pacific, 2003.

Robert, Raymonde, ed. *Contes: Mademoiselle LHéritier, Mademoiselle Bernard, Mademoiselle de la Force, Madame Durand, Madame d'Auneuil*. Paris: Honoré Champion, 2005.

Robinson, David Michael. "The Abominable Madame de Murat." *Journal of Homosexuality* 41, no. 3/4 (April 2001): 53–67. EBSCO.

Roche-Mazon, Jeanne. *En marge de "l'Oiseau Bleu."* Paris: L'Artisan du Livre, 1930.

Sanders, Scott M. "Singing Through the Pain: Murat Riffing on Montaigne." *Eighteenth-Century Fiction* 35 no. 4 (2023): 445–462. http://muse.jhu.edu/article/909733.

Schröder, Volker. "The Birth and Beginnings of Madame d'Aulnoy." *Anecdota* (blog), March 29, 2019. https://anecdota.princeton.edu/archives/995.

Schröder, Volker. "Madame d'Aulnoy and Monsieur le Premier." *Anecdota* (blog), November 7, 2021. https://anecdota.princeton.edu/archives/1654.

Schröder, Volker. "Madame d'Aulnoy's Productive Confinement." *Anecdota* (blog), May 2, 2020. https://anecdota.princeton.edu/archives/1182.

Schröder, Volker. "Marie-Madeleine Perrault (1674-1701)." *Anecdota* (blog), December 31, 2017. https://anecdota.princeton.edu/archives/500.

Schröder, Volker. "On Madame d'Aulnoy." *Anecdota* (blog), last updated April 2022. https://anecdota.princeton.edu/on-madame-daulnoy.

BIBLIOGRAPHY

Seifert, Lewis C. *Fairy Tales, Sexuality, and Gender in France, 1690–1715*. Cambridge, UK: Cambridge University Press, 1996.

Seifert, Lewis C., and Domna C. Stanton, eds. and trans. *Enchanted Eloquence: Fairy Tales by Seventeenth-Century French Women Writers*. New York: Iter, 2010.

Shapiro, Norman. "Catherine Bernard." In *French Women Poets of Nine Centuries: The Distaff and the Pen*, 384–385. Baltimore: Johns Hopkins University Press, 2008.

Sikelianos, Eleni. "Some Greek Girls: On Teaching Sappho and Praxilla." *Teachers and Writers Magazine*, January–February 1999. https://teachersandwritersmagazine.org/some-greek-girls-on-teaching-sappho-and-praxilla/.

Souloumiac, Michel. *Mademoiselle de La Force: Un auteur méconna du XVIIe siécle*. R.A.H., 2004.

Stableford, Brian. "A History of Faerie." In *Tales of Enchantment and Disenchantment*, 7–117. Tarzana, CA: Black Coat, 2019.

Stableford, Brian. Introduction to *The Origin of the Fays*. Tarzana, CA: Black Coat, 2019. Ebook.

Stableford, Brian. Introduction to *The Robe of Sincerity*. Tarzana, CA: Black Coat, 2019. Ebook.

Stableford, Brian. Introduction to *The Tyranny of the Fays Abolished and Other Stories*. Tarzana, CA: Black Coat, 2018. Ebook.

Storer, Mary Elizabeth. *La mode des contes de fées (1685–1700)*. Paris: Librairie Ancienne Honoré Champion, 1928.

Taylor, Helena. "Ancients, Moderns, Gender: Marie-Jeanne L'Héritier's 'Le Parnasse reconnoissant, ou, Le triomphe de Madame Des-Houlières.'" *French Studies* 71, no. 1 (January 2017): 15–30. https://doi.org/10.1093/fs/knw261.

Troll, Jo. "Catherine Bernard: A Question in Studying Asexual History." *Making Queer History* (website), November 27, 2017. https://www.makingqueerhistory.com/articles/2017/11/27/catherine-bernard-a-question-in-studying-asexual-history.

Tucker, Holly. *Pregnant Fictions: Childbirth and the Fairy Tale in Early-Modern France*. Detroit: Wayne State University Press, 2003.

BIBLIOGRAPHY

Unknown. Preface to *The Court of Queen Mab: Containing a Select Collection of Only the Best, Most Instructive, and Entertaining Tales of the Fairies*, by Marie-Catherine d'Aulnoy, iii–iv. London: Cooper, 1752.

Vertron, Claude-Charles Guyonnet. *La nouvelle Pandore, ou Les femmes illustres du siècle de Louis le Grand*. Paris: Mazuel, 1698.

Vertron, Claude-Charles Guyonnet. *Second partie de la Pandore, ou La suite des femmes illustres du siècle de Louis le Grand*. Paris: Mazuel, 1698.

Voltaire, Mr. de. "Ecrivains, dont plusieurs ont illustre le siécle." In *Le siécle de Louis XIV*, 3:237–325. Frankfurt: Veuve Knoch and J. G. Eslinger, 1753.

Wahl, Elizabeth Susan. "Regulating the 'Real' in Fictional Terms: The (Auto) Biography of the Tribade in Erotic and Documentary Texts." Chapter 6 of *Invisible Relations: Representations of Female Intimacy in the Age of Enlightenment*, Stanford, CA: Stanford University Press, 1999.

Warner, Marina. Introduction to *Wonder Tales*, 3–17. New York: Farrar, Straus and Giroux, 1994.

Wikipédia. "Catherine Bernard." https://fr.wikipedia.org/wiki/Catherine_Bernard.

Wikipédia. "Catherine Durand." https://fr.wikipedia.org/wiki/Catherine_Durand.

Wikipédia. "Charlotte-Rose de Caumont La Force." https://fr.wikipedia.org/wiki/Charlotte-Rose_de_Caumont_La_Force.

Wikipédia. "Henriette-Julie de Castelnau de Murat." https://fr.wikipedia.org/wiki/Henriette-Julie_de_Castelnau_de_Murat.

Wikipédia. "Marie-Anne de Bourbon." https://fr.wikipedia.org/wiki/Marie-Anne_de_Bourbon_(1666-1739).

Wikipédia. "Marie-Catherine d'Aulnoy." https://fr.wikipedia.org/wiki/Marie-Catherine_d%27Aulnoy.

Wikipédia. "Marie-Jeanne L'Héritier de Villandon." https://fr.wikipedia.org/wiki/Marie-Jeanne_L%27H%C3%A9ritier_de_Villandon.

Windling, Terri. "Once Upon a Time in Paris . . ." *Myth and Moor* (blog), March 8, 2020. https://www.terriwindling.com/blog/2020/03/once-upon-a-time.html.

Zipes, Jack. Introduction to *Beauties, Beasts and Enchantment: Classic French Fairy Tales*, 1–12. New York: New American Library, 1989.

Zipes, Jack, ed. and transl. *The Original Folk and Fairy Tales of the Brothers Grimm*. Princeton, NJ: Princeton University Press, 2014.

INDEX

A

abuse, of wives, ix, 5
Académie Française, 156
Accademia dei Ricovrati, 6, 156–157
Aesop's fables, xii–xiii
Affair of the Poisons, 88
affairs, ix
anagrams, 190
"Anguillette" (Murat), 67, 69–82, 158
annulments, 90–91
Apollo, 125
aristocracy, 60
aromantic, 159
arranged marriages, ix, 2, 59
Arthurian romances, 59
asexuality, 159

B

Barjot, Louis-Claude, 187–188
Baron, Michel, 87
Basile, Giambattista, xi
Bastille prison, 3
"Beauty and the Beast," 7
"The Bee and the Orange Tree"
 (d'Aulnoy), 158
"Belle-Belle" (d'Aulnoy), 7–8, 32–56, 129
Beringhen, Henri de, 1
Beringhen, Jacques-Louis de, 1, 4
Bernard, Catherine, x, 155–167, 170
 awards won by, 156–157
 d'Auneuil and, 192
 family background of, 155
 financial situation of, 159
 "Florinde," 158, 160–167, 171
 novels by, 156–158
 pension of, 159, 173, 192
 as playwright, 155–156
 poetry of, 156, 159, 172
 religious conversion by, 155
 "Ricquet with the Tuft," 158, 171
 romantic relationships of, 158–159
 sexual orientation of, 159
Bibliothèque Nationale, 191
"Blanche" (L'Héritier), 128–129, 140–152
Boileau, Nicolas, 124, 125
Bossigny, Louise de. See d'Auneuil, Louise
bouts-rimés, 127
Bretagne, Anna de, 67
"Brillante" (Durand), 172, 174–180
Briou, Charles de, 88–91
Briou, Claude de, 89–90
Brothers Grimm, x–xiv, 93, 188
Brutus (Bernard), 156, 157
Brutus (Voltaire), 157

C

cabarets, 87
"The Camel Who Shat in the River"
 (Aesop), xii
Castelnau, Henriette-Julie de. See
 Murat, Henriette-Julie
Catholicism, 86
"The Cat in Love" (Durand), 172
Caumont family, 85
censorship, x, 6, 61

INDEX

Chambre Ardent, 88
Château de Cazeneuve, 86
Château de La Force, 86
Château de Loches, 64–66
Chez Prault, 169
children
   of d'Aulnoy, 3
   fairy tales for, xiv–xv
"Christian Thoughts" (La Force), 92
Comédie-Française, 155–156
comedies in proverbs, 170–171, 172
condoms, xii
conteuses, x–xv, 62
   critics of, xii, xiii, 124–125
Conti, Princess of, 60, 62, 87, 127, 192
convents, 5, 86, 91–92
cour des aides, 89
cross-dressing heroines, 7–8, 59, 65

D

Dame Saint-Balmon, 129
d'Argenson, René, 63–64
d'Aulnoy, Baron, 2–6
d'Aulnoy, Marie-Catherine, x, 1–56, 91
   acclaim of, 6
   arrest of, 4
   as author of d'Auneuil's works, 189–190
   "The Bee and the Orange Tree," 158
   "Belle-Belle," 7–8, 32–56, 129
   children of, 3
   death of, 66, 124
   exile of, 5, 6
   family background of, 1–2
   "Féline," 9–31
   imprisonment of, 4, 5
   "The Island of Happiness," 158
   Judith-Angélique, 2, 3, 4
   kidnapping of, 2
   legal separation of, 5
   marriage of, 2–4, 190
   publishing success of, 6–7
   salon of, 6
   "The White Cat," 7, 192
   writings of, 5, 172, 190
d'Aulnoy, Thérèse-Aimée, 191
d'Aulnoy barony, 2
d'Auneuil, Louise, x, 187–205
   background of, 187–188
   marriage of, 187–188
   "Patientine," 193–198
   publications by, 187, 188
   questions about authorship by, 188–192
d'Auneuil, Marquis, 187–188
The Defense of Women (Murat), 60–61
de Héere, Madame (Marie-Anne), 190–191
Deshoulières, Antoinette, 125
de Villiers, Pierre, 60
"Diamonds and Toads" (Perrault), 128
"The Discreet Princess, or the Adventures of Finette" (L'Héritier), 128
Disney, Walt, xiii
dragonnades, 85–86
dramas, 155–156
Dunamis, 85
"Dunamis" (La Force), 93, 94–114
dungeons, 64
Durand, Catherine, x, 157, 158, 169–184
   "Brillante," 172, 174–180
   family background of, 169
   financial situation of, 173
   Murat and, 170

INDEX

"Ogilire," 172, 181–184
"The Prodigy of Love," 171–172
proverbs of, 170–171, 172
writings of, 169–172, 187

E

education, for girls, 171
"The Enchantments of Eloquence" (L'Héritier), 128–129
Entertainments for Little Ones (Basile), xi
espionage, 4, 5
execution, of Madame Ticquet, 6

F

The Fairy Cabinet (Mayer), 188–189
"The Fairy Lubantine" (Durand), 172
fairy tales
    for children, xiv–xv
    compilations of, 188–189
    credit for writing, x–xi
    plays of, 6–7
    popularity of, x, 172
    principles for writing, 155, 158
    themes for, x
    writing of, x
The Fairy Tales (d'Aulnoy), 6
"Féline" (d'Aulnoy), 9–31
female education, 171
female empowerment, x
Female Falsehood; or, The Life and Adventures of a Late French Nobleman (de Villiers), 60
female storytellers, x–xiii
female writers
    criticism of, 125–126
    defenders of, 129
femininity, x
feminist social clubs, 126
"Finette" (L'Héritier), 131–139, 171
Floral Games prize, 62–63, 156

"Florinde" (Bernard), 158, 160–167, 171
Fontenelle, Bernard de, 157, 159
"The Fortunate Punishment" (Murat), 61
France, repression of agitation in, ix
"The French Amazon" (L'Héritier), 129–130
Fronde, 124

G

gay men, 62
"The Good Woman" (La Force), 92–93
government, oppression by, ix, x
Greek mythology, 125
Grimms' Fairy Tales, xiii
"Grisandole," 59

H

Hachette, Jeanne, 129
"The Happiness of Sparrows" (Murat), 67
Hercules, 85
high aristocracy, 60
homosexuality, 2, 61, 62, 64–65, 126, 127
House La Force, 85, 86
House of Vendôme, 87
Huguenots, 85–86, 88
husbands, ix, 61

I

The Illustrious Fairies, 191
Inez of Cordoba (Bernard), 157–158
Interviews on Fairy Tales . . . a Condom Against Bad Taste (Villiers), xii–xiii, 60, 124
"Iris" (Murat), 68
"The Island of Happiness" (d'Aulnoy), 158

INDEX

J
Joan of Arc, 129
"The Juniper Tree," xiv

K
keeper of the seal, 123, 124

L
La Force, Charlotte-Rose, x, 60, 85–120
    Charles de Briou and, 88–91
    death of, 124
    "Dunamis," 93, 94–114
    exile to convent, 91–92, 172
    family background of, 85–86
    Marquis de Nesle and, 87–88
    marriage of, 89–91
    pension of, 88, 92
    "Persinette," xii, 93, 115–120
    at royal court, 86–87
    salon scene and, 91
    writings of, 91–93
Lambert, Madame, 60
la Motte, François de (Baron d'Aulnoy), 2–6
La Voisin, 88
le Fay, Morgan, 67
Le Jumel, Marie-Catherine. *See* d'Aulnoy, Marie-Catherine
lèse-majesté, 3–4, 7
L'Héritier, Marie-Jeanne, x, 123–152, 159, 172
    "Blanche," 128–129, 140–152
    education of, 123
    family background of, 123–124
    "Finette," 131–139, 171
    Murat and, 126–128
    obituary of, 124
    patronage for, 123–124
    pension of, 124
    prizes won by, 124
    salon of, 126, 157, 158
    Scudéry and, 125–126, 127
    sexual orientation of, 127–128
liberation, x
Little Red Riding Hood, xi
The Little Suppers (Durand), 172, 173
Louis XIV, ix–x, 2
    Affair of the Poisons and, 88
    badmouthing of, by Baron d'Aulnoy, 3–4
    Bernard and, 155, 159
    court of, 60, 63
    death of, 66
    Fronde and, 124
    Huguenots and, 85–86, 88
    La Force and, 88, 89, 91–92
    mistresses of, 170
    political satire and, 7, 91
    Voltaire's literary history of reign of, 157, 170
    wives of, 6, 86, 91, 170–171
love, x, 86–87
love potion, 87–88

M
Mab, Queen, 67
Madrid, 4, 5
magical islands, 158
Maintenon, Madame de, 91, 92, 159, 170–171, 172
male homosexuality, 62
Maria Theresa (queen), 86, 91
"Marmoisan" (L'Héritier), 129–130
marriage
    age for, xv
    annulment of, 90–91
    arranged, ix, 2, 59
    avoidance of, 125, 126, 159
    of d'Aulnoy, 2–4, 190

INDEX

of d'Auneuil, 187–188
of La Force, 89–91
of Murat, 60–61
masculinity, x
mauvaise conduite, 5
Mayer, Charles-Joseph, 188
measles, 188
Melusine, 67
men, x
　gay, 62
Ménilmontant, 87
Mercure galant, 66, 156, 191
metamorphosis, x, 158
Misfortunes of Love series (Bernard), 156
misogynistic writers, 124–125
Mixed Works (L'Héritier), 126
"modern fairies," x
Molière, 125
Mother Goose, xi
Murat, Henriette-Julie, x, 59–82, 91, 158
　"Anguillette," 67, 69–82, 158
　arrest of, 64, 172
　d'Auneuil and, 192
　death of, 66, 124
　diary of, 65–66
　Durand and, 170
　escape attempt by, 65
　fairy tales published by, 61–62, 67
　fame of, 62–63
　family background of, 60
　health issues of, 66
　imprisonment of, 64–66
　"Iris," 68
　L'Héritier and, 126–127
　marriage of, 60–61
　poetry of, 67
　same-sex relationships of, 63, 64–65
　surveillance of, 62–64
Murat, Nicolas de, 60, 65
Muses, 125, 157, 173

N

Nemours, Duchess of, 124
Nesle, Marquis de, 87–88
nested tales, 7
The New Fairy Tales (Murat), 67
The New Pandora, 157, 190–191
nom de plumes, 191

O

"Ogilire" (Durand), 172, 181–184
"old wives," xiii
Order of the Honeybee, 92
"The Origin of Fairies" (Durand), 172
Orléans, Duchess of, 6

P

Padua, 156–157
"The Palace of Vengeance" (Murat), 61–62
Palace of Versailles, 6–7
Paris, ix–xi, 155
"Patientine" (d'Auneuil), 193–198
patriarchy, ix, 2
"Peau d'ourse," 90
Perrault, Charles, x–xiii, 123, 128–130, 158, 171
Perrault, Marie-Madeleine, 129–130
"Persinette" (La Force), xii, 93, 115–120
plays, 6–7, 155–156
plotlines, x
poems
　by Bernard, 156, 159, 172
　by La Force, 91, 92
　of L'Héritier, 127–128

INDEX

by Murat, 67
political satire, 7, 91
Pontchartrain, Countess of, 159, 172
Pontchartrain, Count of, 64–65, 92
Praxille, 126–127
précieuse, 125–126
premier écuyer, 1, 4
"Prince Rosebush" (Bernard), 158
The Princess Bride, 65
"Princess Patientine in the Forest of Erimente" (d'Auneuil), 189–190
prisons, 64–66
"The Prodigy of Love" (Durand), 171–172
Protestantism, 88, 155
Protestants, 85–86
proverbs, 170–171, 172
pseudo memoirs, 1
publication, of fairy tales, x
Puss in Boots, xi

Q

Quarrel of the Ancients and the Moderns, 62, 129, 157
"Queen of Flowers" (de Héere), 190, 192, 200–205

R

rapt de séduction, 90
"Rapunzel," xii, 93
"The Recognition of Parnassus" (L'Héritier), 125, 126
religion, 61, 85–86, 88, 91, 155
"Ricquet with the Tuft" (Bernard), 158, 171
"The Robber Bridegroom," xiv
romance genre, x, 86–87
Rouen, 155
royal censor, x, 6, 61
royal privilege, 6, 61, 63, 91, 156, 173, 188

S

Saint-Lazare, 90
salons, ix–xii, 6, 60, 61, 91, 126, 157, 158
same-sex relationships, 61–65
   See also homosexuality
Sappho, 126, 127
"Satire X," 124–125
satirical pamphlets, 91
Schulz, Friedrich, xii
Scudéry, Madeleine de, 125, 126, 127, 159
secret histories, 91
sex, xv
Shakespeare, William, 59
Sleeping Beauty, xi
"Sleeping Beauty in the Wood" (Perrault), xi
Snow White, xiii–xiv
Society of the Temple, 87
soldiers, 86
storytellers, female, x–xiii
Straparola, 59
Sublime and Allegorical Stories (Murat), 62
"Sun, Moon and Talia" (Basile), xi
Sun King. *See* Louis XIV
sword nobility, 60
symbolism, x

T

The Tales of Tales (La Force), 91–92
teen girls, xv
tendresse, 86–87
themes, x, 158
Ticquet, Madame, 5–6
Titania, Queen, 67

INDEX

"Tortoise and Hare" (Aesop), xiii
torture, 6
Toulouse Academy, 124, 156
tragic endings, 61
transformation, 7–8
tribadism, 63
Troy, 85
"The Tulip" (de Héere), 190
The Tyranny of the Fairies Destroyed (d'Auneuil), 187, 188, 189, 191, 192

U
Urgele, 67

V
Vendôme, Duke of, 2
Villiers, Pierre de, xii–xiii, 60, 124
violence, xv
virtuousness, 128

Viviane, 67
Voltaire, 156, 157, 170

W
"water pot" torture, 6
"The White Cat" (d'Aulnoy), 7, 192
"The Wild One" (Murat), 59
wives, ix, 5, 61
women
    cross-dressing, 7–8, 59, 65
    fairy tales for, xv
    lack of opportunities for, ix
    misbehavior of, 5
    storytellers, x–xiii
    as weak, x
women's education, 128
women's literature, 62
Wonder Woman, 129
writing prompts, at salons, 158, 171, 187

"And that is where our pretty tale ends"